HEARING
Jesus

365 DAILY DEVOTIONS
FOR WOMEN

Rachael Groll

BroadStreet
PUBLISHING

BroadStreet Publishing Group, LLC.
Savage, Minnesota, USA
Broadstreetpublishing.com

Hearing Jesus
© 2025 by Rachael Groll

9781424570492
9781424570508 (eBook)

All rights reserved. No part of this publication may be reproduced, distributed, or transmitted in any form or by any means, including photocopying, recording, or other electronic or mechanical methods, without the prior written permission of the publisher, except in the case of brief quotations embodied in critical reviews and certain other noncommercial uses permitted by copyright law.

Scripture quotations marked NIV are taken from the Holy Bible, New International Version®, NIV®. Copyright © 1973, 1978, 1984, 2011 by Biblica, Inc.™ Used by permission of Zondervan. All rights reserved worldwide. www.zondervan.com. The "NIV" and "New International Version" are trademarks registered in the United States Patent and Trademark Office by Biblica, Inc.™ Scripture quotations marked NLT are taken from the Holy Bible, New Living Translation, copyright ©1996, 2004, 2015 by Tyndale House Foundation. Used by permission of Tyndale House Publishers, Carol Stream, Illinois 60188. All rights reserved. Scripture quotations marked ESV are taken from the ESV® Bible (The Holy Bible, English Standard Version®), Copyright © 2001 by Crossway, a publishing ministry of Good News Publishers. Used by permission. All rights reserved. Scripture quotations marked CSB are taken from the Christian Standard Bible®, Copyright © 2017 by Holman Bible Publishers. Used by permission. Christian Standard Bible® and CSB® are federally registered trademarks of Holman Bible Publishers. Scripture quotations marked NASB are taken from the New American Standard Bible, Copyright 2020 by The Lockman Foundation. Used by permission. All rights reserved. Scripture quotations marked NKJV are taken from the New King James Version®. Copyright © 1982 by Thomas Nelson. Used by permission. All rights reserved. Scripture quotations marked NCV are taken from the New Century Version®. Copyright © 2005 by Thomas Nelson. Used by permission. All rights reserved. Scripture quotations marked TPT are taken from The Passion Translation® of the Holy Bible. Copyright © 2020 by Passion & Fire Ministries, Inc. Used by permission of BroadStreet Publishing®. All rights reserved.

Typesetting and design by Garborg Design Works | garborgdesign.com.
Editorial services by Michelle Winger | literallyprecise.com.
Writing services by Natasha Marcellus.

Printed in China.

25 26 27 28 29 30 31 7 6 5 4 3 2 1

"My sheep hear My voice,
and I know them,
and they follow Me."

JOHN 10:27 NKJV

Introduction

Hey Friend!

I am so thankful you picked up this book.

Maybe you're like me and have wondered if God is speaking to you. You've heard others talk about hearing His voice, but when you try, it just sounds like silence.

For years, I struggled to feel confident in my relationship with God. I longed to hear Him, to be used by Him—I just wasn't exactly sure how. As I sought the Lord, I realized that the primary way He speaks is through His Word. The more I understood Scripture, the more I recognized His voice. And that's when the Hearing Jesus podcast was born.

These devotions come from the heart of that podcast, with the hope of helping you understand that God is speaking. You just need to learn how to listen. Each day includes a verse to focus your heart, a devotion to help you recognize how Jesus speaks, and a prayer to guide your response.

My prayer is that as you go through this book, you'll grow in confidence, learning to recognize God's voice more clearly and follow Him more faithfully.

God loves you. He longs to speak to you personally. He meets you in the quiet, in the chaos, and in the everyday moments of life. Through these pages, may you experience the deep joy of knowing that you can hear His voice.

Praying for you,

Rach

Connect with Rachael at hearingjesuspodcast.com

JANUARY 1

Easily Recognized

"The gatekeeper opens the gate for him, and the sheep recognize his voice and come to him. He calls his own sheep by name and leads them out."

JOHN 10:3 NLT

Although many of us don't live in a farming community, we can grasp the principles displayed in John chapter 10. The way a shepherd cares for his sheep is used to explain how Jesus cares for us. A good shepherd leads his flock with intention and awareness. He calls them, and they follow willingly because they know who he is. The recognition of his voice comes with an association of love, safety, and provision. The flock knows who their shepherd is, and they expect him to take care of them.

When you recognize Jesus' voice, you'll be able to filter out the other noise within your life. Like finding the right station on a radio, you tune out the static until what you are looking for rings clear and true. When your ears are attuned to Jesus' voice, you'll be able to follow Him confidently. You won't have to worry if you're on the right path because you know without a doubt what your shepherd sounds like. His voice calls you, and you trust Him to take care of you as you follow Him.

Jesus, thank You for being my good and faithful shepherd. Fill my heart with truth so that I readily recognize Your voice. Help me follow You closely like a sheep follows a shepherd.

JANUARY 2

Practice over Passion

As the deer pants for streams of water,
so my soul longs for you, my God.
My soul thirsts for God, for the living God.
When can I go and meet with God?

PSALM 42:1-2 NIV

At the beginning of most relationships, passion and emotions are the driving force. We're excited, anxious, and curious as we get to know someone new. The anticipation we feel as we face the unknown motivates us to move forward. At some point, those electric feelings fade, and if we haven't built a firm foundation, we'll struggle to maintain that relationship. Passion must push us to develop healthy habits so a deeper, more sustainable relationship can be created.

This is true in your relationships with others as well as your relationship with God. In the early days of your walk with Him, you may have lived off spiritual highs. Everything you learned was new, and you soaked up truth like a sponge. While passion is beautiful, it can't sustain your walk with God long-term. It's important to intentionally develop habits and practices that promote lasting depth and intimacy. Developing spiritual muscles is a lot like digging a well. The well doesn't feel necessary in seasons of abundant rain, but when drought comes, you'll be grateful for the work that is already done.

Father, give me the fortitude I need to pursue You each day. Draw me close and strengthen my resolve. Help me to build healthy habits that build intimacy with You.

JANUARY 3

After the Mountaintop

Six days later Jesus took Peter and the two brothers, James and John, and led them up a high mountain to be alone. As the men watched, Jesus' appearance was transformed so that his face shone like the sun, and his clothes became white as light.

MATTHEW 17:1-2 NLT

Peter experienced something incredible with Jesus that few others did. He saw Him transfigured, and he heard God's audible voice declaring His love for His Son. Peter had a literal mountaintop experience. Even so, he went on to deny Jesus. The presence of a miracle in his life didn't guarantee he would never stumble. Sometimes, as believers, we seek out emotional experiences because they make us feel like our faith is meaningful. In reality, longevity of faith is built day by day.

Have you put too much weight on mountaintop experiences? Those times are a gift from God, but they cannot be the foundation of your faith. God may use miraculous experiences to encourage you, but they are not meant to be your daily experience with Him. When life becomes mundane or suffering is persistent, you need endurance over intensity. Endurance is built by investing in habits and strengthening your faith bit by bit like a muscle.

God, thank You for the mountaintop experiences I have had. Help me to honor You even when my emotions are not high. As I pursue my daily relationship with You, fill me with truth and help me develop consistency in my faith.

JANUARY 4

Chasing a Feeling

Then we will no longer be immature like children. We won't be tossed and blown about by every wind of new teaching. We will not be influenced when people try to trick us with lies so clever they sound like the truth.

EPHESIANS 4:14 NLT

When we pursue spiritual depth, we protect ourselves from the dangers of making emotional decisions. It's easy to be led astray by our own passions. When we follow our emotions or the whims of our desires, we miss the steadiness that comes from having an identity that is secure in Christ. Seeking to grow spiritually cultivates our relationship with God and gives us a firm foundation to stand on.

Your worth comes from who you are as a child of God. The way you serve, the rules you follow, or the teachings you listen to don't equate to maturity. Maturity is found in developing a personal relationship with God in which you fill your heart with truth and stay soft toward His instruction in your life. Getting to know His voice keeps you safe from following a wayward path.

God, give me the grace to follow You wholeheartedly. Remind me of my worth so my obedience to You is rooted in love. Help me cultivate habits that draw me closer to You.

JANUARY 5

Tenacity and Fortitude

*Let them turn to the LORD that he may have mercy on them.
Yes, turn to our God, for he will forgive generously.*

ISAIAH 55:7 NLT

Culturally, we have become accustomed to doing exactly what we want. We are a society full of short attention spans and the pursuit of instant gratification. We value entertainment over tenacity, comfort over fortitude, and personal satisfaction over sacrifice. If we want a thriving relationship with God, our pursuit of Him must be counter-cultural. We must accept the task of saying yes to God while saying no to what is accepted in the world around us.

Hearing from God and responding to Him is your own responsibility. No one can do it for you, and it won't always be an easy road. There must be a deliberate act of turning away from the ways of the world and turning toward God. The good news is that you are only responsible for your response to Him. The work of sanctification belongs to Him alone. As you turn to Him, He transforms your heart. He is the one who does the hard and miraculous work of redemption.

Lord, give me strength to follow You when I am tempted to go my own way. Give me the grace to surrender even the smallest parts of my life to You. Thank You for transforming my heart as I turn to You.

JANUARY 6

Focus and Engage

> How I love your Law!
> It is my meditation all the day.
>
> PSALM 119:97 NASB

The idea of meditation isn't always readily accepted within Christian circles. Sometimes, we have preconceived ideas of what it means. In reality, meditation is a skill that is necessary in order to discern what God is speaking into our lives. Meditating on God and His Word is mentioned frequently in Scripture. We are taught to focus on God's Word, think about it, and engage in a dialogue with Him.

Meditation, as mentioned in Scripture, is not an attempt to empty your mind. Instead, it is a deliberate attempt to fill your mind with God's Word and Spirit. As you drown out the noise and busyness of your life, you create space to hear what God is saying. As you focus on what He says is true, you detach from the world and grow closer to Him. Meditation can mean listening to His Word, reflecting on His works, and ruminating on His laws. As you fill your heart with these things, God will lead you down the path of hearing His Word, releasing your own ways, and being obedient to what He says.

God, Your ways are higher than my own. Fill me with a desire to know Your law. As I focus on Your Word, transform me more and more into Your likeness. Give me grace to be obedient to Your instructions.

JANUARY 7

Full Confidence

*I cry out the Lord;
I plead for the Lord's mercy.
I pour out my complaints before him
and tell him all my troubles.*

PSALM 142:1-2 NLT

Sometimes, we hesitate to bring negative emotions to God. We associate our intense feelings with complaints or a lack of gratitude. However, complaining to God is not a sin. In fact, it is healthy to bring our worst to God with confidence that He can handle it. God is the only one who can meet us in the depths of our emotions. The only productive way to deal with our deepest hurt is to bring it to God.

There are no emotions that are too big for God. You won't heal from a season of brokenness until you invite Him to move in your heart. He is your good Father, and He longs to comfort you in your heartbreak, chaos, or grief. Open your heart to Him and allow Him to bring light to the darkest corners. He will faithfully move wherever you allow Him to.

Father, thank You for being so kind and gentle with my emotions. When I am tempted to hold back my thoughts, opinions, or feelings, give me the courage to offer You my whole heart.

JANUARY 8

In Alignment

*I lie awake thinking of you,
meditating on you through the night.
Because you are my helper,
I sing for joy in the shadow of your wings.*

PSALM 63:6-7 NLT

We've all had nights where we sat in bed and worried about the previous day or what will happen in the future. We ruminate over our fears and let them dictate the decisions we make. The enemy wants us to stay paralyzed in a state of fear. If we can take our tendency to practice fear and instead turn it toward God's Word, we will find peace, comfort, and joy rather than anxiety.

When you deliberately pursue God's promises rather than the worries of the world, everything changes. Your emotions will come into alignment with God's perfect peace, and your relationship with Him will deepen. As you engage with Scripture throughout your day, it will become rooted in the depths of your heart. Then, when trials arise, His truth will be the first thing that comes to mind instead of worry or fear.

Lord, thank You for meeting me when I choose to be obedient. Thank You for filling my heart with Your Word and giving me peace that overcomes my fears and anxieties.

JANUARY 9

As a Friend

> The Lord would speak to Moses face to face, as one speaks to a friend.
>
> Exodus 33:11 NLT

God speaks to His children. For all of time, He has led His children with a steady and reliable voice. He loves to communicate with us, and He does not withhold His voice. He speaks to us clearly and consistently through Scripture. He longs for us to hide His Word in our hearts and to cultivate a close relationship with Him.

Before the fall of man, God spoke daily with Adam and Eve. In the perfection of the garden, relationship was the top priority. This is still true today. God wants to have an intimate connection with you. He wants to speak to you like a friend, and He wants you to pour your heart out to Him. He is not hiding from you, and He doesn't want you to keep parts of yourself hidden from Him. Through reading the Word, you have unlimited access to the voice of God.

God, thank You for Your steady voice in my life. Give me ears to hear what You are saying and a tender heart to receive Your instructions. Draw me closer to You and give me courage to run to You in every circumstance.

JANUARY 10

Always Near

I can never escape from your Spirit!
I can never get away from your presence!

Psalm 139:7 NLT

God is omnipresent. This means that He is always with us. It doesn't matter where we go or what we do; He is always with us. Meditating on that truth creates an emotional and spiritual space where we can recognize His presence. The more time we spend with Him, the more we will recognize His voice and notice Him moving in our lives. Through intentional, focused time with God we will become more and more familiar with the way He chooses to interrupt our thoughts and daily lives.

The enemy wants you to believe that biblical meditation, or focusing on God, is difficult. He wants you to believe that you can't do it, you're too busy, or you don't need to. The truth is that communion with God couldn't be simpler. He will faithfully meet you every time you look toward Him. He does not hide from you, and He is not difficult to find. Turn your attention His way and build greater intimacy with your kind Father.

Father, Your presence gives me new life. Being with You refreshes my soul and strengthens me from the inside out. Help me prioritize time with You over everything else. You are what I need most.

JANUARY 11

Stay Connected

Never stop praying.

1 Thessalonians 5:17 nlt

Prayer places us in an ongoing conversation with God. It is the deep work that grows our relationship with God, and it's where we get to know Him. Sometimes, we forget that prayer is an ongoing dialogue. We tend to desire a checklist we can move through instead of cultivating an ongoing conversation with our Creator. Like any relationship, this can take time.

Don't be intimidated by prayer. It is not a failure to feel awkward or unsure of how to pray. Getting to know someone isn't something that can be done with one or two meetings. If you want to create intimacy, it takes consistency and a willingness to dig deeper. Each day, you have the opportunity to connect with God as often as you want. Acknowledge His closeness and draw near to His heart through prayer.

God, when I don't know what to say, remind me that connection with You isn't complicated. Fill my heart with Your truth and draw me closer to You each day. Keep me from seeing You as a checklist item and help me cultivate a deeper relationship with You.

JANUARY 12

He Hears

This is the confidence which we have before Him, that, if we ask anything according to His will, He hears us.

1 John 5:14 NASB

There are certain barriers to having an abundant prayer life. One of the most common ones is being discouraged by unanswered prayers. Sometimes, we seek God for something specific and it doesn't happen. This doesn't mean God doesn't hear us or that He doesn't care. If we flip a light switch and the light doesn't come on, we don't automatically assume that electricity isn't real. We likely assume that the bulb is burnt out or there's some sort of connection problem. The same is true with our prayers. Unanswered prayers do not equate to a lack of faithfulness on God's part.

If your prayer life is bound up in ritual and legalism, you will be prone to disappointment and doubt. If your prayer life is based on relationship and intimacy, you'll be prone to trust and steadfastness when trials arise. The ongoing dialogue between you and God is what will carry you through times of difficulty or grief without wavering. Connection leads to trust more than checklists ever will.

God, when doubt fills my mind, help me trust in Your faithfulness. Remind me of the ways You've shown up in my life and teach me how to lean on You in every circumstance.

JANUARY 13

Cultivate Intimacy

No one is abandoned by the Lord forever. Though he brings grief, he also shows compassion because of the greatness of his unfailing love.

LAMENTATIONS 3:31-32 NLT

Trials build intimacy. This is true in our relationships with the people we love, and it's true in our relationship with God. When we are suffering and turn to God, we make our connection with Him even stronger. Through times of grief or intense doubt, He is ready and waiting to comfort us. When He inevitably does, we remember in an even deeper way that His love is what our soul needs most.

When you have nothing left to give, run to God. When you are out of options, He will not fail you. He will meet you in your trials, and He will lead you through them. There is no guarantee that life will look exactly how you want, but you can steadily rely on God being with you through whatever comes your way. Every tear you cry and every problem you face is an opportunity to cultivate intimacy with God. Take your grief and brokenness to Him and let Him give you peace.

Lord, You are my greatest help. Thank You for comforting me when I am troubled and for being steady when life is disappointing or painful. Your presence is enough for me. Please take my brokenness and give me peace.

JANUARY 14

Call to Prayer

Pray in the Spirit at all times and on every occasion. Stay alert and be persistent in your prayers for all believers everywhere.

EPHESIANS 6:18 NLT

As Christians, we know that prayer is powerful. The key is for our knowledge to be translated into action. It's easy to say we will pray for someone, but we often forget about it after leaving the conversation. Scripture is clear that we are meant to engage in consistent prayer. This isn't supposed to be something we read and feel ashamed of our inability to follow through on. God tells us to pray consistently because He knows the abundant goodness that comes from steady communion with Him.

When you think about your prayer life, do you immediately think that you should do better? Instead of viewing it as one more spiritual discipline you haven't mastered, try to shift your thinking. Remember that God wants to hear from you. He longs to speak with you. The call to prayer is not a burden but a delight and a privilege.

God, I don't want my relationship with You to be based on my idea of success. Draw me closer to Your heart and increase my faith. Help me see You as a good Father and a kind friend.

JANUARY 15

Make Space

"Give me your hearts. Come with fasting, weeping, and mourning."

Joel 2:12 NLT

Fasting allows us to deliberately make space for God to move in our lives. When we intentionally remove something, be it food, entertainment, or a habit, we create room for that space to be filled with God's Word and the movement of His Spirit. It's particularly helpful to fast at the beginning of the year because it sets the tone for the months to follow. When we allow God to direct our steps at the beginning of a journey, we are sure to walk in the right direction.

When you fast, it's important to remove something from your life and also replace it with something else. For example, if you decide to give up eating lunch, continue to set that time apart and use it to pray, worship, or read the Word. Fasting is not simply giving up something you like. It's more about what you can add to your daily life that draws you closer to God.

Father, show me how I can use fasting to strengthen my relationship with You. As I give something up, give me the grace to fill that space with Your presence. Meet me in my fast and reveal more of Your truth to me.

JANUARY 16

Quiet the Noise

"This kind does not go out except by prayer and fasting."

MATTHEW 17:21 NASB

Many of us need a breakthrough in specific areas of our lives. We feel tired, overwhelmed, and battle worn. Fasting is an irreplaceable tool in impossible situations. It allows us to quiet the noise in our hearts and make room for God to speak. Fasting does not guarantee our desired outcomes will come to pass, but it does reassure us that God is fighting alongside us.

When you fast, God can give you clarity that you wouldn't find otherwise. He will meet you in your brokenness, and He will comfort you in your grief. If you make space for Him, He will fill your heart with truth. As you trust Him, He will faithfully guide you. As you embrace your weakness and acknowledge His strength, He will give you peace no matter what battle you are facing.

God, I trust You for the clarity I need. As I fast, give me Your perspective. Help me see my life the way You do. When fasting is difficult, help me lean on You. When I am weak, You are strong.

JANUARY 17

Fast and Pray

We fasted and earnestly prayed that our God would take care of us, and he heard our prayer.

EZRA 8:23 NLT

Some of us may have preconceived ideas of what fasting should look like. We might assume that it must be miserable and extreme. In order to know how to properly execute a fast, we must understand what the point is. The point of fasting is to remove something from your life and fill that space with God. This doesn't have to be not eating and only drinking water. We can fast from anything in our lives that takes up space that could be filled with the pursuit of God.

If you feel led to fast, ask the Holy Spirit to guide you. He will show you an effective way for you to fast. It may be that you give up a particular food, but He may also ask you to abstain from a habit or vice that has too much influence on your life. No matter what you give up, the benefits of fasting will far outweigh the discomfort you may temporarily feel. Don't overlook the spiritual discipline of fasting because it feels scary. Embrace the discomfort and allow God to speak to you in your weakness.

God, show me something I can offer You through fasting. Soften my heart and help me seek You through the discomfort of fasting. Give me strength and help me honor You.

JANUARY 18

Intimacy Over Productivity

> "When you fast, put oil on your head and wash your face, so that it will not be obvious to others that you are fasting, but only to your Father, who is unseen; and your Father, who sees what is done in secret, will reward you."
>
> MATTHEW 6:17-18 NIV

Fasting for the sake of fasting isn't helpful. We don't pursue spiritual disciplines in an effort to check off a list or fulfill our own desire for accomplishment. Rather, a fast should be motivated by a desire for deeper intimacy with God. We fast in order to hone in on what God is saying to us. Jesus assumes that we will fast, which tells us that it is a priority in developing our relationship with Him.

Fasting is a declaration of God's strength. It's a physical reminder of your dependency upon Him, and it allows you to focus on what is true. When you fast, you are acknowledging His sovereignty and your weakness. Don't fast because you feel like you have to. Rather, fast because you desire a greater intimacy with Him.

Lord, may my pursuit of spiritual disciplines create a deeper connection with You. Keep me from valuing perfection or productivity over intimacy. As I fast, draw me close and fill my heart with truth.

JANUARY 19

Through His Word

Be transformed by the renewing of your mind, so that you may prove what the will of God is, that which is good and acceptable and perfect.

ROMANS 12:2 NASB

The primary way God speaks to us is through His Word. Even if we know this intellectually, we must allow it to permeate our habits and daily lives. Studying His Word is truly the most effective way to hear from Him. If we fill our hearts with truth, it will keep us steady in times of trial. If we devote ourselves to understanding His ways, we will steadily walk the narrow road.

Studying God's Word allows your mind to be continuously renewed. This is vital if you want to want to faithfully follow God all of your days. It takes discipline to study the Word, and you are well equipped to do it. Start small and focus on a particular Scripture. Let it be deeply rooted in your heart. The more you dwell on His Word, the more you will crave the truth.

Lord, fill me with a desire to know more of Your Word. Give me ears to hear, eyes to see, and a heart to understand Your ways. Give me the tenacity needed to study Scripture even when I don't feel like it.

JANUARY 20

Know the Truth

> "You will know the truth, and the truth will set you free."
> JOHN 8:32 NLT

We all see the world in different ways. Our perspectives are shaped by our unique experiences, positive or negative. The way we interpret Scripture can be influenced by the way we grew up, the trauma we have experienced, or the successes and failures we've walked through. It's important to place a higher value on what Scripture says is true than what our experiences or feelings tell us is true. Our experiences may say that we are alone or unloved, but Scripture is clear that God's love for us is extravagant and unlimited.

The truth cannot set you free if you do not know it. Without a steady reliance on Scripture, you will inevitably rely on your own understanding. The only way to shift your dependence onto God is to fill yourself with the truth of His Word. This can only be done if you take the time to read it or listen to it. When you pay careful attention to what God says, you will reap the benefits of cultivating a deeper trust of His Word.

Father, You have promised me freedom, and I want to experience its fullness! Fill my heart with truth and help me understand Your Word. Give me the desire to read Your Word and faithfully apply it to my life.

JANUARY 21

Pursue Goodness

Whatever is true, whatever is honorable, whatever is right, whatever is pure, whatever is lovely, whatever is commendable, if there is any excellence and if anything worthy of praise, think about these things.

PHILIPPIANS 4:8 NASB

The study of Scripture is an irreplaceable habit in the Christian life. As we deliberately dive into God's Word, we read it, understand it, draw conclusions, and apply it to our lives. The more we learn about God and His character, the more equipped we are to live the way He intended. The things we give our attention to dictate our habits and determine the direction of our lives.

Scripture says to focus on what is true, honorable, just, pure, lovely, and gracious. This is because God knows you will wander toward what holds your attention. Whether you know it or not, you are studying something. You are giving your time and energy to something, whether it's productive or not. Embrace the truth that God knows what is best for your heart.

God, I want to study Your Word with purpose and expectation. I trust You to lead me as I learn more about You. When my attention is captured by something else, draw me back to You and Your goodness.

January 22

Don't Be Distracted

*I will study your commandments
and reflect on your ways.
I will delight in your decrees
and not forget your word.*

Psalm 119:15-16 NLT

We live in a culture that values distraction over concentration. We prefer not to focus on negativity. While this seems like a noble goal, it prevents us from pursuing true healing because it is uncomfortable. A lot of people use distraction to deal with their anxiety or depression when concentration and tenacity are needed. We cannot renew our minds if we are unwilling to confront our weaknesses.

Don't fall into the trap of numbing yourself with distractions. Do the hard work of filling your life with truth. Read the Word and focus on it. Concentrate on what God is saying and what Scripture tells you about His character. The Word can't encourage you if you don't have the attention span to read it. Slowly, as you say no to your whims, you'll develop the fortitude needed to focus on truth.

Father, You know the depths of my heart. Give me the desire to study Your Word when I am overwhelmed. Transform the way I think and encourage me when I am weak. Give me the fortitude I need to focus on the truth.

JANUARY 23

Stay True

His letters contain some things that are hard to understand, which ignorant and unstable people distort, as they do the other Scriptures, to their own destruction.

2 PETER 3:16 NIV

There is a difference between devotional reading and the study of Scripture. Devotionals offer quick encouragement while studying Scripture requires a focused time of learning and understanding God's Word. Studying what we read with intention allows us to uncover the true meaning. We can't understand and interpret Scripture properly if we are unwilling to look at the context. If we rush into application, we might miss the actual intention of what God was saying.

If you want to experience life-transforming truth, you must look beyond what feels good. Scripture is meant to encourage you, but it is also meant to teach you and shape your life. If you are only willing to glance at God's Word, you will miss the depth of intimacy and understanding that can be found through study. This doesn't mean you need to engage in daily intensive study of the Word. Start by setting aside some time each week to really engage with Scripture.

God, help me read Your Word and understand it. Give me the wisdom to know what You are saying and the grace to apply it to my life. Keep me from distorting Your Word to fit my ideas.

JANUARY 24

Live Simply

Stop imitating the ideals and opinions of the culture around you, but be inwardly transformed by the Holy Spirit through a total reformation of how you think. This will empower you to discern God's will as you live a beautiful life, satisfying and perfect in his eyes.

ROMANS 12:2 TPT

The Christian discipline of simplicity allows us to cultivate contentedness in the midst of a culture of excess and extravagance. If we choose to conform to the culture around us, we must realize that we are conforming to sickness. Living simply often requires us to forge a different path. Through simplicity, we diminish the longing for status or position. Everything without eternal value falls away as we pursue a life that is bound up in simple devotion to Jesus.

Sometimes, pursuing a simple life requires sacrifice. As you surrender control of your possessions, finances, time, and energy, you may need to give up comforts you've held onto for years. While this might feel like a great loss, remember that God does not leave His children empty-handed and alone. He will faithfully fill those spaces with contentedness and peace.

God, I surrender my life to You. I give You control over my finances, possessions, time, and energy. I trust You to lead me and provide for me. Help me hold each blessing I have with a loose grip.

JANUARY 25

Seek First

> "Seek first His kingdom and His righteousness, and all these things will be provided to you."
>
> MATTHEW 6:33 NASB

A lot of us are accustomed to indulging our whims and desires. We tend to shy away from a lifestyle of simplicity because it challenges those indulgences. On the other hand, if we overregulate our behavior, it can lead to legalism. The key to walking this line is focusing on the impact of the choices we make rather than the choices themselves. Do our habits draw us closer to God and keep us walking on a path that honors Him?

When you set yourself up for a life of simplicity, you can clearly see habits and tendencies that have been standing in your way. There is a middle road between legalism and a lack of self-awareness. From this place of being willing to make changes, you'll be able to see areas of your life that have room for growth. You can be conscious of how you are living without being bound by a rigid set of rules.

Father, keep my eyes on You. Keep me from being distracted by habits and activities that don't honor You. May my heart be soft toward the voice of the Holy Spirit. I trust You to help me grow and change when I need to.

JANUARY 26

Cracks and Crevices

Godliness with contentment is great gain. For we brought nothing into the world, and we can take nothing out of it. But if we have food and clothing, we will be content with that.

1 Timothy 6:6-8 NIV

Simple devotion to God results in joy. We live in a society that is consumed with entertainment, personal satisfaction, and the pursuit of power, wealth, and status. If we remove those barriers from our lives, our hearts are made light in the presence of God. Choosing to live simply leaves room for Him to move. Deliberately removing distractions from our daily lives can have a huge impact.

Think about what you do to fill the spaces in your day. Do you search for another task to complete, scroll through your phone, or immediately find someone to talk to? What if cracks and crevices in your schedule were instead filled with conversations with God? There is far more satisfaction to be found in the pursuit of Him than there is in the pursuit of your own desires. Ask the Holy Spirit to reveal any distractions in your life and respond to His leadership.

Lord, forgive me for filling my time with everything but You. Help me see where I have space to spend more time with You. You are the source of true satisfaction. Keep me from filling my life with comfort over connection.

JANUARY 27

Take Responsibility

All things are permitted, but not all things are of benefit. All things are permitted, but not all things build people up.

1 Corinthians 10:23 NASB

When we think of addiction, we likely jump right to extreme examples. Just because we aren't addicted to gambling or alcohol doesn't mean our addictions are harmless. Through Scripture we see that we should reject anything that produces addiction in our lives. Put simply, it is wise to watch for undisciplined compulsion. Behaviors and habits that have become coping mechanisms can easily lead to addiction.

You are responsible for your habits and vices. When it comes down to it, you are the only one who can determine the direction of your life. God has fully equipped you to make wise choices. As you surrender to Him, He will gently lead you all of your days. If He highlights an area of your life that is out of control, no matter how big of a deal you think it is, He will give you strength and walk alongside you. Giving up a habit or tendency might be painful at the time, but it is always worth it to be obedient to God's leadership.

Lord, my desire is to honor You in all I do. Give me the courage to take responsibility for my vices and habits. Give me wisdom and keep me from being prideful. As You highlight areas of growth, help me follow Your leadership.

JANUARY 28

You Are Enough

Those who want to get rich fall into temptation and a trap and into many foolish and harmful desires that plunge people into ruin and destruction. For the love of money is a root of all kinds of evil. Some people, eager for money, have wandered from the faith and pierced themselves with many griefs.

1 Timothy 6:9-10 niv

As we embrace simplicity, it will inevitably seep into our finances. Some of us are not constantly consumed with hoarding wealth, but we do have an incessant desire to upgrade what we have. The onslaught of social media comparison has led us to believe that our lives are not enough unless they measure up to an unreachable standard. The messages we hear daily yell at us that our homes are not pretty enough, our wardrobes are not trendy enough, our pantries are not organic enough, and our adventures are not epic enough.

You are enough. The life you have been given is enough. Embrace the blessings you have and refuse to accept the idea that you constantly need more. The deepest longings of your soul can only be met by communion with God. Clearing out the clutter and drowning out the noise will cultivate gratitude and contentment in your life. These two things can help pave the way toward deeper intimacy with God.

God, thank You for the abundant blessings You have given me. Help me to see my life the way You see it. When I long for what I don't have, remind me that You are more than enough. Teach me how to be content with what I have.

JANUARY 29

Silence and Solitude

"Whenever you pray, go into your innermost chamber and be alone with Father God, praying to him in secret. And your Father, who sees all you do, will reward you openly."

MATTHEW 6:6 TPT

As believers we need community and the support of others. Healthy relationships should be prioritized, but we can't ignore the other side of the equation. As much as we were created to be part of a body, we were also created to need solitude with God. We often shy away from this part of Christianity because a lot of us hate feeling alone. The truth is that our personal pursuit of God in times of solitude is the only true remedy to a lonely heart.

A healthy community is a wonderful blessing, but it shouldn't get in the way of embracing solitude. Silence and solitude might feel scary or unsettling, but neglecting it robs you of an irreplaceable experience with God. He longs to draw you away from the crowd and speak directly to your heart. He wants your full attention, free from distractions or the opinions of others. Start small and devote a few minutes of your day to solitude with God.

Lord, help me clear out the noise in my life. Show me how and when I can make space to be alone with You. You are my heart's greatest desire, and You are worthy of my attention and praise.

JANUARY 30

False Connections

*Love the LORD your God, listen to his voice,
and hold fast to him.*

DEUTERONOMY 30:20 NIV

If we engage in consistent social media use, we run the risk of our lives being filled with superficial connections. We are mesmerized by the voices of others, and this limits our ability to hear God's voice. As we listen to what everyone has to say, we become bound by the expectations of the world. If we step back and begin to limit those distractions, we will become more open to God's expectations. Freedom comes when we let go of the opinions of others and instead chase after God's opinion.

It's not very popular to limit phone use, but in today's culture it is necessary. While there are many benefits to technology, it would be unwise not to acknowledge that there are also downfalls. Has your phone become a vice in your life? Has constant access to information created negativity or cynicism in your heart? Has engaging with others online created barriers in your in-person relationships? It is wise to evaluate the things that have captured your time, energy, and attention.

God, give me wisdom and discernment when it comes to the way I use my phone. I want every part of my life to honor You. Show me if there is something I need to change and give me grace to do what You say.

JANUARY 31

Unending Mercy

*"Do not fear, for I am with you;
do not be dismayed, for I am your God.
I will strengthen you and I will help you;
I will uphold you with my righteous right hand."*

ISAIAH 41:10 NIV

The goal of solitude and being alone with God is to help us develop a closer relationship with Him. Many of us avoid solitude because we don't want to be alone with our thoughts, but being alone with God is what fills us up. His presence satisfies our soul in a way nothing else can. We must push past our discomfort and remember the reliability of God's character. He is gentle, kind, and slow to anger. He is merciful and patient. He is delighted when we turn toward Him.

You don't have to worry about how God will respond to you. Any insecurities you have about meeting with Him in solitude can be reassured by remembering His unending mercy toward you. When you run to Him, He will not beat you up about your failures. He will not admonish you or embarrass you. He is gentle and kind. When you turn to Him, He welcomes you with abundant mercy and grace.

Lord, You have my attention. Your presence is all I need. When I am hesitant to run to You, remind me of the goodness and reliability of Your character.

FEBRUARY

FEBRUARY 1

Filled Up

Jesus often withdrew to the wilderness for prayer.
LUKE 5:16 NLT

Serving others is wonderful, but we must prioritize our own time with the Father. Problems arise when we try to lay our lives down without getting what we need from God. We must go to Him in the midst of trying to pour out to others. Jesus was an excellent example of this. As we seek to imitate Him, we learn to run to God for refreshment and direction.

You have probably felt the temptation to help others even when you are emotionally, spiritually, or physically drained. In the moment, you might internalize your overwhelming emotions and try to move forward with your own strength. While this might seem like the right thing to do, the opposite is actually true. God longs to be with you in the middle of your mess. When you are exhausted or overworked, God is the only one who can provide true rest.

Lord, You are my strength when I am weak. Fill me with Your love so I can love others. Keep me from trying to serve out of my own strength. When I am weary, remind me to spend time with You.

FEBRUARY 2

Happily Submit

> "Submit to God, and you will have peace;
> then things will go well for you.
> Listen to his instructions,
> and store them in your heart."
>
> JOB 22:21-22 NLT

Though we often shy away from the topic of submission, it's important to recognize that the world's definition of submission is different from God's. Worldly submission is centered around control, power, and status. Biblical submission results in spiritual freedom and growth. When we take our preconceived notions and willingly change the way we think, we give ourselves the opportunity to experience submission as God intended it.

You may have seen or personally experienced the wrong application of submission. Remember, God can redeem all things. He is merciful toward your hurts. He can heal your greatest disappointments and lead you along a path that honors His Word. Ignoring the idea of submission because of your negative experience will only cause greater pain. As God tends to the wounded parts of your heart, He will show you that submission is not about power or control. When you submit to God, He offers you freedom and grace.

Father, help me recognize anything inside of me that is rejecting the idea of submission. Prepare my heart to submit to You fully. Thank You for the freedom You give when my life is fully in Your hands.

FEBRUARY 3

Give and Take

Recognize the value of every person and continually show love to every believer. Live your lives with great reverence and in holy awe of God.

1 Peter 2:17 TPT

Every relationship consists of give and take. There's a mutual submission that comes from the care and respect we have for each other. A healthy community is filled with people who routinely make sacrifices for each other out of love and kindness. This is the example we see in Scripture. Jesus consistently set aside His own comfort for the good of others. Abuse happens when the motivation for submission is prideful or selfish instead of mirroring Christ's example.

You honor God when you submit to others without pride. Pride insists on its own way. Pride doesn't leave room for the opinions or perspectives of others. Pride refuses to be inconvenienced for the sake of love. Instead, submitting to others means laying down your desires in order to serve those around you. Submitting to others means allowing God to affirm you and care for you as you lay your life down willingly for those in need.

God, show me what healthy submission looks like. Open my eyes to the truth of biblical submission. Help me see Your ways with clarity.

FEBRUARY 4

Recognize Authority

Abandon every display of selfishness. Possess a greater concern for what matters to others instead of your own interests.

PHILIPPIANS 2:4 TPT

When we read Scripture and feel uncomfortable, there should be a red flag in our spirit. It's important to see that flag as a reminder to press in. Discomfort often leads to growth. When we shy away from tension, we rob ourselves of the opportunity to change our perspective and become stronger than we were before. Submission is one of those topics that often causes some discomfort. Biblical submission cannot walk hand in hand with selfishness. When we resist the idea of it, it's often because we don't want to give up our own comfort or control.

True submission is about serving others as you recognize God's authority in your life. When you submit your will to serve others, you are really submitting to God. When Jesus walked the earth, He was constantly submitting to God's authority. If He can do it, you can too. As you relinquish your need for control, you'll find that a lack of control comes with incredible freedom. The more loosely you hold your preferences, the more quickly you will realize you have never been the one holding your life together.

Father, You are in control, and I want my actions to honor Your authority. Help me to see others as more valuable than myself. Teach me how to submit to You and others.

FEBRUARY 5

Free from Pride

Be free from pride-filled opinions, for they will only harm your cherished unity. Don't allow self-promotion to hide in your hearts, but in authentic humility put others first and view others as more important than yourselves.

PHILIPPIANS 2:3 TPT

Biblical submission is not about being forced to give up our thoughts and opinions. Rather, it's about elevating the thoughts and opinions of others. Biblical submission is fueled by consideration for others. As we value and respect others, we experience genuine joy when they succeed. This joy overrides our tendency toward bitterness and jealousy.

When you strive to serve those around you, you identify with Christ through self-denial and servant leadership. Jesus didn't just die on the cross; He also lived a life of service. The way He chose to lift up those around Him gives you an example of how to love well. He lived a life of submission by trusting God's authority, putting the needs of others before His own, and staying obedient to God's instruction even in the face of great suffering. Follow His example and embrace a life of submission.

God, teach me how to serve like Jesus did. Give me opportunities to deny my own preferences in favor of the people around me. As I lay my life down for others, I trust You to take care of me.

FEBRUARY 6

Embrace Pain

Serve wholeheartedly, as if you were serving the Lord, not people, because you know that the Lord will reward each one for whatever good they do, whether they are slave or free.

EPHESIANS 6:7-8 NIV

Building muscles is painful. It doesn't happen easily or accidentally. In most areas, growth requires persevering through difficulty. Pain means progress. The same is true with biblical concepts. The presence of pain or discomfort typically provides an opportunity for growth. Especially in the area of submission, we can only grow when we lean in and surrender.

As you refuse to shy away from pain or inconvenience, you'll find more and more opportunities to submit to others and to God's Word. Your service to others is really service to God. You can put the needs of others before your own because this is what God expects of you. Rather than serving for your own gain, be genuinely kind because God asks you to. As you step out in obedience, He will step in and empower you.

God, I want to honor You with the way I submit to my neighbor. Fill me with Your love for the people around me. When I am uncomfortable, give me the courage to submit to Your ways above my own.

FEBRUARY 7

Purposeful Service

"Even the Son of Man did not come to be served, but to serve, and to give his life as a ransom for many."

MARK 10:45 NIV

We are all called to serve. Scripture is clear that we are meant to lay our lives down for others. This isn't meant to be an indictment or an impossible requirement. We often think we don't have time to serve or that we aren't equipped to do it well. This way of thinking is a barrier to the kind of life God has asked us to live. Service is meant to be an overflow of God's movement in our lives. Our service is meant to be gracious rather than being based on feelings of obligation.

God does not want you to be tired, overworked, and overwhelmed. He doesn't ask you to do something without purpose and reason. Instead, He gives you the grace to accomplish His will, and He equips you to walk in His ways. If your service to others feels forced, it might be time to reevaluate. Ask God to give you His perspective and remember to lean on His strength over your own.

God, thank You for the opportunity to serve You. Help me recognize the areas in my life that are fueled by selfishness. As You reveal my heart, give me the desire to repent and turn toward You.

FEBRUARY 8

Hidden Sacrifice

Constantly love each other and be committed to serve one another.

GALATIANS 5:13 TPT

There is a difference between serving others for our own gain and serving others out of obedience to God. If we want to evaluate our motives, we can look at the desired outcome of our actions. True service is content with hiddenness, while self-righteous service wants recognition and reward. True service is driven by motives which are typically unseen, while self-righteous service is results driven.

When God compels you to serve others, He will equip you to do it. You can confidently embrace opportunities to help those around you, knowing that God is the one who sees your efforts. You don't have to keep track of what you've done, and you don't have to work to ensure a positive outcome. Your love and care for others is simply an avenue for God's love to be magnified. He is the one who will change hearts and guide His children down the right path.

God, thank You for continually showing me Your heart. Forgive me for the times my actions haven't lined up with the way You love and serve people.

FEBRUARY 9

Lifestyle of Service

Do nothing out of selfish ambition or vain conceit. Rather, in humility value others above yourselves.

PHILIPPIANS 2:3 NIV

Godly service is a lifestyle. We aren't supposed to pick and choose who, when, or why we serve. It's not about building a brand or maintaining our own reputation; it's about building the kingdom. True service requires fortitude and longevity. As we experience God's sacrificial love for us, we learn how to sacrificially love those around us. We don't do it out of obligation but out of a desire for others to experience God's love.

When you live a lifestyle of service, you won't be dismayed or disappointed by spontaneous or inconvenient situations. Loving others rarely happens on a predictable and organized timeline. As you practice surrendering to God's will, His agenda will become a delight and a privilege.

Lord, help me cultivate a lifestyle of service. I don't want to view loving others as an inconvenience. Give me grace to joyfully lay my life down whenever I need to.

FEBRUARY 10

Give Credit

"The master of the banquet tasted the water that had been turned into wine. He did not realize where it had come from, though the servants who had drawn the water knew."

JOHN 2:9 NIV

When Jesus famously turned the water into wine, it wasn't a spectacle for everyone to see. It's likely that the only people who knew what had happened were His mother and the people serving the wine. The wedding guests wouldn't have been aware that the wine had run out or that Jesus had performed a miracle. When we serve alongside Jesus, we often get a firsthand view of what God is doing. It is a privilege and an honor to partner with God in His work.

Your service to God is not meant to be glorified. All glory and credit belong to the Father. True service draws others toward Jesus, not toward one person. If your actions have placed you on a pedestal, humbly climb down and lift up the name of the one who deserves all the praise. If you have been blessed enough to have a firsthand view of a miracle, seek to humbly thank God for the encouragement rather than glorifying your own participation.

Lord, thank You for the privilege of seeing Your work in the lives of others. Help me to embrace humility and give You the credit. You are worthy of all my praise and adoration.

FEBRUARY 11

Habit of Confession

There is one God and one mediator who can reconcile God and humanity—the man Christ Jesus.

1 Timothy 2:5 NLT

Sin cuts us off from God. Our propensity to do the wrong thing keeps us from being close to a God who is completely perfect. When we confess our sins and kneel at the cross, Christ's perfection becomes our own. Jesus has made a way for us to be near to the Father. He is our primary means of confession. If we shout our sins from the rooftops, it is meaningless. Trusting in Christ's death and resurrection is our only means of reconciliation.

While an initial confession of sins and declaration of salvation is necessary, it's also important to develop the habit of confession. As the Holy Spirit reveals sin in your life, keep your heart soft and readily bring those things to Jesus. If you approach confession with a growth mindset rather than one of shame, you won't shy away from God's prompts toward change. He desires full and complete freedom for you.

Lord, keep my heart soft and help me remain flexible. When I insist on my own way, remind me of Your wisdom and sovereignty. As You prompt me to make changes, help me to see how gracious and merciful Your leadership is.

FEBRUARY 12

Heal and Grow

Love keeps no record of being wronged.

1 Corinthians 13:5 NLT

Sometimes, we are hurt by others, and we think we can let it go. We convince ourselves that it doesn't matter, and we ignore the pain we've experienced. Glazing over our emotions is not the same thing as forgiveness. If we suppress an issue while continuing to carry it in our hearts, we are not forgiving others; we are lying. Sometimes, it's easier to ignore our pain rather than deal with it. The process of working through conflict is hard, but it is always worth it.

When you willingly address hurt, you give yourself the opportunity to heal, and you give others the opportunity to grow. The entire body of Christ benefits from healthy conflict management. If you pretend your past injuries didn't happen, they will never heal properly. Inevitably, the pain you carry will begin to impact those around you. Learning how to bring your pain to God and allowing Him to heal it properly is an act of service to yourself and everyone around you.

God, thank You for being a God who reveals to heal. Give me the courage to address hurts as You lead me to. May my relationships be honoring to You.

FEBRUARY 13

God's Example

Let us continue to love one another, for love comes from God.

1 John 4:7 NLT

We do our best to love others well, but interpersonal conflict is inevitable. As we walk through life together, we are likely to hurt, offend, or annoy each other at some point. When we live in community, confession must be prioritized. It's important to cultivate an environment in which we are comfortable talking about our failures. When we readily confess our wrongs, we allow God to restore what is broken.

Healthy confession is only possible because of God's love. When you humbly lay your sins at His feet, He eagerly forgives you. His outpouring of mercy and grace serves as an example of how to treat others who confess their sins to you. You can receive others graciously because God has been extravagantly gracious toward you. You can treat the failures of others with tenderness and kindness because God has been infinitely tender toward you.

God, You have been so gracious to me! Help me to extend that grace to others. When people around me make mistakes, help me treat them the way You've treated me. May my reactions reflect Your love and tenderness.

FEBRUARY 14

Live in the Light

Be kind to each other, tenderhearted, forgiving one another, just as God through Christ has forgiven you.

EPHESIANS 4:32 NLT

We've all made mistakes we'd rather not talk about. We've made poor choices, disappointed someone, or even created a deep wound in a relationship. When the problem seems insurmountable, we must rely on God's ability to reconcile. He is fully capable of redeeming even the most broken situation. If we rely on Him and trust His leadership, He will show us what reconciliation looks like in our relationships.

Relationships are made stronger when confession and forgiveness are prioritized. You might assume that conflict causes weakness, but the truth is that healthy conflict resolution actually makes a relationship stronger. Conflict doesn't create nearly as much damage as hiddenness and secrecy. When you live in the light, you leave space for growth and humility. As you seek to imitate Jesus in your relationships, He will restore what seems to be lost.

God, I commit my relationships to You. Help me be honest and forthcoming with each person in my life. Teach me how to resolve conflict in a healthy way that honors You and is a catalyst for growth.

FEBRUARY 15

Close Attention

*"I, even I, am he who blots out
your transgressions, for my own sake,
and remembers your sins no more."*

ISAIAH 43:25 NIV

Most of us have been advised to forgive and forget. We're often told that we should move on from our past pain and never bring it up again. The truth is that God is not telling us to forget the difficult things we've gone through. We are not designed to forget, only He is. We are designed to forgive and heal. The presence of pain in our lives can drive us to deeper intimacy with Jesus. If we forget the hurt we've experienced, we lose the opportunity to grow and change.

If you let Him, God will meet you in your brokenness. He holds the vulnerable parts of your story with great care. He doesn't admonish you to get over it, and He doesn't force you to move on. He is a good Father who pays close attention to the wounds of His children. He is the only one who can fix what is broken and heal what is damaged. If you let Him, He can redeem even the most hopeless situation.

Father, thank You for paying close attention to me when I am hurting. I trust You to heal my wounds and comfort me when I am in pain. Thank You for being a God who redeems.

FEBRUARY 16

All Week Long

"The time is coming—indeed it's here now—when true worshipers will worship the Father in spirit and in truth. The Father is looking for those who will worship him that way."

JOHN 4:23 NLT

Many people have worship preferences, but the Bible doesn't prescribe certain styles of music for worship. If we look at Scripture for guidance in this area, we will see that it is descriptive but not prescriptive. This means that we can find elements of worship but not necessarily a required formula. Instead, worship is more about turning our hearts toward God than the circumstances in which we do it. The form of worship is secondary to the experience of worship. What matters most is that we enter into a place of confession, praise, and adoration of who God is.

Don't limit your worship experience to Sunday mornings. Make space in your day for adoration and praise. Pay attention to what stirs your spirit to worship God and prioritize those things. Maybe it is a specific type of music. Maybe it's reading the Word or processing your thoughts through writing. Maybe spending time in nature or creating something artistically draws your heart toward God. No matter the circumstances, set aside time for your heart to engage with the glory of God.

Lord, You are worthy of my praise every single day. Fill my heart with a greater desire to worship You. Show me how I can pursue a lifestyle of worship instead of limiting myself to Sunday morning.

FEBRUARY 17

When Feelings Fade

I will give you thanks with all my heart;
I will sing your praise before the heavenly beings.
I will bow down toward your holy temple
and give thanks to your name
for your constant love and truth.

PSALM 138:1-3 CSB

There are times when our feelings and our actions line up perfectly. We might be stirred to worship, and we experience the goodness and peace of God's presence. At other times, we might not feel like worshipping at all. As a believer, it's important to know how to handle distraction and a lack of emotion. Our relationship with God can't be based on the whims of our feelings. After all, God's goodness is unchanging, and our adoration of Him should be the same.

When feelings fade, truth remains. If you want your worship of God to be steadfast, it must be based in truth. In order for this to happen, you need a strong foundation to build upon. Read the Word and let the truth of who God is be deeply rooted in your heart. Get to know Him and see how His character is revealed through Scripture. The more you store truth in your heart, the more you will be drawn to worship. Discipline that is cultivated despite how you feel creates long-lasting intimacy.

Lord, You are steadfast and true. No matter how I feel, You never change. May Your Word be the foundation for every decision I make. Help me to cultivate discipline that leads to greater intimacy with You.

FEBRUARY 18

Turn Your Attention

"Holy, holy, holy is the Lord of Heaven's Armies! The whole earth is filled with his glory!"

ISAIAH 6:3 NLT

In this portion of Isaiah, we get a glimpse of the throne room of God. We see the seraphim worshipping Him, and we read about how Isaiah comes face to face with God in the presence of angels. In that place, he is transformed. Through worship, we can also be transformed. We have the opportunity to clear out the congestion of our hearts and turn our attention to our Creator. We focus our eyes on Him and gain a holy perspective for our earthly troubles. Worship has the power to renew, strengthen, and comfort us in our deepest sorrows.

When you experience great joy, run to God in worship. When the sorrows of this life are too much to bear, run to God in worship. When your heart is broken and grief is heavy, run to God in worship. As you fix your eyes upon Him and declare His goodness despite your circumstances, He will comfort, heal, and encourage you. He will lift your countenance and give you strength when you need it most.

God, thank You for the clarity You give through worship. As I fix my eyes on You, I trust You to transform my heart. Your goodness is what gets me through the trials I face.

FEBRUARY 19

Consistent Praise

*Sing to the Lord a new song;
sing to the Lord, all the earth.
Sing to the Lord, praise his name;
proclaim his salvation day after day.*

PSALM 96:1-2 NIV

Instead of thinking of worship as a singular experience, we can think of it as a posture. We don't have to be limited to corporately organized worship experiences. Instead, the way we think, act, and speak can be directed toward God in worship. As we move through our days, we can be in constant communion with Him. We can walk through our lives with a sense of holy expectancy.

When you treat worship as a lifestyle rather than an isolated act, you can experience greater intimacy with your Creator. You are not limited to specific circumstances or parameters. Even when you can't be physically on your knees in a quiet place, you can offer your heart to God as it is. You can interact with Him constantly and expect Him to show up. Today, seek to cultivate opportunities for uninterrupted conversation with God.

God, draw me closer to You as I worship. I offer You my heart, and I trust You to meet me where I am. Fill me with expectancy and help me to cultivate uninterrupted conversation with You.

FEBRUARY 20

Heart Transformation

Rejoice always, pray continually, give thanks in all circumstances; for this is God's will for you in Christ Jesus.

1 Thessalonians 5:16-18 NIV

Worship is not meant to be an antidote for our feelings. True worship results in the transformation of our hearts. When we surrender our thoughts, will, and emotions to God, He leads us steadily on the path to eternal life. When there is a sincere connection between our spirit and God's, He will move tangibly in our lives. In that place of connection, God heals and restores us.

Worship is less like a band-aid and more like a balm. It's not meant to cover up a wound so you can go about your life. Instead, it's like a deep, healing salve that administers exactly what you need and puts your heart in a place where God can change it. His work in your life is about more than how you feel. He wants to see you transformed into His likeness. He wants you to experience the full and abundant life He intends for you. If you have viewed worship as an emotional experience rather than one of deep transformation, ask God to shift your thinking.

Father, You are the only one who can transform my heart. As I meet with You, I trust You to heal every part of me. Be lifted high in every area of my life.

FEBRUARY 21

Overflowing

May God, the fountain of hope, fill you to overflowing with uncontainable joy and perfect peace as you trust in him.

ROMANS 15:13 TPT

God is meant to be enjoyed. In Him is the fullness of joy. It's easy to focus on the dos and don'ts of Christianity, but in doing that, we sacrifice the sweet goodness of who God is. We forget that He is overflowing with joy. He is as joyful as He is holy, mighty, or merciful.

Your days might be filled with grief. You might be overwhelmed by the disheartening reality of our culture. You might have a deep heartache in your personal life. Remember that joy and sorrow can exist simultaneously. Joy isn't something you need to manufacture. Just like grace, mercy, or holiness, it is the result of a healthy spiritual life. Just as God longs for you to experience His abundant mercy, so He longs for you to experience His abundant joy.

Father, remind me of Your glorious joy! It's so easy to focus on the difficult parts of my life. Renew my spirit and fill me to overflowing with uncontainable joy.

FEBRUARY 22

Don't Forget

Let all that I am praise the LORD;
with my whole heart, I will praise his holy name.
Let all that I am praise the LORD;
may I never forget the good things he does for me.

PSALM 103:1-2 NLT

Sometimes, we get caught up in the busyness of our lives, and we forget the abundant reasons to worship God. We view our lives through our own perspective and get lost in our own definitions of success and failure. As a result, we lose sight of who God is and what He says. We sacrifice joy for productivity, peace for anxiety, and submission for a false sense of control. Before we know it, our wheels are spinning, and we've lost the steadiness that comes from being anchored to God in worship.

The quickest route to dissatisfaction and anxiety is to take your eyes off God. Instead, cultivate an intentional posture of worship. The peace, joy, and satisfaction you long for cannot be found anywhere but in the presence of God. Those things are not feelings you can muster up; they are symptoms of a life filled with worship. No matter how busy life gets, the things you need most are found by remembering who God is and all He has done for you.

Lord, You have done wonderful things for me. Forgive me for taking Your blessings for granted. Open my eyes to see the work of Your hands.

FEBRUARY 23

Full of Joy

Taking him by the right hand, he helped him up, and instantly the man's feet and ankles became strong. He jumped to his feet and began to walk. Then he went with them into the temple courts, walking and jumping, and praising God.

ACTS 3:7-8 NIV

Joy is not something you can manufacture in your own life. It is a natural reaction to the incredible goodness of God. This is seen in Scripture several times. When Jesus healed the man in Acts 3, He was filled with joy. He delighted in what God had done, and he couldn't help but experience joyful gratitude. It was out of his control. He turned to God for help and obeyed what was asked of him. As a result, he was filled with joy.

You don't need more joy in your life; you need more Jesus. Joy is the secondary benefit of a genuine interaction with Christ. As you are obedient to His Word, you will inevitably experience the joy that accompanies it. Scripture promises that if you abide in Jesus, you will bear fruit. In other words, the joy you are longing for comes from cultivating a consistent relationship with the one who is eternally joyful.

Lord, I would love to have more joy in my life. Instead of trying to manufacture it on my own, draw me close to You and fill me with joy. As I meet with You, may I bear the fruit of Your Spirit.

FEBRUARY 24

Great Things

The Lord has done great things for us,
and we are filled with joy.

PSALM 126:3 NIV

Lack of trust is a barrier to joy. It's hard to have joy if we are worried all the time. If our thoughts are consumed with what we don't have or what might happen, we will quickly lose sight of what we do have and what has already happened. As followers of Jesus, we have been abundantly blessed. No matter what the circumstances of our lives look like, we cannot ignore the truth that God has done great things for us.

Transitioning your mindset from anxiety to contentment doesn't usually happen overnight. It starts with small steps, and it takes perseverance. Each day, commit to trusting God in a certain area. As you begin to see God's faithfulness revealed in your life, your trust will grow. Each small act of daily obedience is a stepping stone toward contentment and joy. As you continue down that path, you'll begin to notice certain things that previously plagued your thoughts become less as He becomes more.

God, forgive me for my lack of contentment. Open my eyes to see Your faithfulness in my life. Keep me from being worried about things that don't matter and help me recognize the ways You have already blessed me.

February 25

Trust His Guidance

"The Counselor, the Holy Spirit, whom the Father will send in my name, will teach you all things and remind you of everything I have told you."

John 14:25-26 CSB

Developing spiritual discipline is not meant to be an overwhelming task we cannot accomplish. It shouldn't be a burden or generate shame. At the same time, cultivating godly discipline in our lives isn't necessarily easy. If we lean into discomfort instead of shying away from it, God will meet us in the tension. Trials, obstacles, and suffering are not our enemies. Instead, they are opportunities for God to prove His faithfulness.

When it comes to building your spiritual muscles, lean heavily on the guidance of the Holy Spirit. There is no need to focus on every area of your life that needs growth. Doing that will quickly produce shame, a legalistic attitude, and eventually burnout. Prayerfully ask God to show you one thing you can give attention to. Trust His leadership and remember that He is the very best teacher and guide. He knows exactly how to cultivate growth in your life.

God, help me lean on Your guidance instead of my own understanding. Show me areas of my life that need to change, and I will follow Your instructions.

FEBRUARY 26

Gentle and Kind

If we freely admit our sins when his light uncovers them, he will be faithful to forgive us every time. God is just to forgive us our sins because of Christ, and he will continue to cleanse us from all unrighteousness.

1 JOHN 1:9 TPT

As followers of Jesus, it's important to understand the difference between conviction and condemnation. Conviction is from the Holy Spirit, while condemnation comes from the enemy. Conviction leads us to the grace and mercy of Jesus, while condemnation leads us to shame and a focus on self. Conviction is typically the result of a continuous work of God in our lives, and condemnation is an accusatory attack.

God is inherently gentle and kind. He is merciful and gracious. He is patient and long-suffering. His voice echoes each of those qualities perfectly. When He convicts you about a certain area of your life, His character will be on full display. The convicting voice of God is not harsh, critical, overbearing, or full of disappointment. When He brings conviction, He also brings love, mercy, and grace.

God, Your voice reflects Your character. Give me discernment to know when You are speaking to me. Keep me from following the voice of condemnation.

FEBRUARY 27

Seek with Purpose

"Seek first his kingdom, and his righteousness, and all these things will be given to you as well. Therefore do not worry about tomorrow, for tomorrow will worry about itself."

MATTHEW 6:33-34 NIV

God is always at work. Our faith is strengthened when we take the time to pay attention to what He is doing. His faithfulness does not depend on our ability to see what He is doing, yet He longs for us to join Him and be part of His great plan. If we are too busy managing our own lives, we won't notice the everyday miracles that are all around us. It takes intentionality and consistency to partner with God.

Each day, align your heart, mind, and spirit with what God is doing. Take time to purposefully seek Him and He will show you how to partner with what He is already doing. In order to do this, you'll need to set aside your own ambitions and plans. You'll need to deliberately look for God's hand at work instead of trying to coordinate your own success story. As you lay your independence aside, you'll find freedom in the understanding that you cannot do anything apart from Him anyway.

Lord, help me see what You are doing in the world. Remind me of Your faithfulness and show me how I can be part of Your work. I surrender to You and trust that Your plans are better than my own.

FEBRUARY 28

Every Storm

*"We do not know what to do,
but we are looking to you for help."*

2 Chronicles 20:12 NLT

When life is rocky and unsteady, God is faithful. When nothing seems to be going according to plan, God does not waver. When battles rage all around us, God is not dismayed. He does not look at the difficult parts of our lives and cower in fear. He does not see our failures and look at us with disappointment. In every season of the soul, when we wander into messes or create them on our own, God is steady and reliable.

God is with you in every storm you face. His power and provision are enough for you. He has promised not to abandon you, and His Word is dependable. On days when it feels like every part of your life is a battle, remember that the fight is not yours to struggle through. He has gone before you and He has promised to prepare a way for you. Even when you cannot see where the next step will lead, keep your eyes focused on the Lord. He will see you through.

Father, thank You for Your faithful presence in my life. I look to You for help, and I trust You to guide me. You have everything I need. Thank You for being my strength in times of trouble or uncertainty.

MARCH

MARCH 1

He Knows

Jesus reached out his hand and touched the leper and said, "Of course I want to heal you—be healed!" And instantly, all signs of leprosy disappeared!

MATTHEW 8:3 TPT

Jesus touched the leper before He healed him. This is an excellent picture of how Jesus knows our needs, and He meets us there. In a culture that ostracized the sick, He knew the man needed to be touched as much as He needed to be healed. Jesus is the same yesterday, today, and forever. If He understood and met the needs of people thousands of years ago, He can and will do the same today.

God created you in a specific way with specific needs. If you have a lack of healthy touch in your life, Jesus sees you. He is aware of your hurt and He has not abandoned you. Through His Spirit, He can reach the broken parts of your life and heal them with His touch. Through every season of your life, He is capable of compensating for whatever you are lacking.

God, You know exactly what I need. Thank You for seeing me and providing for me. Take the broken parts of my life and make them whole with Your miraculous touch.

MARCH 2

He Provides

As he was sleeping, an angel touched him and told him, "Get up and eat!" He looked around and there beside his head was some bread baked on hot stones and a jar of water! So he ate and drank and lay down again.

1 Kings 19:5-6 NLT

The prophet Elijah was burnt out and tired. He was exhausted to the point that he was ready to die. He called out to God in desperation, and God heard him. He brought Elijah to a hidden place, and He provided for him in an intimate and caring way. God knew exactly what Elijah needed to keep going. He didn't tell him to get over his frustrations, and He didn't ask him to grit his teeth and muster up the strength to go on. Instead, God protected him and provided for him.

Give God the opportunity to meet you in a new way. His gentleness may surprise you. Sometimes, God will change your circumstances, and sometimes, He will give you exactly what you need to walk through them with strength and dignity. You can trust Him to equip you perfectly. No matter what you are facing, running to Him for help is always the right decision.

God, nothing is beyond Your ability. You see my exact situation, and You know precisely what I need. Thank You for faithfully providing for me through every season.

MARCH 3

Ever-present

*I took my troubles to the L*ORD*;*
I cried out to him, and he answered my prayer.

PSALM 120:1 NLT

God's attentiveness does not depend on us having the right approach. He doesn't choose whether or not to listen to us depending on our emotions or tone of voice. Even when we complain, God hears us. He is not intimidated by our feelings, and He is not dismayed by our frustrations. When we feel helpless and alone, God is present. When we feel like no one hears us, we can depend on the reliability of the Word. If we take our troubles to the Lord, He will hear us.

There might be times in your life when other people don't receive you the way you'd like. People don't always react the right way, and we often misunderstand each other. You can't control the way other people perceive you or how well they listen. Even when you are let down by the actions or reactions of others, you can depend on God's unchanging character. He will always hear you perfectly when you call out to Him. He hears you; He sees you, and He loves you.

Father, You are my ever-present help in times of need. I can rely on You because You never change. Thank You for hearing me when I call. Thank You for seeing me clearly even when others don't.

MARCH 4

Lasting Impact

> Look with wonder at the depth of the Father's marvelous love that he has lavished on us! He has called us and made us his very own beloved children.
>
> 1 JOHN 3:1 TPT

Our hard work doesn't draw God any closer to us, and our lack of hard work doesn't push Him away from us. Especially for those of us who are prone to overvalue productivity and performance, this can be a difficult truth to grasp. When we create our own definition of success and elevate the importance of results, we will struggle to understand the unconditional and unchanging love of God. His love for us has nothing to do with the way we perform.

It is good to develop a strong work ethic, but not every moment of your life needs to be consumed by productivity. In fact, lasting kingdom impact will not happen if you are burnt out and exhausted. Good work is meant to be a result of the abundant grace you've been given, not a means to earn God's favor or attention. While your work is probably great, it is not what catches God's eye. He looks at you with great affection simply because you are His child.

Lord, I want to have a lasting impact for Your kingdom. May Your love be the foundation for everything I do. Keep me from focusing so much on my own work that I forget to operate from a place of abundant grace.

MARCH 5

Truly Blessed

*"May the Lord bless you and protect you.
May the Lord smile on you and be gracious to you.
May the Lord show you his favor and give you peace."*

NUMBERS 6:24-26 NLT

God longs to bless His children. Scripture is clear that He loves to give us good gifts. This doesn't necessarily mean our lives will be overflowing with money or resources. Instead, God's blessings come from His outpouring of mercy and grace. He gives us favor and freedom from the inside out. We are cherished, noticed, and made whole because of who our good Father is.

The desire to be blessed is not about what you have. It's about understanding who you are and to whom you belong. When you are confident in your standing before God, you will not be ashamed or embarrassed to ask for His blessing. You will boldly approach His throne because you know what He has already promised you. You are His beloved child, and you are worth all the love and blessings He is capable of giving you.

God, I long for Your blessings. Forgive me for the times that I have wrongly expected material gain. Help me see that Your blessings go beyond anything I can hold in my hands.

MARCH 6

Warning Signs

*"I will be your God throughout your lifetime—
until your hair is white with age.
I made you, and I will care for you.
I will carry you along and save you."*

ISAIAH 46:4 NLT

When we are on a path toward sin, the warning signs might seem small or insignificant. If we aren't paying attention to God, it becomes easy to ignore those small warnings. If we ignore them, we will later ache for the security we passed up. Despite our hesitancy to fully trust God as our guide, He knows what is coming. He knows the obstacles we will face long before we can see them. As we trust Him and allow Him to help us navigate, we will stay safely on the path He has for us.

Only God can rescue you from the reality of your sin. Everyone is prone to drifting toward sin. This truth isn't meant to create shame. Rather, let it stir up diligence and mindfulness in your life. Following God's promptings takes wisdom and humility. If you allow Him to, God will keep you steady because He knows you better than anyone else. He knows your weaknesses and temptations. He knows what is best for you, and He is fully able to lead you toward it.

God, soften my heart and help me see the warning signs You give me. Give me wisdom to follow Your instructions and courage to say no to temptation. Strengthen me when I am weak and guide me on the path to righteousness.

March 7

Chosen

You are a chosen people, a royal priesthood, a holy nation, God's special possession, that you may declare the praises of him who called you out of darkness into his wonderful light.

1 Peter 2:9 NIV

Most of us have experienced rejection or the pain of waiting to be chosen. From the classic example of being picked last in gym class to the heartache of experiencing rejection in our personal lives, the desire to be chosen is universal. The need to be wanted is felt so profoundly because we were created by a God who pursues His children. Our need for belonging can only be truly satisfied in Him.

The way you view God and the way you view yourself can impact every area of your life. When truth is rooted in your heart, it can shape your very identity. Your desire to be chosen and noticed is not needy or weak. It comes directly from being formed by a God who consistently declares that you are His. He sees you; He loves you, and He longs for your heart to be at home in His presence.

Lord, thank You for choosing me. The deepest desires of my heart are satisfied in Your presence. Thank You for seeing me, knowing me, and loving me so perfectly.

MARCH 8

Sacrificial Love

*"Love each other. Just as I have loved you,
you should love each other."*

John 13:34 NLT

There are no prerequisites to being included in Jesus' inner circle. He did not sacrifice His life for a specific group of people or for those who meet certain requirements. All are welcome at His table. Not only does He love those who are hurting and ignored, He searches for them. When He walked the earth, He consistently went out of His way to notice people who were overlooked by the rest of society. If we want to follow His example, we can't ignore the calling to care for people who are hurting, broken, and messy.

You are called to go into dark places and carry the light of Christ. Displaying Christ's sacrificial love is the highest calling you have. Following Jesus isn't about your own desires, comfort, or reputation. Bringing people into God's family and accepting them despite what they look like is holy work. There is great reward in loving others the way Jesus has loved you. Even when the personal cost is great, loving others sacrificially is the way of Christ.

Jesus, teach me how to be like You. Help me lay my life down for others just as You laid Your life down for me. Fill me with compassion and teach me how to love even when the cost is great.

MARCH 9

Original Love

We love because he first loved us.

1 JOHN 4:19 CSB

A good father pursues his children. A good father notices the actions, emotions, and intentions of his child. He sees fully, and he pursues sacrificially. A good father doesn't wait for his child to show him love before he is willing to. God is a good Father. The only reason we can love Him so freely is because He loved us first.

You are a daughter of the King. He has pursued you, and He wants a relationship with you. He doesn't love you because He is obligated to, and He doesn't love you for personal gain. You do not need to chase Him down, and He is certainly not hiding from you. His love for you is greater than you can understand. His entire plan for creation is centered around the redemption of His people unto Himself. Loving you was His idea, and He's not going to give up on it.

God, thank You for Your unending love. When my faith falters, remind me of Your great love for me. Thank You for redeeming me and calling me Your own.

MARCH 10

No Rivals

God created man and woman and shaped them with his image inside them.
In his own beautiful image, he created his masterpiece.

Genesis 1:27 tpt

If pressed, some of us may struggle to list our best qualities. We live in a society that focuses on outward appearance and glorifies a specific version of perfection. We know in theory that we are good enough, but culturally, we are surrounded by unachievable standards. It can be difficult to maintain a positive self-image when we are bombarded with messages that say we just don't measure up.

You are made in God's image. There is nothing in creation that is equal to you in God's eyes. You are His workmanship and His greatest masterpiece. Everything else will fade away, but you have been made to live with Him for eternity. He places more value on you than on anything else. As a result, you do not have to compete for His affection. From God's perspective, nothing in all of creation compares to His children.

God, give me a greater understanding of how You see me. Thank You for making me in Your image. When I view myself in a negative light, give me Your perspective.

MARCH 11

He Sees

> "Never forget that I am with you every day, even to the completion of this age."
>
> MATTHEW 28:20 TPT

Life contains suffering that cannot always be avoided. When we choose to follow God, we are not promised a reprieve from pain, but we are promised a constant companion. God does not leave us alone in our deepest hurts. He is always present and willing to guide us through them. He leads us, and He heals the parts of our hearts that seem impossibly broken.

God sees your pain, and He longs to comfort you. He sees your hurts, and He promises to stay close to you. You have the opportunity to let the difficulties of life shut you down or draw you closer to God. When you let Him heal you, you open the door to be used in the lives of others who need healing. There is no need for you to be satisfied with the brokenness in your life when God offers to restore the ruins.

God, You see my pain, and You promise to comfort me. When I am hurting, keep me from running further away from You. Draw me close and keep me safe. I trust You to heal me in Your perfect timing.

MARCH 12

He Heals

He forgives all my sins
and heals all my diseases.
He redeems me from death
and crowns me with love and tender mercies.

PSALM 103:2-5 NLT

Sometimes, our bodies hold onto stress in ways we don't understand. Prolonged periods of difficulty or trauma can produce long-term problems. Some of us are dealing with physical ailments, and some of us are facing physical symptoms of spiritual or emotional distress. Either way, God's presence in our lives is not limited to our hearts. He wants to heal our bodies as well. Whether we experience healing now or in the age to come, full restoration is promised.

There may be times in your life when you experience miraculous healing. There may also be times when God wisely guides you on a path that leads to healing. This could be through the help of medical intervention or through personal discipline. No matter what healing looks like in your life, God is worthy of your praise. He is not limited to your expectations or preferences. He is good even when His timeline doesn't look like yours.

Lord, You are my healer and my deliverer. I trust Your guidance, and I believe You can heal me. Increase my faith and help me lean on You through every trial I face.

MARCH 13

On His Terms

The LORD scattered them all over the world, and they stopped building the city. That is why the city was called Babel, because that is where the LORD confused the people with different languages.

GENESIS 11:8-9 NLT

If we don't follow God's plans, our success will be temporary. Inevitably, the kingdoms we build on our own will crumble. We can learn from the example of the tower of Babel. Man was desperately searching for a way to get to God. Instead of trusting that God Himself would make a way, they took matters into their own hands. While their intention was good, their mistake was trying to interact with God on their own terms.

You were made to respond to God. You don't need to force His hand or micromanage His plans. Instead, your responsibility is to trust His sovereignty. He is the one who will bring His promises to fruition. He is the one who will lead you on the right path. His greatest goal for your life is for you to be in a consistent relationship with Him. He has already made the necessary provisions for that to happen. Lean on His understanding and trust that He has your life perfectly ordered.

God, Your ways are higher than mine. Help me to acknowledge Your greatness in all that I do. When I am tempted to go my own way, remind me of the perfection of Your plans.

MARCH 14

Grace Over Perfection

*Who could ever find a wife like this one—
she is a woman of strength and mighty valor!
She's full of wealth and wisdom.*

Proverbs 31:10 TPT

While many people hold Proverbs 31 as the ultimate standard for womanhood, it's important to explore it with context in mind. It's possible that it was inspired by a woman who was counseling her son as he entered adulthood. She was telling him the type of woman that he should search for as a wife. Of course, any mother wants what is best and hopes that her son will choose wisely. This doesn't necessarily mean that Proverbs 31 is a standard women should be held to as a whole.

As a woman, you may have felt like you just don't measure up. If you have held yourself to an impossible standard, then you likely feel weary and overwhelmed. While it is good to strive for excellence and to develop a good character, your identity cannot be wrapped up in the opinions of other people. It's more important that you emulate the God of the Bible over the people of the Bible. The idea that you can never live up to the woman portrayed in Proverbs 31 should be traded for a deeper understanding of grace.

Father, I submit my definition of womanhood to You. Help me live by Your standards and not my own ideas of perfection. I trust You to guide me and transform me into the woman You've created me to be.

MARCH 15

Furious Love

I have been crucified with Christ and I no longer live, but Christ lives in me.

GALATIANS 2:20 NIV

There is intense energy that happens at the beginning of a storm. A fury is the electrical charge you can feel in the air. Likewise, the furious love of God is the vitality, energy, and strength that is equated with God seeking a union with man. It's furious. It is incredible that the God of the universe wants to have covenant relationship with us. It's not just a union but an indwelling. God Himself is within us.

God, in all of His perfection, has made a way for you to be with Him. He does not turn you away on account of your sin or refuse to come close to you. He doesn't wait for you to get your life together. Instead, He offers you redemption and eternal life while you are in the midst of your sin. In His great and furious love, He seeks you out and gives you a new life through Christ.

God, thank You for Your furious love. Thank You for making a way for me to be with You for eternity. Thank You for the beauty of Your redemptive plan. I am in awe of the way You pursue me.

MARCH 16

As Jesus Sees

Together with Christ we are heirs of God's glory. But if we are to share his glory, we must also share his suffering. Yet what we suffer now is nothing compared to the glory he will reveal to us later.

ROMANS 8:17-18 NLT

The church doesn't always show up for the broken, but Jesus consistently does. Sometimes, it's easier to be judgmental or critical than to empathize or join others in their suffering. Yet, pain and suffering lead us to experience Jesus in a way that cannot be paralleled. Our lack of perfection is what led us to Christ in the first place, and our continuous acknowledgment of that lack is what keeps our hearts soft.

If you have become calloused toward the sins of others, it might be time for a change of heart. Don't shy away from the discomfort of sitting with others in their pain. The impact you can make in your community is directly correlated to your ability to see others as Jesus sees them. He does not look at a sinner and scorn or create shame. To share in the suffering of Christ is to lay your life down for people who don't deserve it. As you attempt to love in this way, He will equip and strengthen you.

Jesus, I want Your perspective of the broken. When I am tempted to shy away from discomfort, give me the grace to love as You love. Help me see others with compassion and tenderness instead of judgment or criticism.

MARCH 17

Good Father

Love is patient and kind. Love is not jealous or boastful or proud or rude. It does not demand its own way. It is not irritable, and it keeps no record of being wronged. It does not rejoice about injustice but rejoices whenever the truth wins out. Love never gives up, never loses faith, is always hopeful, and endures through every circumstance.

1 Corinthians 13:4-7 NLT

God's ability to be a good father goes beyond our human understanding of the role. He is a kind, attentive, and perfect Father. There is no flaw in His love. There is nothing selfish, manipulative, or lacking in the way He loves His children. Even when we miss the mark, He loves us. Even when we fail, He loves us. His love surpasses our ability to love Him back. This doesn't mean that He doesn't care what we do or how we behave. It simply means that His love isn't dependent on our actions.

God has loved you for your entire life. From the moment you were created, you have been on His mind. He will faithfully pursue you until your last breath. He isn't ashamed of you or disappointed in you. When you make mistakes, His love doesn't lessen. When you fail, His love isn't put on hold. Let His unfailing love transform you and seek to extend it to those around you.

Father, thank You for Your perfect love. Even when I fail, You are faithful. May Your love transform me and make me more like You.

MARCH 18

Every Nuance

*My health may fail, and my spirit may grow weak,
but God remains the strength of my heart;
he is mine forever.*

PSALM 73:26 NLT

A cluttered heart has the same negative impact as a cluttered home. It can cause tension and stress. If our hearts are cluttered, we won't experience the peace God has intended for us. The good news is that it isn't our job to decipher every single thing we carry with us. God is the strength of our hearts. He is our maker, and He knows us inside and out. It's easy to get caught up in treating ourselves like a problem to be solved, but this isn't how God sees us.

God understands every nuance that makes you who you are. He sees each of your days clearly, and He knows how every experience of your life fits together with the rest. He isn't surprised by the way you think or the burdens you carry. You are not broken beyond repair, and your mind is not a mess that He cannot untangle. He longs for you to experience His peace. As you surrender your anxieties to Him, He will lead you perfectly on the path to eternal life. You can trust His guidance implicitly.

Lord, thank You for seeing me. When I feel overwhelmed or misunderstood, help me turn to You. Your understanding is perfect, and Your peace is all-encompassing.

MARCH 19

How to Pray

"Father, hallowed be Your name.
Your kingdom come.
Give us each day our daily bread.
And forgive us our sins,
For we ourselves also forgive everyone who is indebted to us.
And do not lead us into temptation."

Luke 11:2-4 NASB

When we don't know what to pray, we can confidently rely on Christ's example. He approached God with reverence, familiarity, and expectancy. He acknowledged His position, declared His promises, and humbly asked for what He needed. If this is how Jesus prayed, we can do the same. When we are tired and overwhelmed, we can trust God to restore us. When we are burnt out and in need of a break, we can trust God to give us new life. When we are hurting and broken, we can trust Him to mend what is fractured.

When you are in need, run to the Father. Acknowledge that He is the one who made you, and He is the one who will faithfully care for you. The deliberate recognition of who He is will bolster your spirit and soften your heart. When you purposefully turn your heart toward Him, He will meet you with unending mercy and grace.

Jesus, thank You for the example of how to pray. May this truth be deeply rooted in my heart. In times of trouble, bring Your Word to the forefront of my mind.

MARCH 20

Abba Father

You have not received a spirit that makes you fearful slaves. Instead, you received God's Spirit when he adopted you as his own children. Now we call him, "Abba, Father."

ROMANS 8:15 NLT

The Hebrew word *abba* means daddy, papa, or dear father. Much like babies today typically say dada as their first word, children in biblical times would have said Abba. It's a term of affection and endearment meant for everyday use. When Paul referred to God as Abba, this would have been revolutionary. Understanding God as a dear father would have been completely countercultural to the way He had previously been understood. This shift in thinking would change the trajectory of how people interacted with God. It revealed to the listener that God wanted to abide with them.

Through Jesus, you have unlimited access to God. His death and resurrection have made a way for you to interact with Him in a close and personal way. He is your Father, and you are His child. He longs to be near you, and He wants you to know His heart. In times of trouble, He wants to help you. In times of great joy, He wants to celebrate with you. Like a good father wants to share the details of their children's lives, God wants to walk with you through every season.

Father, You are my strength and my provider. Thank You for being such a good Father. Help me see You rightly. In every season of the soul, help me turn toward You.

MARCH 21

The Love of Christ

Jesus stood up and looked at them and said, "Let's have the man who has never had a sinful desire throw the first stone at her." Upon hearing that, her accusers slowly left the crowd one at a time, beginning with the oldest to the youngest, with a convicted conscience.

JOHN 8:7,9 TPT

When we demand vindication, Jesus is an advocate for mercy. His love is attractive because it is different from what we see displayed every day. His love draws us in because it is inclusive, unwavering, and full of mercy and grace. He steadily loves those who we deem to be unlovable. His grace is free for all who turn to Him.

It's easy to look at the brokenness of others and recognize their need for mercy. It's important to recognize your own brokenness as well. When you fail to see yourself clearly, you are more likely to walk down a path of cynicism and shame. It's not your job to reveal the sins of others. Take the pressure off yourself and remember that your job is to share Christ's love with others. You don't have to make sure that every believer thinks and acts the right way. Instead of prioritizing behavior, prioritize healthy relationships that exemplify the love of Jesus.

Lord, forgive me for the times I have tried to change hearts. I surrender my desire for control to You, and I trust Your love to do what I cannot. Instead of being cynical, help me reveal Your love and grace to those who need it most.

MARCH 22

Embrace Grief

Take a new grip with your tired hands and strengthen your weak knees.

HEBREWS 12:12 NLT

When we grieve, we aren't supposed to pretend everything is fine. We don't have to stifle our emotions and continue to go on with our lives. God meets us when we are vulnerable, and He comforts us when we are weak. There are certain aspects of His character that can only be found in the place of suffering. When we call out to Him in our pain, He often validates us and strengthens us to move forward. He doesn't ignore our pain, but He often lifts us up in spite of it.

Multiple emotions can exist simultaneously without negating the value of the other. Just as the rain and the sun can both be present at the same time, so can grief and strength co-exist. You can lean on God for strength in the midst of great pain. Trusting Him to lead you doesn't take away from the reality of your hurt. When you are tempted to bury your pain, cry out to God. Experience the comfort of the Holy Spirit and let Him give you what you need to move forward.

God, thank You for leading me through painful seasons. Help me process my emotions in a healthy way. I surrender my heart fully to You. Fill me with hope as I grieve or experience disappointment.

MARCH 23

In the Midst

Crowds of sick people—blind, lame, or paralyzed—lay on the porches. One of the men lying there had been sick for thirty-eight years. When Jesus saw him and knew he had been ill for a long time, he asked him, "Would you like to get well?"

JOHN 5:3-6 NLT

Even though there was a large crowd of people, Jesus knew exactly who to help. He saw the man's need, and He met him in his brokenness. Jesus is capable of seeing us in the midst of a multitude of suffering. His love is big enough to notice and heal each individual person according to their needs. He is not limited in the same ways we are. His attention is not focused in one direction at a time.

You are not a burden to Jesus. He sees your hurts. He sees your pain, and He is capable of healing you. Don't hesitate to tell Him about your wounds. Don't diminish your needs simply because there are many needs all around you. Jesus is not limited, and He does not triage His children. You are important to Him, and He longs for you to depend on His strength.

Jesus, thank You for seeing me in the midst of a broken world. Your eyes are on each of Your children, and I am thankful for Your ability to heal me. Take the broken parts of my life and make them whole.

MARCH 24

God Knows

*O Lord, you have examined my heart
and you know everything about me.
You know when I sit down or stand up.
You know my thoughts even when I'm far away.*

Psalm 139:1-2 NLT

Each of us gives and receives love differently. There are aspects of our relationship with God that come naturally to us, and there are parts of His character that are more difficult to understand. Some of us feel completely comfortable relating to Him as our father, while others might really struggle with the concept. Some of us delight in His friendship, while some of us are more comfortable thinking of Him as our King. Throughout our lives, we will likely walk through seasons where certain parts of His character are highlighted to us in different ways.

God made you in a specific way. You can trust that He knows the ins and outs of your heart. He knows what you need, and He knows how to love you in a way that makes sense to you. You have your whole life to explore the totality of His character. Whatever season you are in, whether you feel His great affection for you or you are relying on a foundation of truth, remember that His love is big enough to cover your lack of understanding.

God, thank You for Your all-encompassing love. Show me more of who You are. Broaden my perspective of Your character and strengthen my faith.

MARCH 25

Look for Jesus

All Scripture is inspired by God and is useful to teach us what is true.

2 TIMOTHY 3:16 NLT

When reading Scripture, we can look and listen for Jesus. There is a foretelling of the Messiah in the book of Psalms. Throughout each chapter, we see God's promises laid out and His character put on display. We can be encouraged by the way the author's humanity shines through and is always met by the faithfulness of God. We can relate to the troubles the writer describes, and we can find solace in the steadiness of God.

When your wisdom fails, turn to the Word. As you read the Psalms, you'll see Jesus in potentially unexpected places. Through each poem, song, or lament, you can see how God's presence does not fail. If He was with David, Solomon, or Asaph through the most tumultuous times of their lives, He will be with you as well. His faithfulness is the same yesterday, today, and forever. You can lean on His promises and find solace in His presence.

Lord, fill me with affection for Your Word. As I read the Psalms, help me to see Jesus. Thank You for revealing Your redemptive plan long before it even took place.

MARCH 26

Daily Influence

Oh, the joys of those who do not
follow the advice of the wicked,
or stand around with sinners,
or join in with mockers.
But they delight in the law of the LORD,
meditating on it day and night.

PSALM 1:1-2 NLT

As we seek to honor God in every area of our lives, it's important to pay attention to our greatest influences. We shouldn't allow ourselves to be swayed by social media, the news, or a convincing friend without measuring our information against God's standard. His Word and voice are meant to be our constant source of wisdom and guidance. When we turn to other sources to help navigate the world, we will come up short.

In today's culture, there isn't a lack of information or content to absorb. You are influenced daily by the things you see, read, and hear. Do the hard work of testing your sources. Are you swayed by the passion of others regardless of their validity? Do your best to weigh what you hear against the Word. Listen for the voice of God as you navigate your days. As you cultivate a deeper relationship with Him, you'll become more sensitive to the guidance of the Holy Spirit.

God, I surrender my heart to You. I trust You to transform me into Your likeness. Show me what or who has the greatest influence in my life. May Your Word take its rightful place in my life.

MARCH 27

On the Throne

> Why are the nations restless
> And the peoples plotting in vain?
> The kings of the earth take their stand
> and the rulers conspire together
> against the Lord.
>
> Psalm 2:1-2 nasb

Even in biblical times, there was political unrest. While it seems like the world is filled with conflict, it's important to remember that this isn't new. History has always been tumultuous and filled with the uproar of the nations. Kingdoms rise and fall, and leaders rally together to fight their enemies. No matter what the political landscape looks like, Jesus is our one true King. His ways are far above ours, and He will be victorious in the end.

When you are tempted to be swept away by the political fervor of the day, remember that Jesus sits securely on His throne. Since His ascension, He has remained at His Father's side in the height of the Heavens. The Bible is filled with prophecies of His Kingship, and one day, He will return to make all things right. Even when it seems like things can't get any worse, you can trust that no one can overturn the plans of God. Jesus will rule and reign.

Lord, thank You for being steady even when the world is raging. You are the one true King who is worthy of all my praise. When I am tempted to worry or despair over the state of the world, help me to trust in Your faithfulness above all else.

MARCH 28

Impossible Trials

> O Lord, I have so many enemies;
> so many are against me.
> So many are saying,
> "God will never rescue him!"
> But you, O Lord, are a shield around me.
>
> PSALM 3:1-3 NLT

Throughout the Psalms, we see David lamenting to God. He's taking his grief and offering it to the Lord. When we lament, we admit our weakness and depend on God's strength. We recognize that we don't know how to handle the situation we are facing, and we cry out to our Maker for support and encouragement. When we go to God in our heartbreak, grief, and sorrow, we create an opportunity for God to display His faithfulness.

At some point in your life, you will face an impossible trial. You will experience pain you didn't think was possible, or you will face a problem that seems like it cannot be solved. In those humbling moments, God's presence is what you need most. He wants you to cry out to Him and ask for help. He wants to step in and rescue you in your time of need. He promises to be with you in your deepest sorrow.

Lord, You don't despair over the trials I face. Thank You for giving me peace when I bring my troubles to You. Give me the grace to continue trusting in You even when I don't understand what I am going through.

MARCH 29

Trust Grows

*Answer me when I call to you,
my righteous God.
Give me relief from my distress;
have mercy on me and hear my prayer.*

PSALM 4:1 NIV

The unpredictability of life insists that we are in constant communion with God. If we only run to Him when difficult things happen, we rob ourselves of the fullness of His goodness. When we cultivate a consistent relationship with Him, we set ourselves up for success. Trials are inevitable, but God's faithfulness is unchanging. If we spend time cultivating intimacy with our Creator, we will be able to hear Him clearly when it matters most.

When you spend time building a deep relationship with God, your trust in Him will grow. The more you trust Him, the steadier you will be when life doesn't meet your expectations. Even when you experience grief, suffering, or frustration, you will have an unwavering familiarity with God's voice. You will be able to depend on what you know is true because you have built up equity in your relationship with Him.

God, help me to trust You more today than I did yesterday. Thank You for being steady and unwavering in every circumstance. Increase my faith as I lean on You for strength.

MARCH 30

Each Morning

*At each and every sunrise you will hear my voice
as I prepare my sacrifice of prayer to you.
Every morning I lay out the pieces of my life on the altar
and wait for your fire to fall upon my heart.*

PSALM 5:3 TPT

From David, we learn that not only should we engage in prayer each morning, but we should also develop a continuous lifestyle of communion with God. We are meant to start our day with our eyes on the Lord and stay engaged throughout the day. It takes practice to cultivate the discipline of focus. Our schedules fill up quickly, and life can easily become consumed by our own to-do list. It helps to start our day on the right trajectory. When we posture ourselves before the Lord in the morning, we are more likely to maintain that path throughout the day.

Each morning, you have the opportunity to engage with God. Pour your heart out to Him and wait with expectation. Renew your dedication to Him and remind yourself of what is most important. Take the time to talk to Him and wait for His response. This doesn't have to be long, drawn out, or formal. Starting your day in God's presence can be a short practice. He can show up no matter how limited your time is.

Lord, thank You for the opportunity to pursue You in the morning. Give me the grace to start each day in Your presence. When I am tempted to put something else first, help me prioritize time with You.

MARCH 31

Blessed to Be Weak

Have mercy on me, Lord, for I am faint;
Heal me, Lord, for my bones are in agony.
My soul is in deep anguish.

Psalm 6:2-3 NIV

Psalm 6 is a penitential psalm. David is expressing sorrow or severe regret over his sin. He comes to God and is heartbroken over what he has done. Most of us can relate to David's display of emotion because we know what it feels like to regret our actions. It's normal to experience feelings of shame and to wish we could go back in time and behave differently. While we might have a tendency to hide or try to cover up our sin, we must remember that God is already aware of our mistakes, past, present, and future.

God sees every wrong turn you take. He is not disillusioned as to how you will behave. He knows your flaws, and His love is enough to cover all of them. Your mistakes can be an opportunity to draw closer to God. Without weakness, you wouldn't have a need for His great strength. Like David, you can humbly bring Him your mistakes and trust Him to guide you as you repent. Even when the process of healing from sin is uncomfortable or painful, God is merciful and faithful to lead you toward freedom.

God, change my perspective on weakness. Help me see mistakes as an opportunity to grow closer to You. Thank You for Your unending mercy and kindness in the face of my failures.

APRIL

APRIL 1

Faithful Rescuer

YAHWEH, my God, I turn to hide my soul in you.
Save me from all those who pursue and persecute me.
There is none to deliver me but you.
Don't let my foes fall upon me
like fierce lions with teeth barred.

PSALM 7:1-2 TPT

Most of us have experienced a spiritual battle of some sort. We can use David's account in Psalm 7 as an example of how to pray in difficult situations. We can see how surrender during times of unrest can lead us to deeper intimacy with the Lord. As we take refuge in God, He leads us to places of peace. When it feels like there is a battle raging within, God desires to be a source of safety and renewal.

It's important to remember that you are in a war. There is a battle for your soul, and your enemy hates you. He wants you to feel defeated and overwhelmed. Satan's constant desire is to tear you apart like a lion. Because of this, it is always right to pray for rescue from him. You can ask God for help and protection and be confident of His faithfulness to you. Scripture is clear that those who serve and love God can expect Him to rescue them in times of trouble.

God, thank You for being my shield and my protector. Teach me how to run to You at the first sign of trouble. In times of difficulty, You are all I need. Open my eyes to see the battle I am in and give me the strength I need to endure it.

APRIL 2

Mindful of You

*When I look at the night sky
and see the work of your fingers—
the moon and the stars you set in place—
what are mere mortals that you should think about them,
human beings that you should care for them?*

PSALM 8:3-4 NLT

Sometimes we don't fully understand Scripture as it was originally written. The idea that God was mindful of people was revolutionary. The dignity of human beings is stressed in this passage in a way that was unparalleled in Ancient Near Eastern culture. Most people would have understood that they were created for the benefit of whatever god or goddess they served. To be told that the one true God loved them and was mindful of them would have been countercultural.

You are a delight to God. He doesn't love you because of what you have to offer Him. He didn't create you for a utilitarian purpose or because of how you can benefit Him. His love for you is based solely on the fact that you are His child. He sees value in who you are regardless of your weaknesses and shortcomings. God's love for you is steady and reliable when you are at your best and your worst. You are not expendable to Him, and you are not overlooked by Him. In all of creation, you are His most precious possession.

God, thank You for loving me and being mindful of me. Help me see myself the way You do. Remind me of my value and help me find my identity in being Your child.

APRIL 3

All Your Heart

> I will praise you, Lord, with all my heart;
> I will tell of all the marvelous things you have done.
> I will be filled with joy because of you.
> I will sing praises to your name, O Most High.
>
> Psalm 9:1-2 NLT

From beginning to end, Scripture is full of examples of what it looks like to offer our praises to the one who made us. God's children are called to worship. Everything He has created shows His glory and that He is worthy of our praise. There are different methods of praise, and there isn't an exact formula we must follow. We are not limited to our location or our circumstances. Praise can and should be integrated into our daily lives.

When you are consistently aware of God's presence in your life, the natural response is praise and adoration. As you take notice of His unwavering care and provision, both physically and spiritually, praise will be an overflow of your heart. He cares for you, you respond with worship, and He fills your heart with peace and joy. This is one of the many promises you have as a believer. When you turn your heart toward Him, He will not let you down.

God, You are worthy of all my praise. Give me awareness of how You are moving in my life. As I see Your character revealed, stir my heart to worship You.

APRIL 4

Always Good

Why, Lord, do you stand far off?
Why do you hide yourself in times of trouble?

PSALM 10:1 NIV

Praying through Scripture can alleviate tension when it comes to situations we don't understand. Psalm 10 is a heart cry in the midst of injustice. Sometimes, it's difficult to understand why God is delaying His hand of justice. When we see people suffering, it can be hard to maintain the right perspective. We want to see situations resolved in our timing and in a way we can understand. When we can't make sense of how God moves, it can be tempting to question His goodness.

God will be faithful to His children. He promises that perfect judgment is coming, and you can rely on what He says. You might not understand His timing, but you can echo the psalmist's prayer while still trusting in God's faithfulness. You can have confidence that He will deal with every injustice, no matter how big or small. When other believers experience hardship, God is faithful. When the wicked prosper, He is still sovereign. As you wait for God's perfect plan to unfold, you can remain steady and at peace, knowing that He is in control.

God, change my perspective to match Yours. When I am overwhelmed by injustice, help me trust in Your sovereignty. You grieve alongside me when suffering is too much to bear. I trust You to intervene at exactly the right time.

APRIL 5

In His Temple

*The LORD is in his holy Temple;
the LORD still rules from heaven.
He watches everyone closely,
examining every person on earth.*

PSALM 11:4 NLT

If the approval of others is our top priority, we will never reach our goal. We cannot possibly keep up with the world when the definition of truth and goodness isn't based on the firm foundation of God's Word. In Psalm 11, we see that God is always on the throne, no matter what is going on around us. Despite the ever-changing dynamics of our culture, God remains unchanging in His temple. He rules with goodness and mercy no matter what the kingdoms on earth look like.

In the midst of cultural chaos, God is steady. The foundations of society might crumble, but God cannot be shaken. When you find yourself in a place of uncertainty, you can find solace in the certainty of His promises. When you are tempted to compromise biblical principles in light of societal pressure, keep your eyes on Jesus, and He will strengthen you. He will enable you to walk on godly paths even when it's not the popular choice.

God, You are on the throne even when the foundations of society are crumbling. Thank You for Your consistent presence. Help me lean into You when I am overwhelmed by what is going on around me.

APRIL 6

Tested and Flawless

For every word Yahweh speaks is sure and reliable.
His truth is tested, found to be flawless, and ever faithful.
It's as pure as silver refined seven times in a crucible of clay.

PSALM 12:6 TPT

God's Word is tested and tried. When Psalm 12 says that it has been refined seven times in a crucible of clay, it means that it has been purified several times. A crucible of clay is not the same thing as a fireplace or an oven as we know it. In ancient times, a crucible would have been placed in a fire that reached temperatures far above what we are used to. Anything that has been refined in a crucible and brought out is proven to be able to withstand the harshest of circumstances. In a similar way, God's Word is flawless, faithful, and enduring.

It's easy to feel hopeless when you look at everything that's happening in the world. Instead of giving in to those feelings, lean into Scripture. Remember that as the weak are oppressed and the needy groan, God arises and promises protection. You can call out to Him, trusting that He will defend His children and keep His promises. When circumstances seem insurmountable, trust in the tested, flawless, and faithful Word of God.

God, Your Word is always trustworthy. Fill my mind with truth and teach me how to rely upon it in times of uncertainty. Instead of feeling helpless, I cling to what You say is true.

APRIL 7

On Dark Days

I'm hurting, Lord—will you forget me forever?
How much longer, Lord?
Will you look the other way when I'm in need?
How much longer must I cling to this constant grief?

PSALM 13:1-2 TPT

While our range of emotions is vast, there are certain feelings we don't talk about as freely as others. Even though certain things are common to the human experience, we often compartmentalize our feelings into categories of good and bad. When it comes to hopelessness or depression, it's important to remember that we are not alone, no matter how unspoken our thoughts and feelings are. Even when it seems we are lost in the depths of sorrow, God is near to us.

God offers you peace in the midst of your physical and emotional storms. He might not answer your prayers quickly, but that doesn't mean they go unheard. If you experience a delay in response, it does not mean He has abandoned you. Instead, trust that He is capable of weaving together every detail of your life. His plans may be beyond your understanding, but He knows exactly how and when to unveil them to you.

God, You are sovereign even on my darkest days. When I feel hopeless, help me trust in You. Your plans are greater than mine, and I know You will provide for me.

APRIL 8

Perfect Perception

The LORD looks down from heaven on all mankind to see if there are any who understand, any who seek God.

PSALM 14:2 NIV

The Lord looks down on us from heaven, and His vantage point is ideal. He sees each of us physically, spiritually, and emotionally. His vision is clear, and He cannot be fooled. He knows the deepest corners of our hearts, and He understands our thoughts and intentions. He knows all that we lack, and He rescues us from the sin that keeps us from being close to Him. Without Him, we would be foolish and lost.

Instead of leaving you to the consequences of your sin, God graciously offers you freedom you do not deserve. He sees the worst of you and still pursues you because of His great love for you. Through Jesus, He offers you salvation, redemption, and eternal life. He longs for you to turn your heart toward Him, no matter what state it's in. Christ's perfection and lack of sin has paid the price for you to have community with God in this life and beyond.

God, I would be lost without You. Thank You for redeeming me. You see me exactly as I am, yet You love me anyway. Thank You for the gift of mercy through Jesus.

APRIL 9

Who Is Worthy?

*Who may worship in your sanctuary, LORD?
Who may enter your presence on your holy hill?
Those who lead blameless lives and do what is right,
speaking the truth from sincere hearts.*

PSALM 15:1-2 NLT

In the Old Testament, the space surrounding God's temple was sacred. Anyone entering that space was required to be ceremonially clean. God is perfect, and anyone entering His presence must also be perfect. We know that none of us meet that requirement. We are not worthy of dwelling in the sacred space where God is.

While you might not be familiar with Old Testament practices, you probably have your own internal list of rules you follow. You might consider yourself a failure or success based on your ability to meet those standards. Remember that God's standard for perfection can only be met by Jesus. He is the only one who can give you access to the sacred presence of God. When you are tempted to work for God's approval, remember that Christ's death and resurrection have already made a way.

God, keep me from relying on my own perfection. Soften my heart and draw me close to You. Help me follow Your ways and trust in Christ's righteousness.

APRIL 10

Any Good Thing

I said to Yahweh, "You are my Maker and my Master. Any good thing you find in me has come from you."

Psalm 16:2 tpt

There is no meaning in life apart from a relationship with God. Separated from Him, we have nothing. Without His presence and blessing, nothing in this life is going to truly satisfy us. Even if we think we've curated our own joy, it will be temporary at best. Our treasures will fade, and our manufactured security cannot last for eternity.

As you read Psalm 16, you can echo David's prayer. He declares that he will have nothing to do with the false gods of the age. Instead, he pledges his allegiance to his Maker and Master. He acknowledges God's role in his life, and he recognizes everything He has done. Today, you can do the same. Remember God's faithfulness and determine in your heart to offer Him everything you have. Surrender areas of your life where you've sought your own satisfaction and acknowledge the one true God as the source of every good thing.

God, You are all I need. Fill me with a greater desire to be close to You. As I turn to You, help me walk in Your ways.

APRIL 11

Test and Examine

*Let my vindication come from you,
for you see what is right.
You have tested my heart;
you have examined me at night.*

PSALM 17:2-3 CSB

Sometimes, sin keeps us from hearing God clearly. When we have deliberately chosen to disobey Him, it is difficult to remain soft and responsive to His voice. In our stubbornness, we close ourselves off from the goodness He offers. We wrongly assume that we know best, and we forget that His ways are always higher and better than our own. When we look to ourselves or others for guidance rather than Him, we will always come up short.

David knew that God heard the righteous, and he wanted God to make sure his heart was in the right place. He didn't want anything to get in the way of his communion with God. You can follow his example and invite God to test and examine your heart. The more you look to Him for guidance, the more you will recognize His voice as He teaches and leads you. If you let Him, God will faithfully keep you on the right path.

God, I need Your guidance in my life. Search my heart and show me if there is anything in it that isn't right. Help me stay humble and responsive to Your Word.

APRIL 12

Boast in Him

*I called on the L ORD, who is worthy of praise,
and he saved me from my enemies.*

P SALM 18:3 NLT

In ancient times, a victorious king would likely boast about himself. He would take credit when he won, and he would brag about his skills as a warrior and ruler. This is why David's response after being delivered from his enemies was atypical. He didn't boast about his own accomplishments. Instead, he gave all the acknowledgment to Yahweh. David was aware of his debt to God, and he refused to elevate himself above the one true King.

Surely, there are many wonderful things about you. You have skills, talents, and gifts that make you special. Even so, the credit belongs to God. Each of your victories, whether big or small, comes from the hands of your generous Creator. He is the one who saves you from your enemies and is worthy of your praise. He is the one who has faithfully led you for all your days. When you are tempted to boast in yourself, call upon God and acknowledge Him as the victorious one.

God, I give You all the glory. Keep my heart soft and protect me from pride. I praise You and give You all the credit! My victories come only from You.

APRIL 13

Craftsmanship Displayed

The heavens proclaim the glory of God.
The skies display his craftsmanship.
Day after day they continue to speak;
Night after night they make him known.

PSALM 19:1 NLT

Nature reveals God's glory. It's easy to look at something and notice it is beautiful, but it takes deliberate intention to attribute that beauty to God. He created the world with a natural order, and the way everything is interwoven teaches us about His character. As we observe His craftmanship, we can turn our hearts toward Him in worship. Everything He has made declares His goodness, creativity, and sovereignty.

When David gave credit to God for holding the natural world together, he was making claims that were contrary to the common belief of the time. His declaration would have been inflammatory to the cultures around him who believed that various gods and goddesses had dominion over the earth. You can also declare God's goodness in a way that is countercultural. You can give Him credit for the majesty of creation when the world around you tries its best to keep God out of it.

God, thank You for the beautiful world around me. Thank You for how Your character is interwoven in every detail of creation. I give You glory for all You've done! Help me declare Your majesty even when the world disagrees.

APRIL 14

Misplaced Trust

*Some trust in chariots and some in horses,
but we trust in the name of the Lord our God.*

PSALM 20:7 NIV

Psalm 20 is a prayer spoken before going into battle. David declares that while some kings might trust in chariots and horses, he chooses to trust in God. While some might trust in their physical assets, David trusts in the name of the Lord. He knows that God is the one who declares victory over his enemies. God is capable of winning a battle despite the tactical advantages of one side over the other.

It is tempting to use physical circumstances as a gauge for comfort and security. If your bank account is at a certain level, you feel financially safe. If your job is going smoothly, you feel secure in your career. If your kids are well-behaved, you feel successful as a parent. The reality is that your security comes only from God. He is the only one who can guarantee your safety. He is sovereign over each of your days, and He holds your life securely in His hands. Follow David's example and place your trust in God no matter what your physical circumstances look like.

God, I trust You above all else. When I begin to trust in my circumstances, turn my heart back to You. You are the one who holds everything together. Thank You for being my source of protection and security.

APRIL 15

He Fights for You

The king trusts in Yahweh,
And he will never stumble, never fall.
The forever-love of the Most high holds him firm.
Your mighty hands have captured your foes.

PSALM 21:7-8 TPT

Psalm 21 is a prayer of thanksgiving after a victorious battle. The psalmist displays an overwhelming sense of gratitude for who God is and the way He delivered them through difficulty. His prayer reminds us that God doesn't sit back and watch us get attacked. He is not passive, and He does not leave us to struggle on our own. God is both offensive and defensive. He promises not only to protect us but to defend us as well.

Just as God carried David through battle, He will carry you. He is not stagnant or uninvolved in your life. As you cry out to Him, He will step in on your behalf. He fights with you and for you. He protects you from dangers you cannot see, and He shelters you from pain you are unaware of. Whether you see the battle at hand or not, God is your refuge. Like David, you can declare your trust in Him and acknowledge His faithful presence in the midst of your battles.

God, thank You for fighting for me. Thank You for protecting me from enemies, both seen and unseen. I trust You to keep me safe. You are my refuge and strength.

APRIL 16

Agony of Separation

My God, my God, why have you abandoned me?
Why are you so far away when I groan for help?
Every day I call to you, my God, but you do not answer.
Every night I lift my voice, but I find no relief.

PSALM 22:1-2 NLT

Psalm 21 is a Messianic psalm. This means that it prophetically points toward the coming of Jesus. If we pay attention, we can see Jesus revealed through all of Scripture. As the psalmist questions God's nearness, we are reminded of the declaration Jesus makes on the cross. In the midst of physical suffering, the worst part for each was separation from God.

Physical or emotional pain can be endured, but true agony and grief come from separation from God's presence. When Jesus bore the weight of humanity's sin, He was separated from God for the first time. He hung on the cross and cried out in desperation. He felt the full burden of being apart from God, and He bore it so that you would never have to. No matter what physical circumstances you are facing right now, remember that nothing matters as much as your spirit being connected to God.

God, I long to be near You. Thank You for Your consistent presence in my life. You are my source of light and life. I need Your presence like I need air in my lungs.

APRIL 17

He Provides

You prepare a table before me in the presence of my enemies.

PSALM 23:5 CSB

Preparing a table requires intention and purpose. Ingredients must be gathered and prepared accordingly. Plates must be washed and set out. Needs must be anticipated and accounted for. When we prepare a table for someone, it requires forethought and planning. The effort required to be hospitable communicates that there is a relationship between the host and the guest. It shows that the host cares deeply about providing a fulfilling experience for their guest. With this in mind, we can see how meaningful it is for God to prepare a table for us in the presence of our enemies.

Yahweh is a protective shepherd king who provides for His children. His provision for you declares His great love. Even in the presence of your enemies, He is steady and unwavering. He sustains you, and He willingly meets your needs. You are not a burden to Him. His care for you is all-encompassing. Not only does He give you what you need, but He graciously blesses you beyond measure. He loves to share the abundance of His kingdom with His children.

God, thank You for preparing a table for me in the presence of my enemies. Thank You for Your faithful care and for giving me exactly what I need. I trust You to provide for me in all circumstances.

APRIL 18

All Your Days

*Surely your goodness and love
will follow me all the days of my life,
and I will dwell in the house of the Lord forever.*

PSALM 23:6 NIV

Our good shepherd stays with us throughout our life. When we look to Him, we have the benefit of His constant guidance. He is our help and our support. Through every circumstance, He works for our good. As we follow Him, we experience His love and grace. One day, we will abide with Him permanently, but until that day comes, we can trust that He will not leave us or abandon us.

Though heaven is your end goal, don't forget the joy that comes from dwelling with your Shepherd now. Staying close to Him is a gift and a necessity. Life with Jesus is drastically better than life without Him. He longs to spend eternity with you, but He also longs to faithfully lead you through each of your days. Supernatural peace, provision, and rest come from knowing Jesus. Eternity matters but today can also be saturated by the goodness of God.

God, thank You for the promise of Your goodness and love. When I wander, draw me close. I want to spend my days near to You, listening for Your voice and following Your ways.

APRIL 19

Clean and Pure

Who may ascend the mountain of the Lord?
Who may stand in his holy place?
The one who has clean hands and a pure heart,
who does not trust in an idol or swear by a false God.
PSALM 24:3-4 NIV

In Psalm 24, David instructs those who want to worship and serve God. He explains that if they want to approach God, they must have clean hands and a pure heart. In other words, both their internal and external lives must be godly and acceptable. Not only must their actions be honoring to God, but their thoughts and motivations must also be considered pure. Nothing less than perfection is acceptable in God's presence. By those standards, no one can be near Him.

Your lack of perfection disqualifies you from approaching God. This is why Christ's death and resurrection is such an incredible gift. His work on the cross means you get to claim His righteousness as your own. Through Christ, you are perfect. There is nothing you can do to become more perfect in God's eyes, and there is nothing you can do to become less perfect. His great mercy is that Jesus' sacrifice is enough to compensate for your sins now and forevermore. Because of Jesus, your hands are clean, and your heart is pure.

God, thank You for the cleansing power of the cross. Thank You for the blood of Your Son that purifies me from all my sin. Keep my heart soft and give me the grace to confess and repent quickly when I make mistakes.

APRIL 20

No Shame

> I trust in you;
> do not let me be put to shame,
> nor let my enemies triumph over me.
> No one who hopes in you will ever be put to shame.
>
> PSALM 25:2-3 NIV

Shame is a powerful tactic that can leave us feeling powerless and immobilized. The feeling that we are not good enough or that we don't measure up can be crushing. If we are convinced of our failures or that we deserve punishment, we will not experience the freedom that God has intended for us. In order to walk in the fullness of His purposes for us, we must be willing to give our shame to Him.

When Jesus died on the cross, He took your shame upon His shoulders. He paid the price for your sins, and He made a way for you to be free of guilt and embarrassment. There is no need to cultivate shame in your life. When you feel the temptation to speak down to yourself or to wallow in guilt, run to the cross. Give your burden of shame to Jesus and allow Him to handle it. He will lift your head and encourage your heart.

God, thank You for setting me free from the power of shame. When I am tempted to wallow or feel powerless, remind me of the strength that comes from surrendering to You. Thank You for lifting me up and encouraging me.

APRIL 21

Follow the Leader

> Show me your ways, Lord,
> teach me your paths.
> Guide me in your truth and teach me,
> for you are God my Savior,
> and my hope is in you all day long.
>
> Psalm 25:4-5 niv

Throughout the Psalms, we see Yahweh as the teacher and David as the student. Culturally, the rabbi-student relationship was prevalent. It was natural for David to depend on God for understanding. Throughout Psalm 25, David shares some principles for knowing and succeeding in God's ways. Primarily, he opens himself up to receive the wisdom of God. He acknowledges that he needs God to teach him and guide him.

Following God means having a sincere desire for Him to lead you according to His standards. Like a student and a rabbi, you must have respect for your teacher. You can't follow God without having a reverence for what He says and a willingness to be obedient to His Word. When you are tempted to go your own way, remember that God's standards are not meant to limit you. Rather, they are a gift from a wise and loving Father who knows exactly what you need.

God, give me reverence for Your ways. Give me opportunities to humbly submit to Your standards. Teach me how to follow You like a student would follow a rabbi.

APRIL 22

Fix Your Eyes

> Vindicate me, Lord,
> because I have lived with integrity
> and have trusted in the Lord without wavering.
>
> Psalm 26:1 CSB

Psalm 26 is a petition of innocence. David is not bragging or being prideful. Rather, he is surrounded by evil, and he's calling out to God for help. He's declaring that he has done his best, but he still needs God's deliverance. Sometimes, we experience hardship even when we've done all the right things. Following God does not mean we won't experience trials or suffering. Instead of being discouraged by the presence of difficulties, we can use them as an opportunity to worship.

Through worship, God can shape our hearts. Worship allows us to turn our attention to God rather than focusing on our problems. While we might not be able to change the circumstances of our environment, we can change the posture of our hearts. We can focus on God's goodness and provision instead of dwelling on chaos. As we keep our eyes fixed upon Him, God will guide us through situations we thought were impossible to navigate. He will lead us along a straight path even when we are surrounded by wilderness.

God, it can be discouraging to do the right thing and still experience suffering. Whether I am innocent or guilty, I trust You to lead me. Your ways are higher than mine, and I trust You to keep me steady.

APRIL 23

Stronghold

*The LORD is the stronghold of my life—
of whom shall I be afraid?*

PSALM 27:1 NIV

A lot of David's words reflect the constant conflict in his life. This is something we can easily relate to. In our current climate, there is always something negative happening. We hear daily stories of horrific suffering and complicated political situations. Additionally, if we set aside the physical news, we know there is also a spiritual battle happening. There is an undercurrent of war that is always producing tension, whether we notice it or not. Psalm 27 teaches us how we can respond to living with that constant tension.

As much as there is an undercurrent of war, there is an even steadier undercurrent of God's protection. His hand of protection reaches out and reassures us that we are safe in His hands. He is our stronghold and our place of fortification. In His presence, He gives us everything we need to endure the battles we face. He equips us to endure, and He steadily helps us navigate the most impossible circumstances.

God, thank You for equipping me to face my battles. Without You, I would be lost. With You on my side, I am strong and confident. Give me the grace to lean on You through every circumstance.

APRIL 24

No Limits

*The one thing I ask of the Lord—
the thing I seek most—
is to live in the house of the Lord all the days of my life,
delighting in the Lord's perfections
and meditating in his Temple.*

Psalm 27:4 nlt

The sense of being in God's presence is unmatched. Our desire for consistent peace and joy can only be met by Him. Especially when we experience times of tension, His presence is the antidote we need. When we feel the tension of living in the world, God calls us to find refuge with Him. As we spend time with Him, He equips us to endure until the end of our days.

The people who lived during the Old Testament didn't have consistent or easy access to God. They would have had to seek Him in the Temple, and even then, there were strict requirements and sacrifices to be made. You have the gift of the Holy Spirit. Through Him, you can be with God anytime. His presence is always available to you. He won't leave you in the midst of challenging circumstances, and He won't abandon you to figure out life alone.

God, thank You for the gift of Your presence. Being with You is better than anything else in my life. Give me the grace to prioritize my relationship with You above all else.

APRIL 25

Every Emotion

Do not hide your face from me,
do not turn your servant away in anger;
you have been my helper.

PSALM 27:9 NIV

Psalm 27 is a clear picture of the human condition. We see David waffling between emotions. He switches tones and moves from doubting God to trusting in His faithfulness. We can be encouraged by this because it gives validity to the way our emotions can be fleeting and fragile. One minute, we feel confident, and the next, we are filled with fear. This is normal, and there's no need to feel ashamed of our shifting feelings. What matters is how we respond to our thoughts and emotions.

God can handle your most confusing emotions. It's not wrong to experience feelings of frustration or desperation. No matter what you feel, you can cling to the truth. God is your stronghold, and He is steady and unchanging. He never struggles to figure out His emotions, and He is not intimidated by yours. You can take the full spectrum of your feelings and confidently hand them to God. As you spend time in His presence, He will help you shift your perspective as needed.

God, thank You for knowing me and loving me fully. Thank You for seeing my heart and choosing me anyway. When I am overwhelmed by my emotions, give me the grace to run to You. You are my refuge and strength through every season.

APRIL 26

Faithful Father

Though my father and mother forsake me,
the LORD will receive me.

PSALM 27:10 NIV

In a perfect world, parents are committed and faithful. They care for their children with loving kindness, and they protect their family until each person is able to navigate the world without them. Unfortunately, we know that this isn't always the case. Some of us have experienced great pain by the hands of our parents. We've felt abandoned, alone, and forgotten. Those of us who have carried those burdens can relate deeply to the psalmist's words in chapter 27. He says that even if our fathers or mothers forsake us, God will receive us.

Even if the people who are supposed to be devoted to you turn their backs, God will welcome you into His family. He is capable of filling the gaps left by your parents. He is a good Father who is committed to His children. Though you may ache for earthly parents, you can turn that desperation toward your heavenly Father. He will stand in the gap where people cannot. His love is all-encompassing, and He will faithfully guide you through life.

God, thank You for being a faithful father. When I feel lost or abandoned, wrap me in Your arms. When I feel overlooked or forgotten, encourage me with Your presence. Bring healing where it is needed and help me to look to You alone for validation.

APRIL 27

Convinced of Character

To you, LORD, I call;
you are my Rock,
do not turn a deaf ear to me.
For if you remain silent,
I will be like those who go down to the pit.

PSALM 28:1 NIV

In Psalm 28, David pleads with God because he knows he has nowhere else to go. He has great faith in God's ability to rescue him. This is only possible because he is aware of who God is. Without that recognition, he wouldn't bother asking God for help. Without an understanding of God's character, we cannot approach Him rightly or have accurate expectations of how He will answer our prayers.

When you need help, you are likely to ask an expert. A plumber fixes your sink, a carpenter builds a desk, and an electrician rewires a light switch. You wouldn't ask any of them for help if you weren't convinced that they knew what they were doing. Your confidence in their skills is what gives you the ability to have accurate expectations of their work. The same is true in your relationship with God. If you know who He is and how He operates, you will go to Him boldly.

God, I want to see You rightly. Reveal Your character to me through the Psalms and shift my perspective where it isn't right. Show me more of who You are and give me an understanding of how You operate.

APRIL 28

Hands Raised

*Hear my cry for mercy
as I call to you for help,
as I lift up my hands
toward your Most Holy Place.*

PSALM 28:2 NIV

We've all experienced various expressions of worship. Each church has different methods they are comfortable with, and most cultures do at least one or two things differently. The music varies, and the way we respond to it varies even more. Either way, raising our hands in submission is a relatively common display. We see it consistently mentioned in Scripture as a way to humbly declare our surrender to God.

No matter how you choose to worship, the posture of your heart is what matters most. Sometimes, it can be helpful to raise your hands as a reflection of what is happening in your heart. This is never a required standard for worship, but adding a physical element to what is unseen can be helpful. Sometimes, worship can be overly focused on feelings. While it's good to desperately cry out to God, your heart must be actively submitted to God. If your heart doesn't line up with your feelings, your worship has become more about an emotional experience than a truly submitted life.

God, when I come to You in worship, help me focus on what's true. Instead of being led by my emotions, give me the grace to humbly submit my heart to You.

APRIL 29

Carried Tenderly

*The LORD is the strength of his people,
a fortress of salvation for his anointed one.
Save your people and bless your inheritance;
be their shepherd and carry them forever.*

PSALM 28:8-9 NIV

Throughout the Old Testament, God is compared to a shepherd. A shepherd carries lambs on his shoulders or sometimes against his chest. The Hebrew word used for *carry* is the same word used to describe a man who carries his child. It's a picture of tenderness, care, and concern. God, as our shepherd, is present with us in every circumstance. He tenderly looks after us, and He promises to do it forever.

A lamb doesn't worry if it is a burden to the shepherd. A lamb doesn't wonder if it is too heavy or if the shepherd is too busy to take care of it. A lamb simply accepts the faithful care of its shepherd because it has learned to trust the shepherd. In the same way, you don't need to wonder if you are a burden to God. He loves being your shepherd. Caring for you isn't monotonous or burdensome. He isn't too busy for you, and He isn't bored of your constant needs. You can lean on Him with the same simple devotion that a sheep has for its shepherd.

God, thank You for being my shepherd who carries me close. Thank You for walking with me when I am hurting and carrying me when I cannot take another step. I trust You to lead me and provide for me.

APRIL 30

Stand Firm

The voice of the LORD is over the waters;
the God of glory thunders,
the Lord thunders over the mighty waters.

PSALM 29:3 NIV

In ancient times, most people would have been familiar with the god Baal. They knew that he was the god over the waters and that he was believed to have victory over the sea. When David declares that Yahweh is the one true God, the one who thunders over the mighty waters, he was making a claim that would have been incredibly countercultural. He was saying something in direct opposition to the popular belief of the day. David continually reminded people that Yahweh was even higher than Baal.

When you declare that God is holy and worthy of praise, you might come against some opposition. Like David, your belief in biblical truth probably defies the ideas that are most prevalent around you. Don't be discouraged! Stand firm upon God, who is your rock and your refuge. Don't be afraid to speak against what is popular, even if you are the only one doing it. Ask God for wisdom, and He will teach you how to declare truth boldly with the same power and gentleness that Jesus displayed.

God, give me strength to stand firmly upon the truth. When I am tempted to waver, equip me to stay steady. Give me strength in the face of opposition and boldness to declare the truth in love.

MAY 1

He Rescues

*I will exalt you, Lord,
for you lifted me out of the depths
and did not let my enemies gloat over me.
Lord my God, I called to you for help,
and you healed me.*

PSALM 30:1-2 NIV

Sorrow and joy are part of the human experience. We are each familiar with the pendulum swing between those two emotions. In the midst of both, we can trust God. He is with us in every season of the soul. When we trust Him, we can be expectant that joy will come even if we are discouraged by hardship. We can maintain hope even when we are in the depths of grief.

God is capable of lifting you out of the most impossible of circumstances. Call upon Him no matter what you are going through. He might cause the details of your situation to shift, or He may supernaturally encourage your spirit and give you strength to endure. Either way, even if His rescue doesn't fit your expectations, He will never leave you. When you depend on Him, He will step in on your behalf.

God, thank You for rescuing me. You have been faithful to save me so many times, and I trust You will keep being faithful. You are the only one who can truly help me.

MAY 2

Never Abandoned

You hide them in the shelter of your presence,
safe from those who conspire against them.
You shelter them in your presence,
far from accusing tongues.

PSALM 31:20 NLT

David's prayer begins with a desperate cry for help. He finds solace in the shelter of God's presence, and he is changed in that place. When he turns to God, his despair turns to praise. He commits his spirit to God, and in exchange, God faithfully gives him the peace and encouragement he needs.

God is present when you feel alone and rejected. Even if everyone has turned their back on you, He will never abandon you. When you are hurting, you can call upon your faithful Father and find peace in His presence. He longs to shelter you from whatever storm you are facing. You are not the first person to run to Him in emotional desperation, and you certainly won't be the last. Run to God even if you are embarrassed by your feelings or think you should have a better handle on your situation.

God, thank You for sheltering me from the storms I face. When I feel abandoned, may Your presence be my strength. Instead of being ashamed of my emotions, teach me how to call out to You with the expectation that You will bless me with Your presence.

MAY 3

Confess and Receive

*I confessed all my sins to you
and stopped trying to hide my guilt.
I said to myself, "I will confess my rebellion to the Lord."
And you forgave me! All my guilt is gone.*

Psalm 32:5 nlt

In seasons of rebellion, we often experience emotional pain because our sin has caused separation between us and God. Psalm 32 is a beautiful expression of how healing starts with confession. God pursues us while we are entrenched in sin, and He draws us to confession. His pursuit of our hearts does not excuse our behavior; rather, it causes us to humbly accept His mercy and depend upon His grace.

There is great freedom to be found in the confession of sin. When you aren't weighed down by the burden of your mistakes, you will experience a lightness that cannot come from anything else. When you confess your sins, God is faithful to forgive them. Not only that, but He puts your sin out of sight, and He removes your debts from His record. One of His greatest gifts is that you can trust Him with your struggles or the rebellion of your heart.

God, I don't deserve Your mercy, but You shower it upon me anyway. Give me the confidence to boldly bring my sins to You. Thank You for the picture of confession and repentance found in the Psalms.

MAY 4

Creation to Redemption

> By the word of the LORD the heavens were made,
> their starry host by the breath of his mouth.
> He gathers the waters of the sea into jars;
> he puts the deep into storehouses.
>
> PSALM 33:6-7 NIV

From creation to redemption, we are part of an amazing story. It's all tied together with the thread of God's unfailing love. He created the universe, and He regulates and sustains all that He made. As the Creator, He is the only one who can redeem creation. He is the only one with the antidote to our greatest shortcomings and deepest longings.

As your creator, God knows every intricate detail that makes you who you are. He knitted you together with the same power and might that He used to create the starry heavens and the raging sea. He knows everything about you, and He knows exactly what you need. You were made to be with Him, and you will only find true satisfaction in His presence. A need for communion with Him is woven into your very being.

God, the story You've written is glorious! When I am focused on my own problems, remind me that I am part of a story that is bigger than myself. As You draw me close to Your heart, remind me of how creation displays Your majesty, and I do, too.

MAY 5

Mutual Relationship

*I sought the LORD, and he answered me;
he delivered me from all my fears.*

PSALM 34:4 NIV

Every interaction we have with God is an exchange. We can't claim His promises and fail to do our part. Our relationship with Him is not supposed to be a one-sided interaction where we receive the benefits but don't do what He asks. We have to seek God in order to lay claim of what He has said. David didn't passively expect God to meet his needs. He actively sought Him and poured his heart out. He deliberately spent time pursuing a relationship with God, and he delighted in the mutual interactions they had.

The benefits of God's promises often depend on your willingness to seek Him. He longs for you to experience the fullness of everything He has to offer. He wants you to have freedom, peace, joy, and the security that comes from knowing you are eternally cared for. All of these wonderful gifts are offered to you freely as you surrender your life to His love. Seek Him with all your heart, and He will respond. Your devotion to Him will always be met with faithfulness and loving-kindness.

God, I want to lay hold of every good gift You offer me. Thank You for responding to me when I pour my life out for You. Give me strength and fortitude to seek You even when it is hard.

MAY 6

Delight in Deliverance

> I will rejoice in the Lord;
> I will delight in his deliverance.
> All my bones will say,
> "Lord, who is like you,
> rescuing the poor from one too strong for him?"
>
> PSALM 35:9-10 CSB

David often suffered ill-treatment even when he did the right thing. Despite his difficult circumstances, his faith in God's goodness remained intact. While he desired for justice to prevail, he left vengeance in God's hands. He trusted God to deliver him, and he rejoiced in thanksgiving when He showed up.

Like David, you can expect God to show up when you need Him. You can boldly ask for help, trusting that He will not ignore you. When your circumstances are more than you can bear, He is the one you need. When life is disappointing and full of frustration, God is on your side. When you are treated unfairly, you can remain steady because judgment is in God's hands. Whether you see the fulfillment of His justice now or in eternity, He will not fail you.

God, justice is Yours alone, and I trust Your sovereignty. When life is unfair, help me trust You just like David did. Help me lean upon Your perfect judgment and trust that You will deliver me at exactly the right time.

MAY 7

Don't Flatter Yourself

*See how they flatter themselves,
unable to detect and detest their sins.
They are crooked and conceited,
convinced they can get away with anything.*

PSALM 36:2 TPT

Pride can blind us from seeing a dangerous path for what it is. When we are convinced that we alone can discern what is right, we set ourselves up for failure. There is no sin or path to sin that hasn't already been traveled. Thinking that we are uniquely capable of getting away with something only shows that our perspective of ourselves and God is inaccurate. Trusting in our own intelligence is not a sign of success or maturity. Instead, it shows a lack of true understanding and humility.

Don't flatter yourself by trusting in your own discernment. Lean on what God says and actively seek to apply the Word to your life. Following faithfully in His footsteps is the only way to stay on a path that honors Him. As you look to Him instead of trusting in yourself, He will ensure that your steps are steady. When you place your life in His hands, opening yourself up to accountability and correction, He will lovingly and faithfully keep you from falling.

God, help me embrace humility and accountability. Keep my heart soft and sensitive to Your voice. I trust You to lead me in the right direction. You are the only one I want to follow.

MAY 8

Great Riches

> Don't follow after the wicked ones
> or be jealous of their wealth.
> Don't think for a moment they're better off than you.
> They and their short-lived success
> will soon shrivel up and quickly fade away.
>
> PSALM 37:1-2 TPT

If we base our success on the weights and measures of the world, we will come up wanting. It's easy to look at the lives of others and assume that we are failing. We live in a time of staggering contrasts, and the extreme wealth of others can seem frustrating and unfair. If we aren't careful, we can let the stress of comparison eat away at our joy and contentedness. Scripture is clear that this isn't how God wants us to live.

When you surrender your life to God and trust in Christ's work on the cross, you claim an eternal inheritance that far outweighs any earthly success you can imagine. Wealth and material possessions will fade away, but the riches you have as God's child will last for eternity. Instead of spending your time frustrated or annoyed by the circumstances of your life, remember that better days are coming. Follow Jesus faithfully and He will not forget your inheritance.

God, thank You for Your promises. Help me trust in Your plans instead of the injustices I see around me. When I am tempted to compare my life to others, help me remember the great riches I have in You.

MAY 9

Delight in Him

*Take delight in the L*ORD*,*
and he will give you the desires of your heart.

PSALM 37:4 NIV

There is a tendency to read this Scripture and take it out of context. It's common to want to view God like a genie who will grant your every wish. While not abnormal, it is inaccurate. If this is how we view God, we will be disappointed. There are two parts to this verse, and by focusing on one, we miss the overall point. God faithfully gives us the desires of our hearts when we delight in Him.

Your relationship with God is cohesive and two-sided. It's important that you recognize your part in His promises. If you focus on your pursuit of Him rather than what you might get out of it, you will experience the true joy that comes from knowing your Creator. The more you delight in Him, the more your desires will become synonymous with His. His joy will become your joy, and His dreams will become your dreams. Your deepest longings are fulfilled by a relationship with Him because He is the source of true purpose and satisfaction.

God, draw me close to Your heart. May I find true purpose in pursuing and knowing You. Teach me how to love what You love. You are the greatest source of joy in my life.

MAY 10

He Keeps Promises

Commit your way to the Lord;
trust in him and he will do this:
He will make your righteous reward shine like the dawn,
your vindication like the noonday sun.

PSALM 37:5-6 NIV

When we are in right relationship with God, we have the benefit of claiming His promises with confidence. He does mighty and wonderful things for us when we seek righteousness. We know that if we commit our ways to Him, He will answer our prayers. If we trust in what He says, He will lift us up and reward us with His presence. He will lead us through each of our days, and He will not abandon us when we need Him.

Your life may not look exactly how you want. Your physical circumstances might be difficult or even impossible. This does not mean God has left you alone. Even when you are struggling through frustrating situations, God is with you. If you have surrendered your life to Him, He will not forsake you. He is always fighting for you, even when you can't see it. When you commit your ways to Him, you can walk with your head held high, knowing that you have a heavenly inheritance as well as God's sustaining help, guidance, and protection.

God, I don't want to claim Your promises without pursuing You. Today, I give You my heart and trust You to meet me with mercy and grace. Give me confidence in Your Word and remind me to continuously commit my ways to You.

MAY 11

Remorse to Repentance

I am on the verge of collapse,
facing constant pain.
But I confess my sins;
I am deeply sorry for what I have done.

PSALM 38:17-18 NLT

We can relate to David's feelings of anguish in Psalm 38 because we know what it feels like to make mistakes. Sometimes, the disappointment we feel in ourselves is more brutal than the actual consequences we experience. For whatever reason, there are times when we feel enslaved by our inability to pursue God's path. David's experience of God's mercy, even in the midst of grave mistakes, points prophetically to the way we can experience mercy because of Jesus.

When you mess up, God is ready and willing to help you. The beauty of the gospel is that God offers you mercy when you don't deserve it. He sees you struggling to live righteously, and He provides a solution through Jesus. He knows that you aren't capable of perfection, and He does not shame you for it. Instead, He meets you in the anguish you feel over your sin, and He showers you with mercy and grace.

God, thank You for paying the price for my sin. When I make mistakes, teach me how to quickly run to You. Soften my heart and help me to depend on the cross for righteousness.

MAY 12

Double Meaning

*"I will put a muzzle on my mouth
while in the presence of the wicked."*

PSALM 39:1 NIV

When we think of a muzzle, we likely imagine not being able to speak. We might assume that this means we shouldn't fight, argue, or try to persuade the wicked of our opinions. While there is some wisdom in that concept, it's helpful to look at the original language used. The Hebrew word used for muzzle describes an apparatus put on an animal to prevent it from grazing. This was used to keep the animal from eating when it wasn't supposed to.

When you are in the presence of people who don't follow God, don't consume what they are laying out on the table. Your validation is not supposed to come from people who don't honor God with their lives. This doesn't mean that you look down on others or rudely point out their shortcomings. It simply means you should use wisdom by paying attention to the way other people's words and actions affect you. Do you put more stake in the opinions of non-believers than you should? Follow the advice of the psalmist and be mindful of what you consume.

God, teach me to be mindful of who is influencing me. Guard my heart and my mind with Your Word. I don't want to digest anything that doesn't honor You.

MAY 13

Every Moment

*"Show me, Lord, my life's end
and the number of my days;
Let me know how fleeting my life is.
You have made my days a mere handbreadth."*

PSALM 39:4-5 NIV

Life is brief. Even when the days seem to drag on, we can recognize that the years are short. We can use our limited time to seek and honor Him, or we can spend our days in opposition to His plans. Are we going to be faithful to God in a corrupt world, or are we going to carve out our own path? If we choose to be steadfast and follow Him, we have the benefit of leaning on His promises as trials come our way.

You can spend your days living for the pleasures of the world, not thinking about your real home, or you can journey through life with the attitude of a pilgrim. A pilgrim knows their destination and does whatever it takes to reach it. A pilgrim isn't discouraged by obstacles but views their end goal as worthy of any difficulties along the way. With eternity in God's presence as your goal, keep your eyes on Him and deliberately decide to follow His ways. Dedicate yourself to His purposes and seek a relationship with Him above all else.

God, press upon my heart that every moment is a gift. Help me live with eternity in mind. Thank You for the time You've given me to seek and glorify You. Help honor You with all my days.

MAY 14

Even in Failure

> "My hope is in you.
> Save me from all my transgressions."
>
> PSALM 39:7-8 NIV

If we take time to understand David's story, we'll see that he suffered from the consequences of his own sin. He experienced the downside of turning away from God and pursuing his own desires. Even so, we can learn a great deal from the way he handled his situation. Even in the midst of suffering, he stayed in direct communication with God. He didn't lose hope even when he felt the anguish of regret and shame.

There will be times when you make the wrong choice and must find a way to clean up your mess. Even when this happens, God does not leave you alone. When you are tempted to withdraw or lick your own wounds, God is near and ready to help. He does not want you to wallow or fall into despair. You can follow David's example and run to God even when you are the reason for your problems. He is not surprised by your failures, and He doesn't think less of you. When you run to Him, He will offer you hope, peace, and the strength to endure.

God, thank You for the raw emotion found in the Psalms. Teach me how to follow David's example of maintaining hope even when I struggle with sin. Give me the confidence to run to You instead of hiding in shame.

MAY 15

Away From Home

> "Hear my prayer, Lord,
> listen to my cry for help;
> do not be deaf to my weeping.
> I dwell with you as a foreigner,
> a stranger, as all my ancestors were."
>
> Psalm 39:12 niv

Throughout the Old Testament, we see many instances of how God relates to people without a home. As Israel is driven away from their homeland by hardship, we see how God calls His people to His heart no matter their physical circumstances. The Israelites were forced to take refuge in a place that wasn't their own, and they experienced God's faithful provision when they were most vulnerable.

While you may not know what it feels like to be a foreigner or refugee, you can relate with the overarching truth that this world is not your intended home. Whether you are physically displaced or not, you were created to be most at home in the presence of God. You were designed for the perfection of eternity in His presence. Your awareness of the fallen world simply points to the truth that you were made for something more than the world can offer. You were created for communion with God, and He is your true home.

God, You are my home. With You, I am truly alive. When my heart longs for the perfection of eternity, draw me close and comfort me. When I feel like a foreigner, fill me with anticipation for Your return.

MAY 16

Training Time

I waited patiently for the Lord,
and he turned to me and heard my cry for help.

PSALM 40:1 CSB

God rarely moves according to our preferences or timelines. If we choose to follow Him, we will definitely experience seasons of waiting. It only makes sense that we would make the most of those seasons rather than wishing them away. In reality, waiting is an opportunity to open our hearts to doing God's will. God often uses seasons of waiting to prepare us for what is to come. In other words, waiting time is training time.

Throughout your life, you will have many opportunities to wait actively rather than passively. Wait upon God like a servant would wait upon a master. The servant doesn't stand around, assuming the master will summon them loudly or obviously when needed. Instead, the servant pays close attention and is immediately ready for action at the first inkling of necessity. When you are waiting for God to move, you can behave in the same way. Watch, listen, and observe the way He moves.

God, You are always moving, and I don't want to miss it. As I wait for You to intervene, help me keep my eyes trained on You. Teach me how to make the most of every season I walk through.

MAY 17

Relationship over Sacrifice

It's not sacrifices that really move your heart.
Burnt offerings, sin offerings—those aren't what bring you joy.
But when you open my ears and speak to me,
I become your willing servant, your prisoner of love for life.

PSALM 40:6 TPT

Before Jesus died as payment for our sins, people were required to offer sacrifices to God. While they were important, David understood that sacrifices and symbolic rituals were not enough to satisfy the full cost of sin. He knew they would never be able to take the place of a heart that is truly devoted to God. Commitment, obedience, and relationship matter far more than rituals.

You have the benefit of living in a time when you can rely on Jesus' sacrifice rather than your own. He is the one who cleanses you of your sin. His death and resurrection are meant to draw you close to God. Be wary of the tendency to work for your salvation. Remember that God is far less concerned with your checklists and accomplishments than He is with the state of your heart. He wants to be in a close relationship with you more than He wants you to be well-behaved or perfectly put together.

God, thank You for making a way for me to be close to You. Keep me from depending on my own goodness when I should be relying on the perfection of Jesus.

MAY 18

Value the Vulnerable

*Oh, the joys of those who are kind to the poor!
The Lord rescues them when they are in trouble.
The Lord protects them and keeps them alive.*

Psalm 41:1-2 NLT

If we read Scripture faithfully, we will quickly see that God values those who are vulnerable and needy. If we want to live in a way that honors Him, we cannot ignore who He loves or overlook what He says to pay attention to. We must place a high value on caring for those who cannot care for themselves. God prioritizes the weak and the helpless, and we must too.

There is a connection between your response to the needs of others and God's response to you when you are in need. When you care for the weak, you can trust that God will rescue you when you are weak. If He calls you to lay your life down for others, you can believe that He will not leave you empty-handed. He has already sent His son as a sacrifice for you, and He will continue to rescue you when you call out to Him.

God, I want to love others the way You do. Show me opportunities to serve and give me strength to do what is needed. As I lay my life down, I trust You to provide for me.

MAY 19

Faithful in Rejection

Even my best friend, the one I trusted completely, the one who shared my food, has turned against me.

PSALM 41:9 NLT

The Old Testament is not an outdated or unimportant part of the Bible. It's not something we can ignore in favor of the New Testament. God's faithfulness is interwoven into each part of the Bible. The Old Testament's words prophetically point toward Jesus, who is the fulfillment of each of God's promises. Throughout the Psalms, we see several instances where the psalmist's cries are echoed in the life of Jesus later on. We can easily make the connection between David's rejection and the eventual rejection of Jesus.

The sting of rejection hurts in a unique and pointed way. It's painful to feel left behind, unincluded, or overlooked. When you feel alone or abandoned, you can look to Jesus for understanding and compassion. After all, no one has been rejected like He has. He knows exactly what it feels like, and He can comfort you when you experience that type of pain. He will hold your heart gently and bring healing when you need it most. He is full of understanding, and He knows your deepest hurts.

God, help me see the character of Jesus through each part of Your Word. When I feel rejected, remind me to turn to You for comfort and understanding.

MAY 20

Hunger and Thirst

*As a deer longs for flowing streams,
so I long for you, God.
I thirst for God, the living God.*

Psalm 42:1 csb

As humans, we want to feel comfortable, content, and peaceful. It's normal to pursue whatever we think will cultivate joy or happiness in our lives. We tend to fill our desire for happiness with everything from relationships to possessions, from careers to experiences. While none of those things are inherently negative, we will always come up short if pursuing them monopolizes our time, money, and emotions. The longing of our hearts is meant to be met by God.

When you hunger and thirst for God, you are guaranteed to be satisfied. He alone can fill your deepest longings. You will always be most at home in His presence. Living a fulfilling life is directly connected to your pursuit of God. The more you seek Him, the more you will see Him, the more fulfilled you will be.

God, fill me with a hunger and thirst for You alone. Help me remove distractions from my life and keep me from pursuing lesser loves. Time with You is what I need most. Draw me close and give me grace to pursue You with all my heart.

MAY 21

Joy While Waiting

*Send me your light and your faithful care,
let them lead me;
let them bring me to your holy mountain,
to the place where you dwell.*

PSALM 43:3 NIV

We can find joy even when our prayers haven't been answered how or when we want. We can experience the goodness of God's presence at all times. In Psalm 43, the psalmist shifts from complaint about his circumstances to faith-filled worship. He goes from being full of despair to clinging to the hope found in God's presence. He calls upon God to meet him and care for him in his time of waiting because he knows that God is who he truly needs.

God is always moving. Just because you aren't sure what He is doing doesn't mean He is stagnant or uninvolved. He promises to work everything out for your good. He operates in your life even when you can't see it. As you follow Him, He ensures that every detail of your life is perfectly intertwined. While you might be tempted to question God out of frustration, remember that what you really need is time in His presence. It's in that place that your heart will be changed, and you'll shift from frustration to worship and peace.

God, encourage me while I wait for prayers to be answered. Instead of being discouraged, help me maintain hope. Your presence is what I truly need. Fill me with peace and give me grace to rely on Your sovereignty.

MAY 22

Where Is God?

*Despite all of this, we have not forgotten you;
we have not broken covenant with you.
We have not betrayed you; our hearts are still yours.*

PSALM 44:17-18 TPT

At some point, we've all felt the sting of questioning God's presence. It's easy to doubt His goodness when we are surrounded by so much pain. Our natural tendency might be to think God has abandoned us or that He doesn't care. If we allow ourselves to think this way, we won't endure to the end. Instead, we must realize that suffering exists because we live in a world that is hostile to God. Despite this, He has provided us with a great comfort in the midst of our suffering. We have the incredible gift of the Holy Spirit, who is with us at all times.

If your confidence comes from the stability of your physical circumstances, you won't be able to persevere when difficulties come your way. Instead, lean upon God's promises which never change. The truth of who He is and what He has done for you remains steady and reliable. You can endure impossible situations when your eyes are fixed upon the goodness of God and the restoration of all things. Life is filled with trials, but they are an opportunity to stay faithful to the covenant God has made with you.

God, when I am overwhelmed by the suffering around me, help me focus on the truth. I trust You to restore all things in Your perfect timing. Until then, keep me from being bitter and cynical when trials come.

MAY 23

Sacred Commitment

*Let the king be enthralled by your beauty;
honor him, for he is your lord.*

Psalm 45:11 NIV

Psalm 45 outlines the special relationship between Israel and God. Their covenant is compared to a wedding ceremony. The description of the wedding ceremony is later mirrored by Christ's relationship with the church. Jesus, the bridegroom, lays down His life for the church. He wants to be with her forever, and He makes a commitment to her that cannot be broken.

Just like a bridegroom commits to his bride, Jesus has entered into a covenant with you. You can trust that He has your best interests in mind at all times. His love for you is all-encompassing and everlasting. It will never fade, and it is eternal. When you respond to Jesus' sacrifice, you enter into a sacred commitment. It is not simply an infatuation with your bridegroom; instead, it is a lifelong relationship with Him that goes beyond how you feel at any given moment.

God, thank You for the eternal covenant I have with You through Jesus. Thank You for Your everlasting love and steadfast kindness. Remind me of my commitment to You and give me grace to be faithful to what I have promised.

MAY 24

Truth over Emotion

*God is our refuge and strength,
an ever-present help in trouble.*

PSALM 46:1 NIV

God longs to be the highest priority in our lives. He wants our relationship with Him to go beyond superficial interactions. In order for this to happen, we must rely on truth and God's proven faithfulness rather than our own feelings. At the beginning of any relationship, emotions are high, and it's hard to imagine them ever fading. However, we all know that feelings aren't what makes a relationship strong. Overcoming adversity and cultivating intimacy together are much more important.

If you depend on your feelings about God to carry you through life, you will be blindsided by conflicts or roadblocks. Instead, you must rely on the truth of who He is and what He has done for you. As your faith is strengthened, you will experience the richness that comes from His faithful companionship through every season of the soul. Difficult seasons are not a punishment and aren't an indication of your failures. Rather, they are a merciful gift from a loving father who knows exactly what you need to build endurance.

God, thank You for being faithful to me through every season of my life. Help me see all You have done. When I am discouraged, teach me how to rely on truth instead of my emotions.

MAY 25

Sovereign and Strong

God reigns over the nations;
God is seated on his holy throne.

PSALM 47:8 NIV

Psalm 47 is considered an enthronement psalm. It declares that God is the true king, and He reigns over all of creation. He is sovereign over all of history, our present lives, and everything that is to come. His sovereignty is a great comfort to us. When we face trials, God is on the throne. When there is uncertainty in our lives, His position is always certain.

When you choose to trust that God is ruling and reigning over all things, your perspective will shift. Even the worst situation looks better when you view it through God's eyes. He is not surprised by your frustrations, discouraged by your trials, or dismayed by your failures. He knows exactly what each of your days will look like and how you will respond to them. Remember that you serve a sovereign God who is steady and reliable.

God, You are the one true King, and You are worthy of all my praise. When I am discouraged by my circumstances, help me trust in Your sovereignty. Widen my perspective and help me see through Your eyes.

MAY 26

Every Word

All Scripture is God-breathed and is useful for teaching, rebuking, correcting and training in righteousness, so that the servant of God may be thoroughly equipped for every good work.

2 Timothy 3:16-17 NIV

The Psalms reveal the character and nature of God. He is the same yesterday, today, and forever. Therefore, what we read about Him in the Old Testament is also true today. We can be greatly encouraged by the way He moved on behalf of His people because we know that if He did it then, He will do it now. If He rescued the psalmist, He will rescue us. If He comforted the psalmist, He will surely comfort us.

Don't fall into the trap of picking through the parts of the Bible that you like or are easy to read. With the help of the Holy Spirit, you have everything you need to study and understand Scripture. If you don't shy away from it, you will reap a mountain of blessings. Look for glimpses of who God is on every page. As you read through the Word, be encouraged by how God moves and how He is endlessly faithful to His people.

God, thank You for the gift of the Word. Fill me with a desire to know the depths of who You are through Scripture. Give me insight and understanding when I need it.

MAY 27

Stay Focused

*Do not be overawed when others grow rich,
when the splendor of their houses increases;
for they will take nothing with them when they die,
their splendor will not descend with them.*

PSALM 49:16-17 NIV

We place high value on pursuing wealth, influence, and fame. Our culture prioritizes these things often at the expense of character, truth, and sustainability. It's important to remember that we can't take our earthly pursuits with us when this life ends. It's useless to find our security in riches or anything else the world has to offer. Psalm 49 describes the downfall of those who have measured their lives based on how much they earn or how they perform.

It's normal to struggle with the tension that comes from watching the wicked prosper. This is especially difficult when it seems like those who are righteous are suffering as a result. Rather than being discouraged by unfair dynamics, focus on the way God has asked you to live. Instead of comparing your successes and failures to the world, cultivate godly character in your life. Spend your time and energy building something that will last. Pursue God and His righteousness, and you won't be left wanting.

God, sometimes I struggle with comparison and jealousy. When I am discouraged by worldly success, help me focus on what really matters. Give me grace to pursue You with everything I have.

MAY 28

Cultivate What Matters

*I have no need of a bull from your stall,
or of goats from your pens,
for every animal of the forest is mine,
and the cattle on a thousand hills.*

PSALM 50:9-10 NIV

Most of us have fallen into the ritual of Christianity at some point. We do the right things, but our hearts are far from God. Habits that used to be motivated by love become monotonous. We begin checking items off a list out of duty rather than devotion. We might make the right decisions, but we've stopped cultivating a personal and life-giving relationship with God.

God does not expect you to do everything right. He wants you to pursue Him as a response to His loving faithfulness. Without a relationship, your rituals are meaningless. God does not need your sacrifices and offerings. His resources are abundant and never-ending. He can acquire anything He wants. A devoted heart is what He wants from you. He wants a dynamic relationship with you. He wants to dwell with you and interact with you. He longs for unity and intimacy with you.

God, protect me from falling into ritual habits. When my heart becomes calloused by monotony, ignite a fire within me and remind me of Your extravagant love. Help me cultivate what really matters.

MAY 29

Confess and Repent

*Completely wash away my guilt
and cleanse me from my sin.
For I am conscious of my rebellion,
and my sin is always before me.*

PSALM 51:2-3 CSB

Psalm 51 is a personal lament. David is distraught over his sin, and he is crying out to God. He feels regret over his affair with Bathsheba, and he is asking God for help. If we read this Psalm and focus on what David has done wrong, we will miss the point. We are not meant to follow his example. Instead, we should focus on God's reaction to David's sin. David calls out to God in anguish and regret, and God meets him with mercy and grace. David knows that God is the only one who can wash away his guilt.

Admission of sin is the first step toward healing. If you can't humbly recognize what you've done wrong, you won't be able to move forward in repentance. As you confess your mistakes to God, you make space for Him to move within your heart. Don't be ashamed to bring Him your failures. Hesitancy to bring your sins to Him highlights a lack of understanding when it comes to His character. You can boldly confess your sins because you know that God is eager to forgive you.

God, give me boldness when I am tempted to hide in shame. Give me strength to confess my sins quickly. Thank You for taking my guilt and giving me freedom in exchange.

MAY 30

New Life

*I am like an olive tree, thriving in the house of God.
I will always trust in God's unfailing love.*

Psalm 52:8 nlt

God's powerful love can sustain us in every circumstance. When we dwell with Him, we are like an olive tree. Olive trees are unique because they grow new shoots even when they have been cut down. Even when death is looming, olive trees thrive. In the same way, even when circumstances seem dire, God's faithful love brings life and hope. Sin and death cannot hold us down because God has the final say. He produces life and light out of every situation that is handed to Him.

You can be fruitful even when it looks like everything is ruined. When you depend on God's love, you are like an olive tree that thrives even when it seems impossible. As God's child, this is your inheritance and promise. When everything feels like it has gone wrong, when you experience the anguish of your own sin, or when you suffer for what seems like no reason, God's faithful love will carry you through.

God, thank You for Your faithful love. Strengthen me when I am weak and teach me how to rely on You more today than I did yesterday. Thank You for creating new life even when I feel hopeless.

MAY 31

In Your Heart

The fool says in his heart,
"There is no God."

Psalm 53:1 NIV

As we read Scripture, we should pay close attention to accusatory descriptions. There are many places in the Psalms that describe foolish behavior. If our goal is to honor God with our lives, these are the attitudes and actions we want to steer clear of. In Psalm 53, we see the downfall of people who declare that God does not exist. It's notable that the psalmist doesn't say that people are denying God boisterously or even publicly. Rather, he specifies that a fool denies God's existence in his heart.

The state of your heart matters more than your actions. Everything you say and do stems from the attitude of your heart. As you turn to God and surrender to Him, He does the miraculous work of changing your heart. He gives you new life, and He strengthens you when you are weak. His light shines where death and darkness previously thrived. As you follow Him, continuously offer Him your heart. Each day is an opportunity to deliberately choose the object of your greatest affection.

God, I want to honor You with my actions and also with my inward life. Turn my heart toward You and keep me steadily on a path that honors You. Give me the grace to choose You above all else.

JUNE

JUNE 1

When Life Is Unfair

*Come with great power, O God, and rescue me!
Defend me with your might.*

PSALM 54:1 NLT

In Psalm 54 David is being pursued by Saul. He didn't do anything wrong, but he is experiencing persecution. His cry is not just a desperate plea for help but an acknowledgment of his faith. He knows that God will intervene. In times of need, calling to God can change both our circumstances and the state of our hearts as we deal with whatever we are facing. Calling out to Him strengthens us and reminds us of His faithfulness. Even if our circumstances don't change exactly how we want them to, we can experience the blessing of being in a relationship with Him through the ups and downs of life.

You can learn from David's example and cling to God when you are wrongly accused. In times of injustice, God is still sovereign. He is capable of managing tricky situations with wisdom. His perspective is perfect, and His understanding is without bias. Even when things are unfair, you don't need to orchestrate justice. You can depend on God to triumph over evil.

God, You are the perfect judge. When life is unfair, I will still trust You. I know that You will be victorious. Keep my heart soft and help me to continuously depend on You.

JUNE 2

Cast Your Cares

Here's what I've learned through it all:
Leave all your cares and anxieties at the feet of the Lord,
and measureless grace will strengthen you.

PSALM 55:22 TPT

Following God does not protect us from the poor choices of other people. Instead, it offers us an opportunity to cope with the help of the Holy Spirit. We live in a fallen world, and we cannot escape the problems we create for each other. Inevitably, someone will hurt us, or our actions will harm others. In Psalm 55, we see that the best solution is to cast our cares at the feet of the Lord. He alone can take our pain and turn it into something new.

When you take your deepest hurts to God, He promises to strengthen you with unending grace. He knows that life is difficult and that you often face problems you cannot handle. He sees you when you are wounded, and He sees you when your mistakes cause pain to those around you. In both circumstances, He is ready and willing to intervene. He wants you to trust Him with your problems. He doesn't expect you to clean up your own messes or make sure that your life is always orderly. He Himself will strengthen you when you give Him your burdens.

God, I'm so thankful that I am not alone. When I am struggling under the weight of my worries, help me remember that I can cast my cares upon You.

JUNE 3

Trust over Fear

*When I am afraid, I put my trust in you.
In God, whose word I praise—
in God I trust and am not afraid.
What can mere mortals do to me?*

PSALM 56:3-4 NIV

Trust based on measured faithfulness is the antidote for fear. We can trust God because He has proven Himself worthy. He has shown up time and time again to rescue His people. Scripture is filled with stories of how God has fought for His followers, and it all culminates in the life, death, and resurrection of Jesus. God has never failed His people, and He never will.

When trust is the baseline of your relationship with God, you'll experience the freedom that comes from knowing you will be taken care of no matter what. You won't be discouraged by the circumstances of your life, and you won't be shaken by the turmoil of the world around you. If you feel doubtful or unsure, remember that trust is something you can cultivate. Deliberately pay attention to the way God has moved in your life. Make a list of the ways He has been faithful to you. Seek out His character in Scripture and ask the Holy Spirit to give you confidence. The more you acknowledge God's faithfulness, the more you will be assured of it in times of trouble.

God, strengthen my trust in You. I want to lean on You when times are good so that I will be steady when difficulty arises. When I am afraid, help me to turn to You quickly.

JUNE 4

Safe Refuge

Have mercy on me, O God, have mercy!
I look to you for protection.
I will hide beneath the shadow of your wings
until danger passes by.

PSALM 57:1 NLT

When we are in trouble, God offers us the shelter of His wings. Just like a mother hen hides her chicks in order to protect them and keep them warm, God is our shelter in the midst of life's storms. He is fully aware of our vulnerabilities, and He provides us with a place of refuge when we need it most. He does not expect us to weather dangerous circumstances alone. He does not abandon us or use a tough love approach. God offers us His strength and care when we are weak.

While you may never hide in a literal cave like David did, there are likely times in your life when you need a safe place to hide away. When life feels like too much and the worries of the world overwhelm you, God is your safe place. He is always available to wrap you in His arms and strengthen you. Don't withdraw from Him because He is the one you need the most. No matter how messy things seem, God is capable of leading you through.

God, thank You for being my refuge and my strength. I am so thankful for the shelter of Your wings. Strengthen me and prepare me for the battles to come.

JUNE 5

Unbreakable Covenant

*He will send help from heaven to rescue me,
disgracing those who hound me.
My God will send forth his unfailing love and faithfulness.*

Psalm 57:3 NLT

Sometimes, when we hear something over and over, it begins to lose its meaning. We know that God loves us, but we don't always grasp the full and complete meaning of those words. His love for us stems from the covenant He has made with us. His love goes beyond affection; He is committed, faithful, and devoted. Our closest understanding of covenant comes from the use of contracts. While binding, a contract can still be broken. There might be consequences but it's not unbreakable.

There are no circumstances in which God will break His covenant with His people. His promises cannot be changed, voided, or diminished in any way. His love for you is unwavering and eternal. While you might waver in your response to Him, He never will. His faithfulness does not depend on your ability to be faithful to Him. He knows exactly how many times you will turn away or wander down a path you shouldn't. Even so, He is devoted to you for all of eternity. When you call out to God, He sends His unfailing love and faithfulness to rescue you.

God, thank You for Your unending faithfulness. Thank You for Your unwavering love. Your covenant makes me feel safe and cared for. Give me the grace to respond to You with my whole heart.

JUNE 6

A Coming Reward

> "There is a reward for the righteous!
> There is a God who judges the earth!"
> PSALM 58:11 CSB

A day is coming when evil will be fully defeated once and for all. As believers, we have the benefit of looking forward to that day with great anticipation. We have surrendered our lives to God and are safe from judgment because Christ has taken our judgment upon Himself. Because of that, we can look forward to eternity, knowing we are safe and provided for. A perfect and wonderful reward is coming for those of us who have put our trust in God.

No matter how difficult your life is, you have the glory of eternity to look forward to. The pain you experience on earth will not last forever. The grief you carry and the frustration you experience cannot compare to the goodness of what is coming. As you trust in Christ's righteousness, He will give you the strength to endure until He comes back. He has promised to be with you until the end of the age, and you can trust that He will not break that promise. He will guide you through each of your days, and He will reward you for your life of faithfulness.

God, fill me with anticipation for eternity spent with You. When I am discouraged, remind me of Your glorious plan of redemption. Give me strength to endure until the end.

JUNE 7

Only God

*You are my strength, I sing praise to you;
you, God, are my fortress,
my God on whom I can rely.*

PSALM 59:17 NIV

God is the only one we can rely on for justice. We see suffering everywhere, and it's painful to watch the innocent be taken advantage of. As much as we want to change the world, we must remember that true justice is in the hands of God. No matter how we think we can help or make a difference, we must depend on God to intervene. Our desire for change must begin with prayer and humility. Alone, we are powerless and helpless.

You might remember a time in your life when you felt like you had all the answers. As you've gotten older, you've likely realized that most situations are more complicated and nuanced than they seem at first glance. When you come face to face with an impossible situation, there is no option other than to cry out on behalf of the hurting and trust faithfully in God's sovereignty. Let your desire for justice drive you to your knees in acknowledgment of God's faithfulness and strength.

God, help me turn to You when I am overwhelmed by the suffering of the world. You are the only one I can rely on. Keep me from pridefully thinking I have all the answers.

JUNE 8

Beyond the Physical

*Save us and help us with your right hand,
that those you love may be delivered.*

Psalm 60:5 NIV

Psalm 60 outlines David's reaction after a daunting defeat in battle. We can relate to his tendency to look at physical circumstances while forgetting what God has promised spiritually. Even when things seem impossible, we must listen to God's voice calling us to a deeper level of understanding. He reminds us to set our eyes on the reality that is beyond our physical circumstances. Even in earthly defeat, we have eternal victory. Even in earthly frustration, we have eternal clarity.

When you call upon God for help, He lifts you out of your physical circumstances. He gives you His perspective and reminds you that things aren't always what they seem. When you turn to Him rather than wallowing in defeat, He will remind you of His promises and help you maintain hope. He alone will save you at exactly the right time. He knows which victories you need and which defeats you can endure. Just because you don't understand the situation you are in doesn't mean God is not able to help you navigate it.

God, when nothing makes sense, I turn to You. When I am overwhelmed by defeat, I turn to You. I trust You to save me and guide me along the right path. Help me honor You even when I don't understand my circumstances.

JUNE 9

Temporary Home

*I call to you from the ends of the earth
when my heart is without strength.
Lead me to a rock that is high above me,
for you have been a refuge for me,
a strong tower in the face of the enemy.*

Psalm 61:2-3 csb

As believers, heaven is our home. We were created to experience the perfection of God's presence for all eternity. Until then, we do our best to persevere and depend on God for strength. In this lifetime we will inevitably experience things that are contrary to His original created order. This creates some internal tension because we know intuitively that this is not how it's supposed to be.

Living in the chaos of the world feels wrong because it is wrong. When you feel overwhelmed with the suffering you see around you, let it push you closer to God. Find your refuge in Him and remember that one day, He will make all things new. Let your frustration over injustice fill you with anticipation for the perfection of eternity. Let it motivate you to love those around you with the sacrificial and life-changing love of Jesus.

God, help me find hope in the midst of chaos. Open my eyes to see Your hands at work even when there is suffering everywhere. Thank You for protecting and guiding me as I seek to honor You.

JUNE 10

Unwavering Hope

*Yes, my soul, find rest in God;
my hope comes from him.
Truly he is my rock and my salvation;
he is my fortress, I will not be shaken.*

PSALM 62:5-6 NIV

Psalm 62 is laced with the overarching theme that God is our all in all. He is everything we need, and He is the fulfillment of every longing we have. This idea is completely countercultural to the way society functions today. We see the pursuit of personal happiness and success everywhere we look. We see great despair and emotional distress. We see horrifying news stories and unending desperation. In general, the world can seem dissatisfied and hopeless.

You are called to live differently than the world. You are not hopeless. Even when nothing seems to be going the right way, your hope is intact because it isn't dependent on physical circumstances. As a child of God, your hope does not come from who the president is, what the economy looks like, or how the government operates. Your hope does not come from society functioning the way you want it to or people making choices you agree with. Your hope comes from the steady and unwavering truth that God is in control.

God, thank You for being an unwavering source of hope. When I am tempted to be discouraged by the world around me, help me turn to You. When I am frustrated by the circumstances of the world, encourage my heart and give me strength.

JUNE 11

Fully Equipped

By his divine power, God has given us everything we need for living a godly life.

2 Peter 1:3 NLT

Most of us have felt overwhelmed with our relationship with God at some point. We've let insecurities become irrationally large, and we've convinced ourselves that we are praying or serving the wrong way. We worry that God isn't speaking to us and that we aren't as spiritually mature as the people around us. Part of the problem is that we are overcomplicating the way God speaks and moves. He has given us everything we need to follow Him perfectly. He has fully equipped each believer to live a life that is honoring to Him.

It's common to feel like you aren't hearing God's voice. If that has been your experience, you aren't alone. While it's normal to feel that way, you don't need to stay in that mindset. When you entered into a covenant with God, He gave you the gift of the Holy Spirit. Through His guidance and the truth found in the Word, you have everything you need. The power within you to know God is the same power that rose Jesus from the dead. You are not limited in your faith, and you are not weaker than anyone else.

God, thank You for giving me what I need to follow You. When I feel weak or ill-equipped, remind me that I have the power of Christ within me. Empower me to live in a way that honors You.

JUNE 12

Thirst After God

> I thirst for you,
> my whole being longs for you,
> in a dry and parched land
> where there is no water.
>
> PSALM 63:1 NIV

David spent a lot of time either running or hiding from enemies. He spent time in the wilderness, and he knew what it was like to be desperate and thirsty. While many of us don't necessarily identify with running away from our enemies, we do understand the analogy of being in a dry and parched land. We know what it feels like to be searching for something we cannot find. The deepest longings of our hearts can only be filled by having a close and personal relationship with God.

Especially if you've been a believer for a long time, your sense of devotion to God might become more about your actions than the longings of your heart. While having a sense of purpose or duty isn't a bad thing, it's important to remember you were created for a deep and fulfilling relationship with God. This isn't because it's the right thing to do, but because you were made in His image. His very being is woven into every part of who you are.

God, I need You more than anything else. Fill me with a hunger and thirst for Your presence. You alone can satisfy the longing of my heart.

JUNE 13

Better than Life

*Because your love is better than life,
my lips will glorify you.
I will praise you as long as I live,
and in your name I will lift up my hands.*

PSALM 63:3-4 NIV

David declares that God's love is better than life. We might know that truth conceptually, but what really matters is if we allow it to have an impact on our daily lives. We all tend to pursue something other than God. Some of us chase after a career, while others might relentlessly pursue relationships or material possessions. No matter what the object of our affection is, we will never be satisfied. Pursuing God wholeheartedly is the only way to find true satisfaction.

If you are dissatisfied and lacking contentedness, it might be time to evaluate your pursuits. What has become the most important thing in your life? Where are you spending the majority of your time, money, and emotional bandwidth? If the pursuit of God doesn't make the top of your list, it's time to rearrange your priorities. He is worthy of your life and all your praise.

God, search my heart and show me where I have my priorities mixed up. I surrender my life to You. I want to experience Your life-giving love in the same way David did.

JUNE 14

God the Warrior

*All will stand awestruck over what God has done,
seeing how he vindicated the victims of these crimes.
The lovers of God will be glad, rejoicing in the Lord.*

PSALM 64:9-10 TPT

When we think about God's character, it feels easy to see Him as a father, shepherd, or king. These roles fit neatly into our perspective of Him. However, we can't ignore the parts of His character that we might be less comfortable with. God is a warrior who fights on behalf of His children. Our hesitancy to grapple with that aspect of who He is doesn't change the truth of it. Scripture is clear that He will vindicate the righteous, and they will rejoice in what He has done.

God promises to defend you when you need it. He doesn't just shelter or protect you. He is offensive as well as defensive. He doesn't stand by passively while you are attacked. He will vindicate each of His children. When you enter into a covenant with Him, you can be assured of His ability and willingness to fight for you. He is a good father who cares deeply about your suffering. When you feel weak, remember that the Creator of the entire universe is on your side.

God, when I feel alone and weak, help me remember that You fight for me. Deepen my understanding of who You are as a warrior. Thank You for defending me when I cannot defend myself.

JUNE 15

Nothing Too Heavy

*When we were overwhelmed by sins,
you forgave our transgressions.*

PSALM 65:3 NIV

God's forgiveness is not dependent on the gravity of our sin. He isn't less gracious when we really mess up, and He isn't more willing to forgive us when our sins seem less grievous. There is no sin that is beyond His ability to forgive. Whether we are drowning in guilt, dealing with very serious consequences, or simply know we haven't lived up to God's standard, His ability to forgive us is the same. He takes our transgressions in equal measure and hands out mercy without limitation.

You are not equipped to carry the weight of your sin. It is too heavy for you to bear. Take your burdens and boldly give them to the Lord. No matter how big or small you might categorize your wrongdoings, all sin causes separation in your relationship with God. When you become aware of sin, you have the opportunity to run to Him and let Him restore what is broken. Don't hide your sin or insist on carrying it alone. Instead, respond wholeheartedly to His invitation of redemption.

God, soften my heart and reveal any sin in my life. I give You my failures and mistakes, and I trust that You will redeem me. Thank You for Your continuous gift of forgiveness.

JUNE 16

Creator and Redeemer

The whole earth is filled with awe at your wonders;
where morning dawns, where evening fades,
you call forth songs of joy.

PSALM 65:8 NIV

In Psalm 65, we see the idea that God's forgiveness and the wonders of nature come together as dual witnesses of His grace. This is a common theme that is found repeatedly in the Psalms. Redemption and creation are intrinsically linked. As a result, only the Creator can redeem His creation. The very DNA of redemption is written into the story of creation. When we meet the Creator in Genesis 1, we are also meeting the Redeemer. These two roles are simultaneously intertwined.

Every single thing God has made bears witness to His character. When you look outside, there is evidence of His goodness everywhere. Even if you don't have endless Scripture memorized or you struggle with in-depth study of the Word, you can look at creation and worship the Creator. His design for the universe is ideal, and He will make everything perfect again. When Jesus comes a second time, He will make all things new. He will return things to the way they were intended to be. Rejoice because you will be included in the eternal redemption of creation.

God, thank You for the way creation tells me about who You are. Open my eyes to see Your plan of redemption. I worship You as my Creator and Redeemer. You are worthy of all my praise.

JUNE 17

Come and See

Come and see the wonders of God;
his acts for humanity are awe-inspiring.
He turned the sea into dry land,
and they crossed the river on foot.

PSALM 66:5-6 CSB

We each have the opportunity to utilize our stories for the glory of God. Our testimonies have great power. With boldness and selflessness, we can explain to others what God has done in and through us. Our experiences matter, and if we think about them deliberately, we will see countless examples of how God has shown up. Just as the Israelites were able to share their wonders about what God had done for them, we can purposefully share how He has intervened on our behalf.

You might not have miraculous stories about the sea drying up, but God has undoubtably done great things for you. He formed you in your mother's womb, and He faithfully led you to a place where you chose to devote your life to Him. Sharing the love of God with others is as simple as sharing your story. As you give credit to God for weaving your life together, your testimony will be an overflow of your praise.

God, thank You for my unique story. Help me see all You have done so I can share it with others. Give me boldness and opportunities to testify of Your love and faithfulness. Be glorified when I share my testimony.

JUNE 18

Tested and Refined

*You, God, tested us;
you refined us like silver.*

PSALM 66:10 NIV

If we look at the long period of Israel's slavery, we might assume that God was punishing them. In reality, He was refining them as a nation. The trials they faced are compared to the process of refining silver. Purifying metal is a slow process that requires an incredibly hot furnace. The metal must be melted down multiple times in order for the impurities to be thoroughly separated and easily discarded. As more impurities are removed, silver becomes more and more valuable. This process is similar to the process of refinement we experience as believers.

When you experience trials, it helps to see them as an opportunity for refinement. Even when incredibly painful things happen, God can use your circumstances to make you stronger and more like Him. Remember that even in refinement, God is gentle and kind. He is not harsh, and He does not stand by and watch emotionlessly as you suffer. He does not orchestrate painful or demeaning circumstances; rather, He redeems them and uses them for your good and His glory.

God, I trust Your ability to refine me. Help me lean on You in seasons of difficulty or grief. Give me grace to trust the process of becoming more like You.

JUNE 19

Proven Faithful

May the nations be glad and sing for joy,
for you rule the peoples with equity
and guide the nations of the earth.

PSALM 67:4 NIV

Faith is not blind trust. We aren't expected to declare our allegiance to God for no reason. Rather, our faith is supported by the evidence of God seen throughout history, both in our own lives and in the life of the church. As we lean into the knowledge of God's faithfulness, our trust in Him grows. Our dependence on God is based on the reliability of His character and nature.

From the beginning of time, God has faithfully guided the nations of the earth. He has proven Himself to be kind, just, merciful, and mighty. If you search Scripture, you will find endless examples of how God has shown up for His people. You can also do that in your own life. Deliberately take note of how God has shown up for you. Keep track of God's goodness and let it encourage you to continue to serve Him.

God, help me remember how You've been present throughout my life. You have been so faithful and kind to me. Encourage me when trials arise and help me depend on what I know is true.

JUNE 20

Good Father

To the fatherless he is a father.

PSALM 68:5 TPT

Some of us feel the painful sting of being fatherless. God is mindful of all who are hurting and needy. He is our kind Father, and we can trust His ability to love us well. When we are lonely, He will provide us with families. When we are hurting, He will comfort us and hold us close. When we are lost, He provides guidance, wisdom, and direction.

No matter what your earthly experience has been, God is your perfect heavenly Father. Your relationship with God as a father far exceeds any kind of relationship you could have with an earthly father. He delights in fulfilling this role, and He longs for you to feel at home in His presence. As you experience His delight and affection, let His love overflow to those around you. He defends you when you are weak so you can be a defender of the weak. He showers you with mercy and grace, so you can extend that same grace to those around you.

God, show me who You are as a good Father. Teach me more about the way You see me. As I experience Your love, help me to love others well. Show me opportunities to care for others who are needy or overlooked.

JUNE 21

Set Free

He sets the prisoners free and gives them joy.

PSALM 68:6 NLT

When we read about God setting the prisoners free in the Old Testament, we can compare it to how Jesus sets prisoners free through His death and resurrection. Most of us don't know what it's like to be physically imprisoned, but we can certainly relate to the idea of being spiritually, emotionally, or mentally imprisoned. Without Jesus, we are trapped by the weight of our sin and are unable to earn freedom. There is nothing we can do to pay the debt we owe.

When you surrendered your life to God at the foot of the cross, you were given freedom you don't deserve and cannot earn. No matter how many good choices you make, they will never outweigh your guilt. No matter how competent you think you are, you will never compare to the perfection of Christ. The truth of this reality is not meant to cause shame but to provoke confidence in Jesus' mercy. You cannot meet God's standards, but Jesus is your willing Savior and Redeemer.

God, give me awareness of my sin and iniquity. I don't want to take my freedom for granted. Thank You for taking the weight of my burdens and giving me mercy instead.

JUNE 22

Shame and Scorn

*I endure scorn for your sake,
and shame covers my face.*

PSALM 69:7 NIV

As followers of Jesus, it's likely that most of us have experienced scorn of some kind. Sometimes, our worship of God and passion for truth evoke misunderstanding or even judgment from others. This is not a new concept. For all of history, believers have experienced ridicule and persecution. The psalmist declares several times that he endured scorn for God's sake. He was rejected because of his belief and trust in God.

When you experience rejection, God is near. When you are scorned or insulted because of your faith, His love will sustain you. Remember that God sees each situation clearly. He sees your heart and intentions, and those of others. Sometimes, other people reject or ridicule you because they are challenged by the way you live. It's possible that your worship of God makes them uncomfortable and highlights something they feel guilty about. No matter what the details are, God is worthy of your praise.

God, You are worthy of my life and my praise. No matter how other people react, I want to remain faithful to You. Even if I am scorned, give me grace to follow You.

JUNE 23

Until Then

Hasten, O God, to save me;
come quickly, Lord, to help me.

PSALM 70:1 NIV

Psalm 70 is a declaration that the Lord is great, and despite being in a season of waiting, there is hope of deliverance. Even when our circumstances haven't changed yet, we can declare the unchanging truth of who God is. We can look forward and rest in God's faithfulness. We can proclaim His greatness and wait patiently for His deliverance.

Every believer is waiting for God to restore all things. All of creation is anxiously waiting for the day that He comes back and makes all things new. Declare God's goodness even as you long to spend eternity in His presence. Proclaim His worthiness until that glorious day when you are free from the sting of death and the weight of sin. May the promise of perfection fill you with hope as you endure living in a place that isn't your home.

God, I can't wait to be with You forever. Fill me with hope while I wait. Give me strength to endure every trial that comes my way. Give me the grace to fulfill Your purposes until You call me home.

JUNE 24

Aging Gracefully

> In my old age, don't set me aside.
> Don't abandon me when my strength is failing.
>
> PSALM 71:9 NLT

Our culture doesn't always value the elderly, and we seem to have a disdain for aging. Unfortunately, our dislike for getting older can seep into our relationship with God. It's not abnormal to fear that He might forget us or set us aside as we get older. If we buy into the lie that our value decreases as we age, we might struggle to maintain an accurate picture of how God sees us.

God longs to be present through every moment of your life. He will never leave you or forsake you. Look beyond your insecurity and lean into what you know to be true. God is faithful, and He does not overlook even one of His children. Your entire life is a beautiful culmination of God's faithfulness. Your age is a gift that should be honored and valued. Every year you live declares the sustaining grace of God.

God, You see the entirety of my life clearly. You know exactly how many days I will live, and You know what each of them will look like. Thank You for the gift of life. Help me see my later years as a precious gift.

JUNE 25

Prophecy Fulfilled

May he vindicate the afflicted among the people,
help the poor,
and crush the oppressor.

PSALM 72:4 CSB

Hundreds of years before His arrival, Jesus is prophetically announced over and over again. As King Solomon prays about his reign over Israel, we can see similarities to how Jesus prayed in the New Testament. King Solomon asks for vindication for the afflicted, and Jesus asks for God's will to be done and for His kingdom to come. In both instances, we see a desire for the hand of God to intervene on behalf of His people.

As Solomon prayed about his reign, he foreshadowed the kind of reign that Jesus would have. He alluded to the truth that Jesus would defend the afflicted and take notice of the needy. He knew how important these things were as a king and also as a follower of God. Living on this side of history, you can attest to the fact that caring for the oppressed is exactly how Jesus defined His life and ministry. King Solomon declared that a good king helps the poor, and Jesus came with humility and fulfilled that promise for all eternity.

God, thank You for the picture of Jesus found in the Psalms. Help me learn more about Him as I read through Your Word. Fill my heart with truth and draw me closer to You as I dwell on what You've said.

JUNE 26

Heart Shift

*My flesh and my heart may fail,
but God is the strength of my heart,
my portion forever.*

Psalm 73:26 csb

In Psalm 73, David experiences the pain that comes from watching the wicked prosper while the righteous suffer. He himself is trying to please God, and he is attempting to shift his attitude in the midst of an unfair situation. Toward the end of the Psalm, he grasps ahold of the only truth that can carry him through what he is facing. He recognizes that even if everyone around him has abundant riches, he has all he needs in God.

God is the strength of your heart. He is all you need. It's easy to declare this truth during seasons of ease or comfort, but it's much harder when your circumstances are difficult. You can try to muddle through your challenges, or you can lean on the Lord and trust His strength over your own. When everything seems to be going wrong, having an authentic interaction with God is the only thing that will change your perspective. As you call upon God to sustain you, He will shift the attitude of your heart.

God, You are the only one who can change my heart. Show me how I can depend on You when my circumstances are frustrating or difficult. You are all I need, and I want to be satisfied in Your presence.

JUNE 27

Unanswered Questions

Why do you hold back your hand, your right hand?
Take it from the folds of your garment and destroy them!

PSALM 74:11 NIV

Many of us have at least a few unanswered questions. We've walked through unexpected grief, unmet expectations, and unforeseen trauma. When life doesn't unfold the way we want, the disappointment can be crushing. While it might seem like a frustrating solution or no solution at all, we must come to terms with the fact that there are certain things we simply won't understand.

You won't always be able to make sense of the details of life. There might be aspects of your story that are not resolved on this side of heaven. Part of living in a fallen world is embracing the tension you find yourself in when circumstances don't line up with your expectations. It's not wrong to ask God why something is happening or how long it will last. The key is shifting your perspective from accusatory questioning to reverent submission. His sovereignty doesn't depend on your understanding.

God, You are in control, and You see details I don't. Keep my heart soft and willing to submit to Your ways. When I am tempted to be critical, help me trust in Your sovereignty.

JUNE 28

Standard of Justice

*No one from the east or the west
or from the desert can exalt themselves.
It is God who judges:
he brings one down, he exalts another.*

PSALM 75:6-7 NIV

Just like David experienced when he wrote the Psalms, we are experiencing political and cultural turmoil. There are new conflicts everywhere we turn. It seems like everyone is screaming their opinions, and we are constantly being fed an overload of information. It can be daunting to navigate the world while maintaining a sense of peace and confidence.

Instead of feeling despair over the state of the world, you have an opportunity to trust God. His standard of justice is in perfect alignment with His character. Because of this, you can be confident that the choices He makes are inherently better than yours. You can find comfort in the fact that you aren't responsible for solving the world's problems. While you might think a certain situation should be managed a certain way, it's important to recognize that God sees things more clearly than you do. You can trust Him to work out the story of the world in the best way possible.

God, You are in control of the story of the world. When I am tempted to question what You are doing, help me trust Your sovereignty.

JUNE 29

Fulfill Your Vows

Make vows to the Lord your God and fulfill them.

Psalm 76:11 niv

Throughout Psalm 76, we see four declarations of who God is. He is the God who is known, the God who is light, the God who is awesome, and the God who is feared. The psalmist is prompted to surrender to God because He is worthy. He describes how God has faithfully brought victory in battle and that He is deserving of all honor and praise. He declares that God's character is reliable, and our response should be to faithfully follow Him.

When you surrendered your life to God, you made a covenant with Him. You vowed to follow Him, and you trusted that He would fulfill His end of the bargain. Just as you trusted Him then, you can trust Him now. He is the same yesterday, today, and forever. The God you serve today is the same God who was declared mighty by the psalmist. His character is still the same. Today, take a moment to renew your devotion to God.

God, thank You for the treasures found in Psalm 76. Help me seek You out in all of Scripture. Highlight Your character and give me understanding as I read. Give me grace to fulfill my vows to You.

JUNE 30

When He Is Quiet

*As I thought of you I moaned, "God, where are you?"
I'm overwhelmed with despair as I wait for your help to arrive.*
PSALM 77:3 TPT

Most of us have experienced a season when we are convinced that God isn't listening. When we're going through something difficult, we think we need to be able to hear God's voice loud and clear. When that doesn't happen, we can feel ignored or forgotten. In those moments, it's important to recognize the unchanging truth of God's character. If we say we believe what He says, we must believe it despite how we feel.

God is faithful despite your questioning. He is steady despite your tendency to doubt Him. Even if you can't hear His voice, He is present. If you let your feelings dictate your beliefs, you will quickly find yourself wandering down the wrong path. Instead, do the purposeful work of filling your heart and mind with the Word. Become intimately acquainted with God's promises. When doubt arises, your instinctive reaction will be to rely on the truth rather than your feelings.

God, there have been so many times that I've let my emotions dictate my actions. Keep me steady when I am tempted to rely on my feelings. When doubt rises within me, remind me of Your faithfulness.

JULY 1

Good Example

*He decreed statutes for Jacob
and established the law in Israel,
which he commanded our ancestors
to teach their children.*

Psalm 78:5 niv

As believers, we are expected to teach our children about God. If He has blessed us with children, we have the responsibility of equipping and training them. It's important to realize we are always teaching our children something. Even when we don't realize it, we are communicating with them about what's important and how to live. They will learn from our example, whether it's good or bad.

Even if you don't have children of your own, the idea of passing down God's story still applies. You won't always be a perfect example of God's character, but you can strive to be a reminder of His grace and mercy to all who see you. Your goal isn't to live perfectly but to humbly accept God's lordship over your life and follow His ways with all of your heart. As you do this, the people around you will witness the way He moves in your life.

God, I want my thoughts and actions to reflect Your character. Help me be an example to the people around me. Give me grace to teach them about Your love.

JULY 2

Don't Forget

*They forgot what he had done,
the wonders he had shown them.*

PSALM 78:11 NIV

One of the reasons Israel struggled spiritually was because they forgot what God had already done for them. They were so focused on their immediate problems that they couldn't recall God's proven faithfulness. He had been present throughout their history, and He continuously intervened on their behalf. Instead of recognizing that and being encouraged by it, they allowed themselves to question who God was and why He wasn't doing what they wanted Him to.

Israel's lapse in memory serves as a powerful lesson to remember the works of God in your own life. He has done great and miraculous things for you. If you are intentional, you can be continuously encouraged by the way He has been faithful for generations. It's easy to become shortsighted when you focus all of your energy on your current circumstances. Instead, allow yourself to look up and see the bigger picture. God's faithfulness has been proven long before you were even born.

God, You have shown that You are reliable and good. You have proven that You will rescue and redeem Your people. Refresh my memory and help me see all the wonderful things You have done.

JULY 3

Pattern of Mercy

*He gave a command to the skies above
and opened the doors of the heavens;
he rained down manna for the people to eat,
he gave them the grain of heaven.*

PSALM 78:23-24 NIV

Even when the Israelites failed to honor God, He provided for them. Even when they wandered away from Him, He was faithful to His promises. He did not abandon His plan just because they didn't stay true. God's provision for Israel in the desert is a beautiful picture of His enduring love. We can be assured that if He loved Israel through their disobedience, He would have the same mercy toward us.

Your mistakes don't dictate God's faithfulness. He is eternally gracious and merciful. This is not meant to be a permission slip to continue sinning. Instead, let the promise of His provision drive you toward continued faithfulness. May His grace draw you closer to Him in devotion and obedience. May His mercy cause you to worship Him with wonder and reverence. He provides for you because He loves you and wants to have uninterrupted fellowship with you.

God, You have done so much for me. Thank You for Your provision and for being faithful despite my failures. As I read about the disobedience of the Israelites, help me to be humbly aware of my own wanderings.

JULY 4

Mighty and Merciful

He was merciful;
he forgave their iniquities
and did not destroy them.

Psalm 78:38 niv

Throughout the Old Testament, we see many instances of God withholding His power. He could have destroyed the Israelites when they were disobedient, but He didn't. We do ourselves a disservice when we fail to recognize that His mercy and grace do not come from a lack of strength or might. He is capable of doing exactly as He pleases. If His desire were for destruction, it would happen. Yet, everything He does comes from a foundation of everlasting loving kindness. He is merciful because He loves us, not because He is weak.

God will faithfully offer you grace every time you ask for it. You can approach His throne with confidence, knowing that He will give you mercy in your time of need. He will also equip you to start over as you surrender to Him. You are not meant to rush in, claim a snippet of forgiveness, and then hurry along your way. God longs to draw you in, heal your heart, and teach you how to live in a way that reflects His character to the world around you.

God, help me understand the fullness of Your character. Help me surrender when I am wrong and humbly accept Your correction.

JULY 5

Intercession

*O Lord, how long will you be angry with us? Forever?
How long will your jealousy burn like fire?*

Psalm 79:5 nlt

As believers, we have the opportunity to advocate for other people and situations through intercession. When we notice a need, we can call upon God to intervene. Even when we are physically helpless, we can move mountains through prayer. Even when we are miles away, we can fight spiritual battles because there is no distance in the Spirit.

Especially when you feel helpless, intercession is a powerful tool. Life is full of situations that don't always have practical solutions. You might not be able to single-handedly solve every problem you come across, but you can confidently bring it to God. When you see injustice, you can plead with Him to intervene. When you know something doesn't line up with God's standards, you can call upon Him and ask difficult questions. Through prayer, you can pour your heart out to Him without fear. Through prayer, the Holy Spirit can align your heart with God's and give you peace that comes from knowing He is in control.

God, thank You for the opportunity to intercede on behalf of others. Stir my heart to pray for situations that are out of my control.

JULY 6

Many Warnings

*Pour out your wrath on the nations
that do not acknowledge you,
on the kingdoms
that do not call on your name.*

PSALM 79:6 NIV

In certain parts of the Old Testament, we might wonder why God seems so harsh. There are situations where His discipline looks violent or cruel. It's important to understand the full context and history of Scripture. Otherwise, we won't get an accurate picture of God's perfect character. In the case of Psalm 79, the Israelites had been incredibly unfaithful to God's covenant. They turned their backs on what they knew was right, and they continuously acted in a way that dishonored God.

The Israelites were given many chances to change their ways, and they didn't. God's eventual intervention is actually a display of His patience. He longed for them to surrender, and He did what was best for them in the long run. This shows that God is patient and slow to anger. It also shows that sometimes, He will let you experience the consequences of your own actions. Like any parent, He can only warn you of danger so many times before you have to learn a lesson the hard way.

God, keep me from the foolishness of my own actions. Give me the desire to repent at the first sign of sin in my life. Help me hear Your voice clearly and choose obedience over my own desires.

JULY 7

With Humility

Help us, O God of our salvation!
Help us for the glory of your name.
Save us and forgive our sins
for the honor of your name.

Psalm 79:9 NLT

Psalm 79 is a post-exile glimpse into the mindset of the Israelites. Their community has been devastated, and they're taking an inventory. They're recognizing that God allowed certain events to happen and some of their experiences were the result of their own sins. This is such a relatable situation because we all know what it feels like to pick up the pieces of our lives in the aftermath of our own mistakes.

It takes a lot of humility to admit our weaknesses and rely on God for restoration. It would be so much easier to pridefully refuse we've done anything wrong and ignore our problems. While you might feel better temporarily, that approach will never result in true healing or restoration. Like the Israelites, you need to declare your need in order for God to rescue you. He alone can take your biggest mistakes and turn them into something that will glorify Him. When you surrender to Him, He will save you and forgive your sins.

God, protect me from pride and stubbornness. When I mess up, give me the grace to run to You quickly. Instead of burying my mistakes, help me surrender them to You with humility. I trust You to fix what I cannot.

JULY 8

Not an Adversary

Hear us, Shepherd of Israel,
you who lead Joseph like a flock.

PSALM 80:1 NIV

We've all experienced God's hand of discipline in our lives. Just like Israel had to deal with their sin, we need to deal with the consequences of our own actions. It's important to understand that when God disciplines us, He isn't our adversary. He is our kind shepherd who knows exactly what we need. He loves us and wants what is best for us. He knows how we operate, what our strengths and weaknesses are, and what we need to change and grow.

God always knows exactly what you need. He knows what each of your days will look like, and He knows how your story will unfold. He knows every battle you will face and every tear you will cry. In His sovereignty, He is capable of preparing you for struggles you aren't even aware of yet. He is an expert teacher, a faithful shepherd, and a beloved father. When you are humbly surrendered to His ways, He will continuously intervene on your behalf.

God, give me confidence in Your ability to guide me. Thank You for the reminder that You are a faithful and attentive shepherd. I trust Your leadership in my life.

JULY 9

Shine Your Light

*Restore us, O God;
make your face shine on us,
that we may be saved.*

PSALM 80:3 NIV

Throughout Psalm 80, the same sentiment is repeated multiple times. Anytime this happens in Scripture, it is wise to pay attention. In this case, the psalmist asks God to restore them so they might be saved. It's a repeated acknowledgment that God is the only one who can bring restoration. When our lives are a mess, or our circumstances are painful, God is the only one who can bring healing and revival. We need His intervention more than anything else.

Just like the earth needs the warmth of the sun to sustain life, you need God's face to shine upon you. You need His presence in order to be fully alive. His light is your source of comfort, warmth, and illumination. Life is infinitely colder, darker, and more confusing without Him. You were created by Him for His glory. His presence is the only place you will find true fulfillment and belonging. When you turn to other less worthy sources of light, you will inevitably be disappointed. The light of God's face is truly what you need most.

God, shine Your light upon my life. I need You more than anything or anyone else. Restore me and give me grace to have an unhindered relationship with You. You are worthy of all my devotion and praise.

JULY 10

Master Gardener

*You transplanted a vine from Egypt;
you drove out the nations and planted it.
You cleared the ground for it,
and it took root and filled the land.*

PSALM 80:8-9 NIV

Psalm 80 is full of imagery comparing Israel to a vine. As we read through it, we see a picture of how God is the one who planted the vine, and He is the one who tends to it. As the gardener, He knows what is best for the vine, and He is capable of protecting it. Everything He does is for the health and well-being of the vine. He provides for it, nourishes it, and keeps it safe from harm. God's love and care for Israel is thorough and intentional, just like a gardener's care for his garden.

In the same way that God tended to Israel, He tends to you. He knows what you need, and He is capable of providing it. He protects you, nourishes you, and keeps you safe. You can trust His expert hands to shape and transform your life so that it bears as much fruit as possible. When He prunes you, it is for your good. When He pulls weeds of sin from your life, it is so they don't overtake healthy growth. If you allow Him to, He will faithfully tend to you just like He did Israel.

God, You are the master gardener of my life. I trust You to help me grow and flourish. Soften my heart and give me grace to daily place my life in Your hands.

JULY 11

Natural Consequences

> Watch over this vine,
> the root your right hand has planted,
> the son you have raised up for yourself.
> Your vine is cut down, it is burned with fire;
> at your rebuke your people perish.
>
> PSALM 80:15-16 NIV

In Psalm 80, we read about the destruction of Israel through the comparison of a vine being cut down, burned, and taken from. The vine is ruined because it's no longer being protected by the strong walls of the city. It became vulnerable and easy to attack. In the same way, Israel was destroyed and without protection. Israel suffered at the hands of others, but they also suffered because of their own sin. God removed His hand of protection because Israel refused to be faithful.

While difficulty is not always a result of your sin, it could be. If you have been living in a way that is contrary to God's design, you might be experiencing some of the consequences of your own sin. It's not healthy to shoulder unnecessary guilt, but it's also not healthy to be oblivious to the natural outcomes of your actions. Ask the Holy Spirit for guidance and search Scripture for instructions. As you remain humble and open to correction, God will keep you on the right path.

God, thank You for Your guidance in my life. I cannot do it alone. Keep me from being too prideful to admit when I am wrong. Give me the strength to listen to Your correction when You give it.

JULY 12

Listen Well

*"Oh, that my people would listen to me!
Oh, that Israel would follow me, walking in my paths!
How quickly I would then subdue their enemies!"*

PSALM 81:13-14 NLT

When reading through Psalm 81, we can almost hear the ache of God's heart. He longs for Israel to listen to His voice. He wants them to understand that everything He does is for their good. He wants them to submit to His ways so He can keep them safe and help them thrive. He knows they don't want to listen, but like any good father, He wants them to see that He knows what's best.

God's ways are always better than your own. When you choose to wander away from His plan for your life, you are doing the same thing Israel did. When you are tempted to ignore what God is saying, remember that He knows best. It is never too late to change direction and move toward Him. No matter how far you think you've wandered, His mercy is available when you surrender and seek forgiveness.

God, I don't want my thoughts or actions to be a source of grief for You. May the words I say and the things I do be honoring to You. Help me hear Your voice clearly and follow Your instructions diligently.

JULY 13

Reward for Obedience

*"I would feed you with the finest wheat.
I would satisfy you with wild honey from the rock."*

PSALM 81:16 NLT

We were created to have a dynamic relationship with God. He longs to communicate with us and be involved in our lives. As we listen to His voice and are obedient to His plans for us, we experience the blessings that come from having His hand upon our lives. He does not ask us to follow rules simply for the sake of obedience. Instead, every single standard He has set has a purpose. His ways are best even if the road is narrow and difficult to travel.

In Psalm 81, God tells the Israelites that if they follow Him, He will satisfy them. The same is true for you today. When you honor God's instructions, He gives you a multitude of gifts. Sometimes, you will experience physical blessings, and sometimes, you will experience spiritual or emotional blessings. The rewards you get for obedience might be evident in your life now, or sometimes you won't see them until the other side of heaven. Either way, He will not leave you empty-handed. Obedience is always a blessing.

God, thank You for the way you bless me and provide for me. Help me live a life worthy of the calling You have given me. I don't deserve the good gifts You give. Thank You for being so generous and kind.

JULY 14

Without Discrimination

*"Provide justice for the needy and the fatherless;
uphold the rights of the oppressed and the destitute.
Rescue the poor and needy;
save them from the power of the wicked."*

PSALM 82:3-4 CSB

Social justice is not optional for the believer. We don't get to decide whether or not we will advocate for the poor and needy. God has a heart for the marginalized of society, and so should we. It's easy to let our social or political opinions carry more weight than God's call to be compassionate and servant-hearted. Instead, we should take every opportunity to set aside our own comfort in favor of sharing God's grace and mercy with those who need it most.

God places incredible value on every human life. He does not pick and choose who deserves His love, mercy, or grace. Showing partiality or favoritism does not reflect God's love. Instead, do your best to cherish each person regardless of ethnicity, social status, or economic position. While the labor of loving others can be inconvenient and even painful at times, it is a worthy calling.

God, forgive me for the times I have overlooked people who deserve to know You. Fill my heart with compassion and show me opportunities to lay my life down for others.

JULY 15

Quietly Faithful

O God, do not remain silent;
do not turn a deaf ear,
do not stand aloof, O God.

PSALM 83:1 NIV

By reading through the Psalms, we can find validation for some of our emotions. When we realize that it's a common human experience to feel discouraged by God's perceived silence, our faith is strengthened. If the psalmist felt like God wasn't helping him, then we don't need to be ashamed when we feel that way. Instead, we can put our energy into focusing on what we know is true about God's character.

Just because you can't see how God is moving doesn't mean He isn't at work. Just because you would deal with a situation differently doesn't mean God is uninvolved. His stillness is not a lack of faithfulness. As you cry out to Him in desperation, remember that His answer might be different from what you want. His faithfulness does not depend on your perspective or understanding. Just like He was faithful to Israel, He will be faithful to you.

God, thank You for the reassurance I find in the Psalms. Encourage me when I think You are silent or uninvolved. Help me depend on the truth rather than how I feel. Teach me how to be faithful to You even when I don't understand how You are moving.

JULY 16

Spiritual Battles

Our struggle is not against flesh and blood, but against the rulers, against the authorities, against the powers of this dark world and against the spiritual forces of evil in the heavenly realms.

EPHESIANS 6:12 NIV

Throughout the Psalms, we read about physical enemies who threaten David's life. Even as he deals with those circumstances, he often recognizes that there is a spiritual element to the battles he faces. Later, in the New Testament, we are reminded that the struggles we encounter are often because of an unseen enemy. Our troubles might be physical, but they are also spiritual. Until Jesus returns and redeems all things, we must stand strong against the enemy's attacks.

As long as you proclaim allegiance to God and seek to follow His ways, you will have spiritual opposition in your life. It isn't a matter of if but when and how. As you seek to remain faithful despite the attacks of the enemy, remember that God will protect you and equip you to endure every trial you face. He does not leave you alone to suffer under the hand of an enemy you can't defeat.

God, give me eyes to see my battles clearly. Help me remember that there is often more going on than I can perceive. Give me strength to endure whatever the enemy throws at me. Fight with me and for me as I seek to remain faithful to You.

JULY 17

Where You Belong

How lovely is your dwelling place,
O Lord of Heaven's Armies.

PSALM 84:1 NLT

In ancient times, the temple was the place where God's people could experience His presence. It was a sacred space, and there were specific rules to follow in order to enter it. God's dwelling place could not be accessed by anyone at any time. When the psalmist declares that there is no better place to be than in God's presence, it shows an understanding of how people needed to be with God. As a society, they centered their lives around the hope that heaven would touch earth. The psalmist longs to spend all of his days in the dwelling place of God.

Built within you is an inherent desire to be with God. Now, because of Jesus, there is nothing holding you back from continuously experiencing God's presence. Jesus' death on the cross has given you eternal access to the throne room of God. Jesus walked the earth and willingly laid down His life so that every barrier between you and God would be removed. You don't have to enter a temple, follow rules of worship, or use sacrifices to sanctify yourself. There is nothing in the way of connecting with God.

God, fill my heart with a desire to be in Your presence. Remind me of the satisfaction and joy that can only be found with You. Thank You for giving me eternal access to Your presence through Jesus.

JULY 18

Barriers Removed

What joy for those who can live in your house, always singing your praises.

Psalm 84:4 NLT

As modern readers, we can't understand the full impact of what it was like for the Israelites to worship in the temple. In the temple there were two main spaces: the inner court and the outer court. God's presence was found in the inner court, inside the Holy of Holies. Separating the Holy of Holies and the inner court was a curtain that could not be passed by anyone but the high priest. It was a physical barrier between God's presence and the people.

When Jesus took His last breath, the curtain was torn in half. This curtain was not a typical piece of fabric as you might imagine it. It was four inches thick, and it tore from top to bottom. No one removed it or cut it; it supernaturally ripped in half. Through Christ, the barrier between people and God was physically and spiritually removed. Now, you can experience the joy of continually living in God's presence.

God, thank You for making a way for me to be close to You. Thank You for tearing the curtain and drawing me into Your presence forever. Give me a fresh revelation of the gift of Your presence.

JULY 19

Better than Anything

*A single day in your courts
is better than a thousand anywhere else!*

PSALM 84:10 NLT

When we have an eternal perspective, our priorities naturally fall into order. As we surrender our lives to God and seek to be obedient to His ways, we will find that nothing is better than staying on the path He chooses. There is nothing as satisfying as spending time with Him. There is nothing as fulfilling as cultivating a relationship with Him. If we allow ourselves to be distracted by the things the world values, we will miss out on what is best for us.

God's presence is better than anything else the world can offer. Being with Him is better than having an overflowing bank account, a wide circle of influence, a top-notch education, or a home full of material possessions. Being with Him is better than checking off a travel bucket list, eating at a five-star restaurant, or seeing your favorite artist in concert. None of those things are inherently bad, but they simply can't compare to the joy and satisfaction that comes from knowing and being known by God.

God, knowing You and being known by You is such a gift. Draw my heart toward You and remind me of the satisfaction that can only be found in Your presence. Give me the grace to cultivate a relationship with You above all else.

JULY 20

Everlasting Light

The Lord God is our sun and our shield.

Psalm 84:11 NLT

God is a light for those who yearn for His presence. When we seek Him, He shines on our hearts and our lives. He illuminates the darkness and helps us see the truth clearly. He provides warmth, comfort, and goodness when we are loyal to His name. He gives us protection, provision, and safety when we seek Him with everything we have. There is no limit to the blessings that come from knowing Him and being known by Him.

While life isn't always easy, and following God means walking a narrow path, remember that there is unimaginable blessing involved as well. You will face trials, but you can also know the kind of joy that doesn't make sense to the world. You will experience suffering alongside Christ, but He will also be your sun and your shield. If your priority is to develop an ongoing relationship with your Creator, He will be with you every step of the way, shining His everlasting light on every part of your life.

God, thank You for being my sun and my shield. I long for more of Your presence in my life! Guide me along the path You have chosen for me.

JULY 21

Keep Meeting

Let us not neglect our meeting together, as some people do, but encourage one another, especially now that the day of his return is drawing near.

HEBREWS 10:25 NLT

While we have God's Spirit to guide us and His presence is always with us, it's important that we don't ignore the corporate worship experience. It is good and right to experience God's presence together. Through corporate worship, we can carry each other's burdens, encourage one another, and call each other toward greater obedience to God's plan for our lives.

The benefits of a healthy community cannot be replaced in your life. While you can find a lot of richness and truth through social media or online church, it's important to see those things as tools rather than your primary means of connection. Meeting face-to-face allows for fellowship that is authentic, vulnerable, and real. If this is an area of your life that is lacking, bring your needs before the Lord. Ask Him to show you a place where you can find the kind of relationships your soul needs.

Lord, thank You for the gift of community. Thank You for the way other people can point me toward truth and teach me about new aspects of Your character. Thank You for accountability and the ability to worship You together.

JULY 22

Always Good

*You forgave the guilt of your people—
yes, you covered all their sins.*

PSALM 85:2 NLT

This Psalm is a proclamation made after the Israelite people returned from exile. Even though they endured terrible circumstances, they acknowledge God's faithfulness. It would have made perfect sense for them to dwell on the awful things they went through, yet there is a consistent theme of God's goodness woven throughout the Psalm. Despite his circumstances, the psalmist is thankful for God's forgiveness and redemption.

Even when you walk through difficult seasons, there are opportunities to praise God. Acknowledging what He's done for you does not make your hurt or frustration any less valid. In fact, praise and worship are tools that can lift your spirit and broaden your perspective. As you hold tightly to what God has done, it can encourage you and help you persevere until your circumstances change.

God, help me remember Your faithfulness in times of trouble. Help me focus on Your goodness with a heart that trusts in You, even when it would make sense for me to complain. Help me have a heavenly perspective rather than an earthly one.

JULY 23

Over and Over

Restore us again, O God of our salvation.
Put aside your anger against us once more.

PSALM 85:4 NLT

We are each prone to wander toward different sins. We have different propensities and desires. None of us come close to God's standard of perfection. Instead of comparing the ways we choose to sin, it can be more fruitful to focus on the fact that God is faithful to restore each of us no matter how many times we fail. Each of us are in desperate need of the continued mercy of God.

If you've followed God for any amount of time, you have likely experienced victory over certain sins in your life. It's also possible that you have habits or struggles that are more difficult to change. Today, take a moment and thank God for the way He has continued to love you despite your weaknesses. Every single time you run to Him and humbly ask for forgiveness, He is faithful to help you. He doesn't keep a list of how many times you've failed. Be encouraged by His mercy and strengthened by His grace.

God, sometimes I'm discouraged by the mistakes I seem to make over and over. Strengthen me by Your grace and help me honor You with my actions. Thank You for being merciful and kind whenever I ask You for forgiveness.

JULY 24

Ask For Revival

*Won't you revive us again,
so your people can rejoice in you?*

PSALM 85:6 NLT

When we repent from our sins, the end goal is to be restored to uninterrupted communion with God. Sin stands between us and the relationship we were created for. When God restores us it's not so that we simply feel better or look better; He restores us so that we can experience the fullness of His presence once again. We were created to rejoice in Him, and sin gets in the way of that.

Continued sin often causes a lack of spiritual vitality. When you humbly surrender, ask for forgiveness, and repent, God restores you. He gives you new life. He heals what is broken, and He makes dry land flourish again. He takes hard hearts, and He softens them. He takes impossible situations, and He makes a way through them. All of this is miraculous and more than you deserve. The key is that you must ask. God won't intervene in your life without your permission.

God, I want more of You in my life. Fill me with Your spirit and give me new life. Revive me and draw me closer to You.

JULY 25

Embrace Weakness

Lord, in my place of weakness and need, I ask again:
Will you come and help me?
I know I'm always in your thoughts.
You are my true Savior and hero,
so don't delay to deliver me now, for you are my God.

PSALM 40:17 TPT

God always hears prayers that are offered in humility from a place of hardship. He takes special care of His people who are broken, needy, and dependent on Him. He pays attention when we call Him, and He is mindful of us when we are weak. He is compassionate, kind, and always ready to intervene on our behalf.

When you are aware of your weaknesses, God is always ready to help. He will not turn you away when you call on His name. There is no need to clean yourself up or figure out your problems alone. In the middle of a trial, when your attitude is wrong and your emotions are a mess, call upon God. Allow Him to guide you through whatever you are facing. Don't be ashamed to ask for help. Remember that He willingly offers you His peace, wisdom, and comfort.

God, help me develop the habit of calling upon You when I am overcome by weakness. Forgive me for the times I have let pride stand in the way of asking for help. Remind me that it is okay to be needy when I am clinging to You.

JULY 26

Righteousness and Peace

*The Lord will indeed give what is good,
and our land will yield its harvest.
Righteousness goes before him
and prepares the way for his steps.*

PSALM 85:12-13 NIV

In Scripture, righteousness is first and foremost associated with justice. When the justice of God prevails, peace is the result. In other words, when we follow God's example of what is right and wrong, we experience peace or well-being. When we disregard God's example and allow our actions to fall outside of His standards, we won't experience God's best for us.

God's plan for righteousness is fulfilled in Jesus. Through Christ, everything that's wrong is made right. He is the answer to everything you lack. His example is the only one worth following. When you surrender your life at the foot of the cross, Christ's perfection becomes your own. Through His death and resurrection, you are aligned with God's idea of perfection as Jesus stands in the gap. Through Jesus, your relationship with God is made right.

God, thank You for the righteousness I have in Christ. Strengthen me to keep living according to your ways. Give me the peace that comes from living a life that lines up with Your standards.

JULY 27

Ask for Help

Hear my prayer, Lord;
listen to my cry for mercy.
When I am in distress, I call to you,
because you answer me.

PSALM 86:6-7 NIV

In Psalm 86, the psalmist is in trouble, and he handles it by asking God to give him wisdom. This is helpful because it reminds us that we aren't meant to operate with our own understanding. In all things, it is best to call upon the Lord. His wisdom is far above ours. His understanding is perfect and complete. Even the advice of other people can be faulty, but God's wisdom is what we need. When we face troubles of any kind, the best solution is to pause and ask God for guidance, strength, and perseverance.

You are not meant to manage life on your own. You aren't expected to master every aspect of Christianity and execute it flawlessly. You were created to be dependent upon the one who made you. Leaning on Him is not a sign of weakness. In fact, you show incredible strength when you remain dependent on God. Asking Him for help shows that you see Him rightly.

God, soften my heart and teach me to be dependent on You. When I begin to lean on my own strength, draw me back to You. Give me grace to seek Your understanding above my own.

JULY 28

Undivided Heart

> Teach me your way, Lord,
> that I may rely on your faithfulness;
> give me an undivided heart,
> that I may fear your name.
>
> PSALM 86:11 NIV

Throughout Scripture, we see a continuous call to be devoted to God. We are called to show the highest respect for our Creator. His ways are higher than ours, and He alone is worthy of our praise. In Psalm 86, David shows us an example of what it means to have undivided devotion to God. Just as he sought wisdom and tried to stay on the path God had for Him, so should we.

If your heart is divided, you will find it difficult to serve God. You can't give yourself fully to more than one thing. You can't serve God and love the ways of the world. You can't love others fully but put your own needs first. A divided heart is ineffective and unsustainable. Follow David's example and humbly ask God for help. Do your best to learn His ways and rely on His faithfulness. Ask Him for an undivided heart, and He will give it to you.

God, You alone are worthy of all I have. I don't want to run after more than one thing. Show me if there are areas of my life that are divided. Give me grace to be loyal and committed to You alone.

JULY 29

Fear and Faith

Give me a sign of your goodness,
that my enemies may see it and be put to shame,
for you, Lord, have helped me and comforted me.

PSALM 86:17 NIV

The presence of fear does not mean our faith is weak. David is an excellent example of being afraid and having faith simultaneously. He was consistently in the midst of difficult circumstances, yet his faith did not waver. He expressed his fear and frustration, and he also faithfully declared God's goodness despite his situation. He called upon God in the presence of his enemies and trusted that He would show up.

There is nothing wrong with you if you are afraid. You aren't weak or broken. It's a natural human emotion, and you don't have to be ashamed of it. Instead, let fear be a red flag that it's time to deliberately declare God's truth over your life. As you call upon Him in the midst of fear, He will strengthen you to endure whatever you are facing. He will be with you every step of the way. The more you lean on His strength over your own, the less power fear will have in your life.

God, thank You for the example of David. Thank You for holding my fear gently and strengthening me when I need it. Teach me how to call upon You no matter how afraid I am. I surrender my worries to You and trust You to lead me.

JULY 30

Citizens of Heaven

He has founded his city on the holy mountain.

PSALM 87:1 NIV

God has prepared a place for us to spend eternity. We are not meant to live in the chaos of this world. Our true home is with Him, in the city He has made for His people. No matter what it says on our passport, our citizenship is with Him. This can be a great comfort to us when we feel out of place in this world. When the news is overwhelming, and everything feels wrong, we can find hope knowing that one day we will live in a place of peace with our Creator.

If you are discouraged by the state of the world, don't despair. A day is coming when everything will be made right. If you are overwhelmed by what the future might hold, don't let your faith in God's plan waver. He is not surprised by the current state of affairs. In His perfect timing, He will fix everything that is broken. When you struggle to live as a foreigner in this world, remember that it is temporary. Your time here will pass, and you will spend forever in your true home.

God, thank You for making a place for me. Thank You for welcoming me into Your kingdom and giving me a home. When I am overwhelmed by the world, help me lean on You.

JULY 31

You Belong

*The Lord will write in the register of the peoples:
"This one was born in Zion."*

PSALM 87:6 NIV

As believers, we belong to Zion. When we made the choice to follow Yahweh, we were given a new identity. It doesn't matter what our birth certificate says, where we live, or what our family history looks like. God made each of us new when we surrendered to Him. We are part of His family and His kingdom. The titles we have now were given to us by the one who has all authority in heaven and earth; they can't be taken away by anyone less worthy.

You belong in God's family. With Him, you are provided for, accepted, and loved. You are not out of place. You have the privileges and responsibilities that come with being in any family. You have an eternal inheritance, and you have the opportunity to love what God loves and hate what He hates. As you embrace your identity as His child, He will teach you to live in a way that reflects His character. He is a good father who loves to guide and equip His children.

God, thank You for the home I have in You. Thank You for welcoming me into Your family and kingdom. Teach me how to live in a way that reflects Your values. I want to represent my family well.

AUGUST

AUGUST 1

When You're in Pain

> Hear my prayer;
> listen to my cry.
> For my life is full of troubles,
> and death draws near.
>
> PSALM 88:2-3 NLT

Psalm 88 bears a striking resemblance to the story of Job. Job experienced great suffering yet remained faithful to God. Even when he lost everything, he declared God's goodness. The psalmist seems to be experiencing something similar. He is full of grief and is walking through a season of darkness. Both situations remind us that sometimes God allows us to experience great difficulty. He doesn't always lift us out of our pain, but He does equip us to endure it.

It's important to recognize that just because God allows difficulty, He isn't the cause of it. He does not create it, but He mercifully gives you what you need to persevere. He is not your enemy; He is your refuge and strength. He is a kind father who grieves when you are in pain. He sees you and is gentle with your hurts. You may never fully understand why you experience certain things, but you can have unshakeable confidence that God will be with you through it all.

Father, thank You for the gift of Your presence. Thank You for keeping me steady even when life feels unbearable. Help me to trust You, even when I don't understand the trials I am facing.

AUGUST 2

In Darkness

Darkness is my closest friend.
Psalm 88:18 nlt

Sometimes circumstances are out of our control, and we feel overcome by grief that we cannot overcome. Sometimes, our knees buckle under the weight of our trials, and we struggle to remain steady and upright. If we view these seasons as a personal failure or the abandonment of God, we won't be able to endure them.

When it feels like darkness is your closest friend, God is closer. If depression feels like a heavy blanket, you are not alone. If you have experienced a significant loss or heartbreak and feel as if you can't go on, you are not a failure. God sees your pain, and He promises to be gentle with you. He is not frustrated by your weakness or disappointed by your inability to conquer it. Instead, He longs for you to call upon Him and allow Him to help. He longs to comfort you, strengthen you, and lead you through whatever you are experiencing.

Heavenly Father, You see my greatest pain. You know me inside and out, and You are aware of my needs. Meet me when I am broken and comfort me as I grieve. Thank You for staying close to me when I feel overcome by darkness.

AUGUST 3

History of Faithfulness

I will sing about the Lord's faithful love forever;
I will proclaim your faithfulness to all generations
with my mouth.

PSALM 89:1 CSB

When the Israelites disobeyed God and experienced the consequences of their actions, they didn't know that God would fulfill His promises. They trusted Him, but they didn't have the physical proof that we have. They didn't see Jesus walk the earth, and their hope was completely dependent on what they had already seen God do. They clung to His already proven faithfulness.

The Israelites didn't know how God would fulfill His promises, yet they trusted Him. You have the benefit of hindsight and the guiding truth of Scripture to lead you through life. You have thousands of years of documented divine intervention. You have the life and death of Jesus, and you have your own personal story of how God has shown up in your life. The resources available to you are vast. When you are tempted to doubt, take advantage of everything at your disposal. Dive into the Word, be encouraged by the testimonies of others, and lean upon God's faithfulness in your own life.

God, I am thankful to live in a time when I have so much access to biblical truth. Help me to take advantage of the resources I have. Remind me of Your faithfulness throughout my life.

AUGUST 4

Stepping Stones

Lord, where are the former acts of your faithful love that you swore to David in your faithfulness?

Psalm 89:49 csb

Throughout the Psalms, we see that each writer depends on God's history of faithfulness. They knew what God had done in the past, and they believed that He would show up in the future. They trusted Him because they were well-versed in stories of His provision, care, and divine intervention. We can utilize the same tools to strengthen our faith. When we notice God's presence in our lives, we can record it and look back on it when we need encouragement.

Every time God shows up in your life, you have the opportunity to build stepping stones of faith. Deliberately take note of what God is doing and choose to remember it when times are hard. When you study a book, you might put sticky notes on the pages so you can easily reference them when needed. In the same way, you can create bookmarks or stepping stones in your own life. Then, when trials come, you can be encouraged that the God who showed up for you in the past is the same one who will show up in your present.

God, I know my life is filled with instances of Your faithfulness. Help me deliberately record them. I don't want to forget all You've done for me. When trials come, help me lean on Your already proven goodness.

AUGUST 5

Natural and Expected

> Lord, you have been our dwelling place
> throughout all generations.
>
> Psalm 90:1 niv

Some of us didn't grow up in homes that used eternal language. We didn't grow up attributing the glory of creation to a god of any kind, let alone the one true God. This wasn't the case for Israel. Culturally, they were very familiar with the idea of God as their eternal dwelling place. Stories of God's faithfulness were passed down through generations, and people grew up hearing about how their ancestors worshiped Yahweh.

There is a constant fight in today's culture to remove God from every aspect of society. Just because society as a whole doesn't operate the way it used to doesn't mean you can't follow Israel's example in the Old Testament. Your home and the way you live can declare God's goodness. You can pass down stories of His faithfulness to the next generation. You get to decide the language and tone of your household. Make discussions of God's faithfulness natural and expected.

God, I want my family to be familiar with eternal language. Help me set the tone for my household. May we honor You as our eternal dwelling place in everything we do. Help us declare Your goodness every day.

AUGUST 6

Everlasting God

*Before the mountains were born
or you brought forth the whole world,
from everlasting to everlasting you are God.*

Psalm 90:2 niv

God has no beginning and no end. He is everlasting. He created everything we see, and He will exist for eternity. Our concept of time and creation is so limited compared to God's. Scripture teaches that He transcends space and time. This means that God has full knowledge of the past, present, and future. He is fully present in all of time.

God is as much in your future as He is in your present. You see time as linear, but God sees it in its entirety. He sees the whole picture at once, and He is present in each part of it. There is nowhere you can go that He isn't. This is why you can trust Him so willingly with everything that is yet to come. Your understanding is limited, but His is perfect and complete. Trust in Him, the God who exists from everlasting to everlasting.

God, I trust Your eternal existence. When I begin to worry or fret over the details of my life, help me lean on Your perfect perspective. Give me understanding when I need it and wisdom to make choices that honor You.

AUGUST 7

Limited Time

> Teach us to number our days,
> that we may gain a heart of wisdom.
>
> PSALM 90:12 NIV

The average lifespan isn't very long. We each have approximately 70 to 80 years on this earth. In comparison to the time we will spend in eternity, it's very short. The challenge we all face is to use the time we have with wisdom. Are we making investments that really matter? Are we living with eternity in mind? Our lives don't end when we take our last breath. Rather, our current lives are preparation for the life that is to come.

If you ask God what He wants you to accomplish with your life, He will tell you. If your plans are committed to Him, He will make sure they have a kingdom impact. It's not your responsibility to orchestrate His will; it's your responsibility to be obedient when He calls you. Keep your heart soft and listen when He gives you instructions. He is capable of managing your time if you let Him.

God, I want to faithfully serve You. I want my time to matter and make a difference. I trust You to guide me. Give me grace to be obedient when You call me to action.

AUGUST 8

Presence Equals Peace

*Whoever dwells in the shelter of the Most High
will rest in the shadow of the Almighty.*

Psalm 91:1 niv

There is a direct connection between the amount of time we spend in God's presence and how much peace we experience in our lives. When we have complete trust in God, it assures us that He will be our refuge in times of trouble. He will give us rest when the world feels chaotic, or our circumstances don't make sense.

God is your ever-present help in times of trouble. He will give you peace and rest when you trust Him. One of the greatest blessings of following Him is that you are no longer dependent on your circumstances to experience joy, peace, or contentment. Even if your life is full of turmoil, God is your source of goodness. Everything you truly need is found in Him. While the world trusts in details that shift and change, your security comes from the one who never changes. He is always reliable, steady, and available to you.

God, You are all I need. Thank You for giving me rest and shelter even when life feels chaotic or full of storms. Help me rely on the steadiness of who You are rather than my ever-changing circumstances.

AUGUST 9

Foundation of Truth

*No harm will overtake you,
no disaster will come near your tent.*

PSALM 91:10

Nothing can happen to a faithful servant of God unless He allows it. This can be difficult to believe when we are dealing with suffering, heartache, and difficult circumstances. When we are in danger or walking through times of trouble, it's easy to assume God has abandoned us. Instead, we must rely on the truth rather than our feelings. When difficulties come up, we lean on the foundation that has already been built.

Filling your heart with the Word is like making sure there is water in your well. When droughts happen, you won't despair if your well is full. Likewise, when problems happen in your life, you won't despair if you have a solid foundation of biblical truth to lean on. God says that no harm will overtake you. If you believe this with all your heart, you will stand firm even when your circumstances are shaken.

God, fill my heart and mind with truth. When problems come up, help me lean on what You have said. Thank You for the promise of protection. I trust You to work everything out according to Your will.

AUGUST 10

Angel Commander

He will command his angels concerning you to guard you in all your ways.

Psalm 91:11 niv

When we choose to follow God, He does not leave us alone to fend for ourselves. He commissions angels to watch carefully over the lives and interests of people who are faithful to Him. He takes special notice of people who are deeply committed to knowing and serving Him. Angels guard believers both physically and spiritually. Protection is promised to those who are pursuing a relationship with God.

Even when no one understands what you are going through, you are not alone. God is with you, and He has commanded His angels concerning you. With your life committed to Him, you are safe in His hands. As you trust God and follow His purposes, He promises to fight with you and for you. As you are obedient to Him, He is working everything out for your good.

God, thank You for protecting me even when I don't understand. Thank You for keeping me safe in the midst of trials and for fighting battles I cannot win. I am so thankful for Your protection and provision.

AUGUST 11

He Will Answer

"He will call on me, and I will answer him;
I will be with him in trouble,
I will deliver him and honor him."

PSALM 91:15 NIV

God is greater than any threat you face. The Almighty has the power to confront and destroy any enemy you have. Having a relationship with Him provides assurance that He is with you in any circumstance. The Lord Most High is on your side. He has all authority in heaven and earth, and you are His treasured child. He has loved you with an everlasting love, and He will always be with you.

God is your shield and defense. He is the God of the entire universe, yet you are the object of His greatest affection. He loved you long before you even had the capacity to love Him back. Everything you do is a response to what He has already done for you. If you call on Him, He will answer you. If you are in trouble, He will be with you.

God, thank You for Your protection and help. I would be lost without You. When I am in trouble, remind me I can call upon You.

AUGUST 12

Enduring Praise

*It is good to give thanks to the Lord,
to sing praises to the Most High.*

PSALM 92:1 NLT

Praise and thanksgiving are basic elements in the life of a believer. The very foundation of our relationship with Him is worth an attitude of thanksgiving. The salvation He has provided through Christ is reason enough to praise Him on a daily basis. Even if the circumstances of our lives are difficult, the gift of the gospel remains.

You will have plenty of days when you don't feel thankful. You might be annoyed, frustrated, discouraged, or full of grief. No matter what emotion you are experiencing, the truth of the gospel does not change. It is steady through the ups and downs of life. In all things, you can choose to be thankful for the redeeming love of Jesus. When you focus on the unchanging truth of the gospel, the shifting circumstances of life won't seem as catastrophic.

God, I want to praise You faithfully and with endurance. Give me grace to turn to You in the midst of trials. As I focus on Your goodness, transform my perspective and help me persevere through the difficulties of life.

AUGUST 13

Dynamic Relationship

You thrill me, Lord, with all you have done for me!
I sing for joy because of what you have done.
PSALM 92:4 NLT

Praise is an overflow of our hearts. When we experience God's hand in our lives, it only makes sense that worship and praise pour out of us. In order for that to happen, we must be willing for God to intervene. We have to participate in a dynamic relationship with Him where He speaks, and we respond. When the cry of our hearts is for Him to be Lord of our lives, we will not have a shortage of reasons to praise Him.

Your relationship with God is not meant to be one-sided. He won't work where you have not given Him permission to. If you want Him to move in your life, you must invite Him to be involved. Surrender your heart to Him and let Him transform it. Give Him the details of your days and commit your plans to Him. Listen to His instructions and obey His commands. When your desire is to faithfully honor Him in all you do, you will more clearly see the way He is moving in your life.

God, soften my heart today. Fill me with a greater desire to honor You in all I do. I want You to be involved in every part of my life. May my heart overflow with praise as I follow You.

AUGUST 14

Fully Surrendered

*The LORD reigns, he is robed in majesty;
The LORD is robed in majesty and armed with strength;
indeed, the world is established, firm and secure.*

PSALM 93:1 NIV

We know that God is in control. This is a truth that is easy to proclaim but more difficult to live out practically. Even though we declare God is sovereign, have we really given Him control of our lives? Have we included Him in the details of our days? Are we giving Him space in every part of our lives? If not, what can we do about it?

When you allow God access to every part of your life, you are celebrating His kingship and recognizing His character. You can trust Him because You know He is reliable. You can follow His lead because you know He is eternally wise, kind, and loving. You can bow down to His sovereignty because you know He is worthy of your praise.

God, I want my heart to be fully devoted to You. You are worthy of every part of my life. Show me any areas I have withheld from You out of pride, fear, or selfishness. Soften my heart and give me grace to surrender all I have to You.

AUGUST 15

Partner with Him

The Lord is a God who avenges.
O God who avenges, shine forth.
How long, Lord, will the wicked,
how long will the wicked be jubilant?

PSALM 94:1, 3 NIV

God does not ignore or overlook injustice. We are faced with news of wars and awful crimes on a daily basis. It can be tempting to doubt Him or question His ability to intervene. It's important to remember that He is a God who avenges. The injustice in this world does not go unnoticed. Instead, He asks us to partner with Him to stop the progression of evil. We are called to pray and intercede as well as to stand firm as protectors of the oppressed.

The enemy would love you to believe that you are helpless. He would love you to believe that your place at the kitchen table, with your Bible in hand, is a place of weakness. The truth is that You are strong and capable of creating change in the world. Filling your mind with truth, declaring Scripture over situations of injustice, and interceding on behalf of the oppressed is powerful. You have the ability to partner with God as He works toward peace and righteousness on earth.

God, I don't want to stay silent in the face of injustice. Fill me with a sense of urgency to see Your will be done on earth as it is in heaven. When I feel helpless, remind me of the power of prayer.

AUGUST 16

Grow and Change

*Blessed is the one you discipline, LORD,
the one you teach from your law;
you grant them relief from days of trouble,
till a pit is dug for the wicked.*

PSALM 94:12-13 NIV

Sometimes, we look at God's sovereignty through the lens of judgment. We see Him as the authority over all things who has a standard of perfection we must live up to. If this is how we view Him, we've missed the big picture. God's sovereignty is a blessing. Everything He does comes from a foundation of love. Even when we experience the consequences of our own actions, we can trust that God's love is still present, and He knows what is best for us.

Receiving discipline is rarely easy. It can be painful to work toward changing habits or learning from past mistakes. It takes wisdom and humility to recognize that growth is difficult but necessary. You aren't meant to be stagnant, complacent, or trapped by sin. God is an attentive Father who longs to see you experience the fullness of His goodness and love. In order to do that, you must be willing to surrender your sin, repent, and faithfully walk along the path God has laid out for you. God's discipline is a blessing.

God, thank You for being a kind Father who disciplines perfectly. I trust Your guidance and Your ability to cultivate growth in my life.

AUGUST 17

Mercy of Exposure

Unless the LORD had given me help,
I would soon have dwelt in the silence of death.
When I said, "My foot is slipping,"
your unfailing love, LORD, supported me.

PSALM 94:17-18 NIV

There is mercy in the exposure of sin. While it might seem more comfortable to keep our sin secret, it will eventually be our downfall. It's not uncommon to see unfortunate situations in ministry where the sin of church leaders is brought to light. It can be painful to watch everyone involved struggle through the aftermath. Even so, it's better for sin to be brought to light than to be kept hidden. When our own mistakes are revealed, we get to choose how we will react. Will we humbly repent? Or will we stubbornly insist on self-preservation?

When you willingly admit your faults, God reaches in and lifts you up. He supports you with His unfailing love and gives you a firm place to stand. Your desire for repentance is always met with mercy. It's in your best interest to allow Him to help you rather than trying to keep your sin a secret. Even when it's difficult, living in the light is so much less painful than hiding in the dark.

God, have mercy on me! Give me strength to confess and repent when I sin. I want to depend on Your mercy and help rather than insisting on my own way. Protect me from the temptation to hide my sin.

AUGUST 18

Natural Response

*Let us bow down in worship,
let us kneel before the Lord our Maker;
for he is our God
and we are the people of his pasture,
the flock under his care.*

PSALM 95:6-7 NIV

Psalm 95 is a challenge and an encouragement to engage in regular worship. Worship is an outward expression that honors God's worthiness. It's a physical acknowledgment that He is great and deserves our devotion. Worship is an opportunity to respond to God's faithfulness. He has provided for His people from beginning to end. He created us with intention, and He will care for us for all our days.

Worship should be a natural response to God's proven love and provision. You are part of the flock under His care, and it only makes sense to express how thankful you are. As you kneel before the Lord, He blesses you with His presence and transforms your heart. He gives you what you need, and He teaches you how to live. When you turn to Him, He equips you to live in a way that displays His character and honors His purposes.

God, as I come to You in worship, transform my heart to be more like You. As I kneel before You, help me be obedient to Your voice. As I lay my life down for Your purposes, help me honor You in all that I do.

AUGUST 19

Just You and Him

*Sing to the Lord, praise his name;
proclaim his salvation day after day.
Declare his glory among the nations,
his marvelous deeds among all peoples.*

PSALM 96:2-3 NIV

The Israelite people placed a lot of importance on music as a means of worshipful expression. This is even more meaningful when we imagine a society with far less access to information than our own. There wouldn't have been widely available books, social media, or even shared art. Their artistic gift to God was music. They expressed their devotion to Him through individual and corporate songs.

You live in a time when you are overwhelmed with information, opinions, and expressions. Everyone has something to say, and everyone believes their platform is worth listening to. Remember that you don't need anything other than a surrendered heart to worship God. The song within you is a beautiful act of worship when it is presented to God in humility. As you offer Him your life, you bring Him glory.

God, thank You for the gift of music. Thank You that I can worship You anytime, anywhere. Help me remember that my communion with You doesn't depend on external sources.

AUGUST 20

Stand Firm

Let those who love the LORD hate evil,
for he guards the lives of his faithful ones
and delivers them from the hand of the wicked.

PSALM 97:10 NIV

A natural symptom of being close to God is loving what He loves and hating what He hates. Our culture loves a lot of things that God despises. The current trends of our society are in opposition to Scripture. It's not always easy to stand up against those things, and it takes great courage to maintain our convictions in the face of injustice and wrongdoing. Psalm 97 is encouraging because it reminds us that we are not alone in our attempts to remain faithful in the presence of evil.

God has not left you alone to be strong against evil. He is on your side, and He is with you. He strengthens you as you lay your life down and do your best to show His character to the world. When you face challenging situations, the Holy Spirit will equip you to boldly stand firm. If your goal is to courageously adhere to God's standards, He will help you when you ask. You don't have to muster up strength, you simply need to rely on the one who is strongest.

God, teach me to love what You love and hate what You hate. When I am tempted to compromise to fit in, give me strength and courage.

AUGUST 21

For You

> Sing a new song to the LORD,
> for he has performed wonders;
> his right hand and holy arm
> have won him victory.
>
> PSALM 98:1 CSB

If we read Scripture and skip over the Old Testament, we will lose the details and information about why Jesus was needed in the first place. The Psalms consistently point us back to Israel's story, which reflects our own story. Israel's history is our history. By understanding their experiences, we can learn more about how God interacts with His people.

While the Word was not originally written to you, it was written for you. While the original audience is far removed from current culture, there is so much you can learn about God's character and nature. There is a parallel between Israel's victory over their enemies and your victory over sin through Christ. Psalm 98 is a prophecy that is fulfilled through the empowerment of the Holy Spirit in your life as Christ's follower. You sing a new song to the Lord not because He has delivered you from an actual exile but because He has set you free from the power of sin and death.

God, thank You for the universal nature of Scripture. Thank You that I can learn about who You are even though it wasn't written directly to me. Give me understanding as I read and fill my mind with truth.

AUGUST 22

All Things Redeemed

Let the rivers clap their hands;
let the mountains shout together for joy
before the Lord,
for he is coming to judge the earth.
He will judge the world righteously
and the peoples fairly.

PSALM 98:8-9 CSB

Jesus came to redeem humanity, and He will come again. After He rose from the dead, He promised that when He returns, He will make all things new. Scripture says that even nature will rejoice because it, too, will be liberated from corruption. When Christ rules the earth, death, sin, and brokenness will be no more. Everything will be exactly as it was originally intended to be.

The restoration of creation can bring you great joy. Imagine living in the perfection God intended when He created Eden. All of nature will be at peace. Scripture says that the wolf will lay with the lamb, and a little child will lead them. Death, destruction, and pain won't exist. This is what you have to look forward to as a child of God who has been redeemed by Jesus. When your days are difficult, turn your eyes toward what has been promised to you.

God, fill me with anticipation for Christ's return. May the promise of perfection bring me hope and encouragement on difficult days. Thank You for Your plan of redemption.

AUGUST 23

Exalted Above All

> The LORD is king!
> Let the nations tremble!
> He sits on his throne between the cherubim.
> Let the whole earth quake!
>
> PSALM 99:1 NLT

As believers, we cannot overlook God's holiness. Our culture tends to gravitate toward living however we want, but that doesn't always line up with God's standards. He is meant to be elevated above all. His definition of perfection should be the measuring stick we use for our thoughts, words, and actions. When we compare ourselves to Him, we quickly realize that it's impossible for us to be as perfect and holy as God is. This is why we need Jesus.

When Christ died and rose again, He bridged the gap between your humanity and God's perfection. He made a way for you to stand before a holy God and be invited into His presence. The nations should tremble before His majesty, but through Christ, you are given access to Him. Let the realization of His holiness bring you to your knees in thanksgiving and worship.

God, thank You for making a way through Jesus. Thank You for mercifully inviting me into Your presence even when I fall short of Your perfection. Help me be aware of my continuous need for Jesus' sacrifice.

AUGUST 24

He Is Holy

Exalt the Lord our God!
Bow low before his feet, for he is holy!

PSALM 99:5 NLT

God's holiness distinguishes Him from humanity, and it summons us to become more like Him. It's not uncommon for churches to be hyper-focused on grace and mercy. Of course, God is extravagantly merciful, but He is also holy. If we focus on only one aspect of His character, we won't have a full picture of who He is. God's holiness is what makes Him worthy of our worship and praise. He is pure, perfect, complete, and separate from evil. His name is to be treated with the highest honor and respect.

God should never be treated as though He is on the same level as people. While Western culture doesn't embrace the idea of reverence or respect, this is something you can cultivate in your own relationship with God. You can lift His name high in every area of your life. Each day, you have the opportunity to approach Him with awe. Today, ask Him to teach you about His holiness, and He will. Ask Him to give you a full and accurate picture of His character, and He will.

God, I want to be continuously aware of Your holiness. I want to see and know the fullness of Your nature. Show me how I can revere You in a greater way than I have before.

AUGUST 25

Perfect Discipline

> O LORD our God, you answered them.
> You were a forgiving God to them,
> but you punished them when they went wrong.
>
> PSALM 99:8 NLT

God can forgive and discipline people at the same time. He can forgive our sins and restore our relationship to Him yet still allow us to experience the consequences of our actions. When we learn a lesson the hard way, it doesn't mean God isn't being merciful. In fact, experiencing consequences now is infinitely better than the eternal consequence of being separated from His presence. It's not easy to work through the aftermath of sin, but it is worth it.

Just like a wise parent doesn't always rescue their child from a lesson that needs to be learned, sometimes God doesn't rescue us from our own mistakes. He knows exactly what we need to learn and grow, and He is capable of guiding us through those lessons. If we are surrendered to Him, He will mercifully teach us to live in a way that honors Him and reflects His character and love to the world around us.

God, I trust Your guidance in my life. Give me Your perspective when I am walking through a season of difficulty. Help me to lean on You when I face the consequences of my own actions. Help me learn each lesson I face with humility and fortitude.

AUGUST 26

All the Earth

Shout for joy to the Lord, all the earth.

PSALM 100:1 NIV

Psalm 100 is a celebration psalm. It highlights that the gospel was given not just to the Jewish people but to the entire world. All nations are able to take part in God's saving gospel. His grace is universal, and His love knows no boundaries. In God's eyes, we are not divided by ethnicity, country of origin, status, or class. Scripture says that He has poured out His Spirit on all flesh. Separation from God does not come from His end. We decide whether or not we will be close to Him. He opened the door in equal measure for every single person.

Shout for joy because God has not withheld His presence from you. Shout for joy because you have the opportunity to worship and adore the King of Kings. Shout for joy because there is nothing holding you back from experiencing His everlasting love and faithfulness. Any barrier between you and God has been fabricated on your end. His Word says that there is nothing that can separate you from His love.

God, thank You for Your all-inclusive gospel. Thank You for making Your love available to each of us equally as we turn to You in repentance. Give me grace each day to surrender my life to You and lean on what You say is true.

AUGUST 27

Posture of Worship

Worship the Lord with gladness;
come before him with joyful songs.

Psalm 100:2 niv

One of the greatest opportunities we have, both on an individual level and as the corporate body of Christ, is to praise God through songs. We can celebrate His goodness and His guidance in our lives. The act of worship creates space for us to think through the fact that God has created us and has restored our relationship with Him. We celebrate that we belong to Him, and He leads us through life. As we worship, He reminds us of these truths.

When you turn your heart toward God in worship, it's like a declaration that you are available and paying attention to His voice. You are recognizing that He is God, and you are not. As you posture yourself in that way, He can speak to you and transform your heart in His presence. Worship is the foundation for God to move within your life. It turns your eyes toward Him instead of being focused on yourself or the people around you.

God, thank You for the opportunity to worship You. Show me how I can incorporate praise and worship into my everyday life. As I turn my attention toward You, transform my heart to be more like You.

AUGUST 28

Enter with Thanksgiving

> Enter his gates with thanksgiving
> and his courts with praise;
> give thanks to him and praise his name.
>
> PSALM 100:4 NIV

In the Old Testament, when the temple was the primary place for worship, there would have been a gatekeeper who allowed people in and out of the courts of the temple. This verse in Psalm 100 is alluding to that idea. However, it is saying that we enter God's courts with thanksgiving. Thankfulness and praise are the primary methods for being near to God. We don't depend on someone else to give us access. Instead, we posture our hearts to be close to Him.

With thanksgiving as the means for entering God's temple, everyone has access. No one is excluded because everyone has the same opportunity to worship. Each person alive has the ability to direct their thanksgiving and praise toward God. There is nothing holding anyone back. No matter what your life looks like, you can praise Him. No matter how your days are ordered, you can praise God for what He's done and what He promises to do.

God, I praise You for all You've done and have yet to do. Thank You for each good gift You've given me. When I am discouraged, fill my heart with worship.

AUGUST 29

Already Not Yet

*The LORD is good and his love endures forever;
his faithfulness continues through all generations.*

PSALM 100:5 NIV

We live in the tension between already and not yet. God is always good, yet we haven't experienced the fullness of His goodness. God is always faithful, yet we haven't physically seen the fulfillment of every promise He's made. Israel knew God would redeem His people, but Jesus hadn't come yet. They were dependent on His promise. We know that God's heart is for all people and that He desires restoration for everyone, but we also live in the reality of a fallen world. We are waiting for Christ's second coming.

Like Israel, you are dependent on God's promises. Unlike Israel, you have the comfort and encouragement of the Holy Spirit. You have a constant companion who will remind you of God's goodness and love as you wait for Jesus. If you allow Him to, the Holy Spirit will point you toward truth and bring to mind God's previous and present faithfulness. He will strengthen you when you are weak and give you what you need to endure the trials of life. He will remind you of what God has already done and will bolster your faith to look forward to the eternal fulfillment of His promises.

God, thank You for Your goodness and enduring love. Thank You for leading me through each of my days. Fill me anew with Your Holy Spirit and strengthen me to follow You well.

AUGUST 30

At All Times

> Lord, hear my prayer!
> Listen to my plea!
> Don't turn away from me
> in my time of distress.
>
> PSALM 102:1-2 NLT

When we are on our knees begging God to hear us, He does not turn away. He is attentive and available whenever we call upon Him. Psalm 102 is a desperate plea to have an audience with God. The psalmist knew that in his time of distress, God was his only hope. We can follow his example and position our hearts toward God when we are in need. As we pour our hearts out to Him, we are reminded of His faithfulness and willingness to intervene on behalf of His people.

Through the Holy Spirit, you have continuous and uninterrupted access to God. In every circumstance, He will be your advocate and counselor. You don't ever have to wonder if God hears you or if you have access to Him. Through the spirit, you can be in communion with your Father every minute of every day. When you humbly surrender at the cross and call upon Jesus, there is nothing standing between you and His presence.

God, when I doubt Your attentiveness, remind me of what's true. Thank You for the gift of the Holy Spirit. Thank You that I can call upon You anytime and You hear me. Draw me close to Your heart and bless me with the comfort and peace of Your presence.

AUGUST 31

Misplaced Hope

*You, O Lord, will sit on your throne forever.
Your fame will endure to every generation.*

Psalm 102:12 NLT

We each find hope in different things. Some of us feel steady and secure when our relationships are in order. Some of us feel full of hope when our bank account is exactly where we want it to be. Some of us feel confident when our home is neat, tidy, and perfectly presented. No matter what we turn to, it's important to realize that hope found in anything other than Jesus is temporary and superficial. Feelings of security are not the same thing as the guaranteed security found in a relationship with God.

Be wary of finding comfort and hope in your daily circumstances; they are unreliable and will surely change. The only thing that can be truly relied upon is God's character and nature. He will remain King for all eternity. He will sit on His throne forever. If you find hope in religion, human relationships, or material possessions, you will be disappointed. If your hope is found in God, it will never be shaken. Everything around you might change, but God remains the same.

God, search my heart and show me where my hope lies. Help me turn away from things that won't bring eternal satisfaction. I want my hope to be found securely in You and Your unchanging character.

SEPTEMBER

SEPTEMBER 1

Mercifully Unbalanced

Praise the Lord, my soul;
all my inmost being, praise his holy name.

PSALM 103:1 NIV

Psalm 103 starts and ends with the same phrase—*praise the Lord, my soul*. This Psalm expresses feelings of thanksgiving and praise to the Lord because of the benefits and blessings His people enjoy. One of the blessings we gain from Him is the faithfulness of His relationship with us. He is forever present with us, even in the moments when we are not aware of His presence.

There are unending reasons for you to praise God. He deserves to be worshipped because of His great and unfaltering love. His love, expressed through mercy, kindness, compassion, and justice, is more than enough to be worthy of your life-long devotion. He offers you peace, healing, joy, and rest, not to mention eternal security, salvation, and the forgiveness of sins. Praise Him because the blessings He offers you far outweigh what you can give to Him.

God, I am so aware of how little I can offer You. May my worship and praise be honoring to You. I don't deserve all You've done for me. Thank You for loving me so faithfully.

SEPTEMBER 2

Rescued and Redeemed

He redeems your life from the Pit;
he crowns you with faithful love and compassion.

PSALM 103:4 CSB

God has redeemed each of us from the pit. In other words, He has rescued us from the power of sin and death. We have been set free and no longer need to worry about where we will spend eternity. When we devote our lives to God and faithfully follow His commands, He gives us a security that cannot be taken away from us. Through Christ's death on the cross, we have been redeemed. Death is no longer the end of the story.

Jesus has paid the price for you. You were once bound to a life of slavery and captivity, but now you are set free. When you surrendered your life to Him, you acknowledged that He did what you could not. He lifted you out of the pit, and He set your feet on solid ground for the rest of your days. He made a way where there wasn't one. On days when you feel overwhelmed, dry, or discouraged, remembering the basic truth of the gospel can refresh your spirit. No matter what the circumstances of your day look like, you have been redeemed, rescued, and crowned with the love of your Savior.

God, thank You for the reminder of all You have done for me. Turn my heart toward You and fill me with the peace that comes from knowing I am redeemed. I am so grateful for all You've done.

SEPTEMBER 3

Love and Compassion

> The LORD is compassionate and gracious,
> slow to anger and abounding in faithful love.
>
> PSALM 103:8 CSB

Love and compassion are two attributes of Yahweh that we see echoed throughout the Psalms. They are both foundational to the way God operates. His merciful love and abundant compassion are woven into everything He does. He does not treat us how we deserve to be treated. He treats us with great love according to His unchanging character. His actions are always in perfect alignment with His nature.

Your sins do not dictate how God feels about you or how He treats you. He lovingly forgives you, and He has mercy on you as you come to Him in prayer. Even though your actions make you guilty, Jesus took on your guilt. As you pursue a relationship with Him and recognize His lordship in your life, you have unlimited access to His compassion and kindness.

God, thank You for Your abundant love and compassion. Thank You for not treating me according to my actions. Your unchanging nature gives me peace and security. When I am tempted to believe You are harsh or domineering, remind me of Your unending compassion.

SEPTEMBER 4

Immeasurable Love

*As high as the heavens are above the earth,
so great is his faithful love
toward those who fear him.
As far as the east is from the west,
so far has he removed
our transgressions from us.*

PSALM 103:11-12 CSB

God's love for us is as high as the heavens are above the earth, and He has removed our transgressions as far as the East is from the West. Both of these things are immeasurable. We don't have the capability to quantify them. The psalmist is making the point that we can't possibly understand how great God's love is, and we cannot possibly grasp how much distance He puts between us and our sins.

God's love for you is steady, reliable, and faithful. He will not change His mind about you, and He will not give up on you. His love for you is greater than you can understand and more expansive than you can grasp. Even if you spent each of your remaining days exploring how God feels about you, you'd barely scratch the surface. Let His vast and unchanging love draw your heart toward Him in worship.

God, give me a greater revelation of Your love for me. Thank You for being steady, unchanging, and endlessly compassionate. I will never be able to thank You enough for Your love.

SEPTEMBER 5

Made of Dust

> He knows what we are made of,
> remembering that we are dust.
>
> PSALM 103:14 CSB

Our lives are like grass. In the greater scheme of things, they are short and frail. None of us know how many days we will have. Our response to the vulnerability of life should be to cherish it, value it, and use our time wisely. While we walk the earth, we are each part of a tiny glimpse of God's story. Humanity is temporary, fragile, and held together perfectly by an eternal God.

God is not unaware of your humanity. He knows exactly who you are, where you came from, and what you are capable of. He is not surprised by your weakness or disappointed by your limitations. His understanding is perfect, and His perspective is always clear. He knows what each of your days will look like; He knows how your life will unfold. Take a deep breath and let your soul rest, knowing that your life is securely in the hands of God. He is the one who weaves everything together perfectly.

God, when I am tempted to worry, help me remember that You are in control. Give me awareness of my weakness compared to Your greatness. I trust that You hold each of my days securely.

SEPTEMBER 6

Caring Creator

> They all depend on you
> to give them food as they need it
> When you supply it, they gather it.
> You open your hand to feed them,
> and they are richly satisfied.
>
> PSALM 104:27 NLT

Psalm 104 is a parallel to the creation story. It describes how God formed each part of creation and how He continues to care for it. He is not an uninvolved creator. He did not make the world and leave us to our own devices. He holds each part of His creation together perfectly. He satisfies the needs of every living thing, and He orchestrates every natural pattern and system. He is mindful, attentive, and skilled at keeping the world exactly as it should be.

If God satisfies the needs of all creation, that includes you. He knows exactly how to provide for you. Put your life into His hands and He will not leave you wanting. He wants to be included in the details of your day. Commit your heart to Him and He will be with you every step of the way. He wants to be close to you, walking alongside you for the entirety of your life. He created you, and no one knows you better than He does.

God, thank You for caring for Your creation so perfectly. Thank You for being a God who longs to be close to us. Walk with me throughout my days and help me see how You have always provided for me.

SEPTEMBER 7

Pray Through Scripture

I will keep on praising you, my Lord, with all that is within me. My joyous, blissful shouts of "Hallelujah" are all because of you!

Psalm 104:35 tpt

Psalm 104 marks the first time the word *hallelujah* is used in the Psalms. It's a Hebrew word that means to praise God. It's used a few other times in the Psalms, but it isn't seen anywhere else in Scripture. This is confirmation that many of the Psalms were originally written with the purpose of worship in mind. As we read through them, we can use them as a springboard for our own worship. When we are unsure of how to praise God, we can turn to Scripture for examples.

If you are ever in a season where you feel at a loss when it comes to prayer, pray through the Psalms. They were written as a form of praise to God, and you can utilize them in your prayer life. Praying Scripture over your life is a powerful way to agree with the heart of God. As you declare truth, especially when you feel unsure or lost, your spirit will find rest and steadiness in God's presence.

God, thank You for the gift of the Psalms. Thank You that I can always rely on the Word to guide me. As I declare truth over my life, change my heart. Align my thoughts and actions with Your purposes.

SEPTEMBER 8

Remember the Wonders

*Remember the wonders he has done,
his miracles, and the judgments he pronounced.*

Psalm 105:5 NIV

Psalm 105 is a call to praise God and pursue a deeper relationship with Him. It's a reminder to the Israelites that God miraculously directed their individual lives and their history as a nation. He led them faithfully in order to establish and preserve them as a people who were set apart for His purposes. This Psalm is a call to remember the ways God intervened on their behalf.

In the same way, you can look back on your history with God. You can take note of each act of faithfulness and provision. Make a list of how God has shown up for you and taken care of you. As you take note of those things, let them inspire you toward gratitude. Let God's faithfulness cause you to be more loyal and devoted to Him. You have been under God's watchful care, and remembering His provision can encourage you to endure current or future struggles.

God, thank You for being so faithful to me. Help me recall everything You have done for me. I don't want to forget a single instance of Your provision. You deserve all glory and honor.

SEPTEMBER 9

Unbreakable Covenant

*He remembers his covenant forever,
the promise he made, for a thousand generations,
the covenant he made with Abraham,
the oath he swore to Isaac.*

PSALM 105:8-9 NIV

Psalm 105 summarizes God's story of faithfulness to the Israelites. He made a promise, and that promise was fulfilled over a span of hundreds of years. Even when the Israelites were unfaithful, God did not go back on His word. In the same way, His ability to be faithful does not depend on our ability to be faithful.

You will not follow God perfectly. You are likely to make mistakes, and you will probably choose your own way some of the time. This is not a surprise to God. He knows every wrong turn you will make, and He still chooses to pursue you. Just like He was faithful to the Israelites, He will be faithful to you. He will not break the covenant He has with you through Christ. Until your very last breath, God will fight for you.

God, thank You for Your faithfulness. Thank You for the unbreakable covenant You have made with me. I don't deserve Your mercy and grace. Thank You for opening Your arms to me whenever I need You.

SEPTEMBER 10

Top Priority

*They exchanged their glorious God
for an image of a bull, which eats grass.
They forgot the God who saved them,
who had done great things in Egypt,
miracles in the land of Ham
and awesome deeds by the Red Sea.*

PSALM 106:20-22 NIV

Israel's pitfalls and mistakes seem so obvious, and God's faithfulness seems so obvious. It's easy to assume we would do better if we were in their situation. The reality is that we are often just as oblivious. God is constantly showing up in our lives, and we are too busy to notice. We overlook His provision and His faithfulness just as often as the Israelites did.

If you ask the Holy Spirit for a greater level of awareness, He will give it to you. With a humble heart, ask Him to show you any areas of your life where you have traded your affection for God for anything less worthy. Evaluate your priorities and pay attention to the way you spend your time, money, and resources. When you wholeheartedly offer yourself to Him, God will faithfully and gently guide you just as He did the Israelites.

God, You alone belong on the throne in my life. Help me see where I have replaced my devotion to You with lesser loves.

SEPTEMBER 11

Slippery Slope

*They worshiped their idols,
which became a snare to them.
They sacrificed their sons
and their daughters to false gods.*

PSALM 106:36-37 NIV

As we read through Israel's history, we quickly realize that their sins became more and more grievous. They eventually came to a place where they were sacrificing their own children to false gods. Their disobedience didn't start out that extreme, but it slowly worsened. This is often true in our own lives as well. When we choose to lower our standards, we are more likely to continue to let them slide. Typically, sin is the result of many small compromises along the way.

You don't need to be afraid of sin, but you do need to be aware of it. There is a big difference between legalism and using wisdom. Legalism says that you must behave a certain way in order to gain God's favor. Wisdom says that you live according to God's standards because He loves you and knows what is best for you. Be wary of disregarding wisdom in an effort to avoid legalism. God knows what is best for you, and He always has a purpose for the standards He calls you to.

God, I don't want to follow the same path as the Israelites. When I deviate from Your standards, gently draw me back to You.

SEPTEMBER 12

His Plan Is Better

Many times he delivered them,
but they were bent on rebellion
and they wasted away in their sin.

PSALM 106:43 NIV

Israel repeatedly rebelled against God and His Word. They were unfaithful to His instructions, yet He continued to provide for them. He delivered them many times despite their unfaithfulness. When God's people, either individually or as a group, confess failures with a humble heart, God will not turn them away. If He delivered Israel over and over again, He can be confident that He will also deliver us.

When you humbly ask God for forgiveness, He will always respond with mercy and grace. When you bring Him your failures and admit your need for Him, He will meet you with love and compassion. Sin is not the biggest potential problem in your life. Rather, the refusal to admit when you have sinned is a much bigger issue. If you willingly admit your weaknesses to God, He will strengthen you and equip you to navigate them. He is not worried about you living a perfect life. He is much more concerned with you living a life without Him.

God, when I am weak, You are strong. When I am humble, You are quick to forgive me. Keep me from pridefully insisting on my own way. Protect me from stubbornly progressing down a path of sin. When I begin to wander, soften my heart and draw me back to You.

SEPTEMBER 13

Covenant Love

*He took note of their distress
when he heard their cry;
for their sake he remembered his covenant
and out of his great love he relented.
He caused all who held them captive
to show them mercy.*

PSALM 106:44-46 NIV

God keeps His promises to us because His love for us is so great. He remains faithful to His covenant because He doesn't want any of us to be enslaved to sin and death. He created us to be fully alive in His presence, and He wants to spend eternity in communion with us. His desire for a relationship with His children is the foundation of the covenant He made with Abraham and fulfilled in Christ. He will never turn back on it, and He will never change His mind. We belong with Him, and He will make sure we receive what He has promised.

If you are a parent, you might understand how it feels to love someone even when they mess up or turn away from you. That feeling is a small glimpse of how God feels about you. Even when you fail to meet His standards, He loves you. Even when you make deliberate mistakes, He pursues you. You will always be His child, and He will always be faithful to His covenant. Your job is to respond to what He has already done.

God, thank You for pursuing me even when I'm making the wrong choices. Thank You for loving me as Your child so faithfully and consistently.

SEPTEMBER 14

Impossible Transformations

He turns a desert into a pool,
dry land into springs.
He causes the hungry to settle there,
and they establish a city where they can live.

Psalm 107:35-36 csb

God is the only one who can calm the chaos in our lives. He is the only one who can do the impossible. He brings order out of messes, and He creates life out of death. He fills the darkness with light, and He gives hope to the lost. God's ability to transform our lives should produce a response of thankfulness within us. As we realize that He is the antidote for every ailment we have, we can do nothing less than praise Him and devote our lives to Him.

When you surrender your life to God, He can make flowing springs come out of dry land. This could be literal or figurative. Sometimes, He might change your actual circumstances. Other times, He might change your heart instead. He is capable of giving you peace, even if your circumstances don't immediately change. Whether you experience His faithfulness internally or externally, He is still worthy of a lifetime of worship.

God, You can do the impossible. I surrender to You, and I put my life in Your hands. Thank You for all the ways You've moved on my behalf. You have been so good to me.

SEPTEMBER 15

Steadfast Love

My heart, O God, is steadfast;
I will sing and make music with all my soul.

PSALM 108:1 NIV

To be steadfast is to be resolute or unwavering. Scripture describes God's love for us as steadfast, and the psalmist describes his response to God in that way as well. Another definition of steadfast is to be dutifully firm or loyal. When we choose to love God in this way, we align ourselves with the way He loves us. We acknowledge His unending love for us, and we do our best to respond in a way that is fitting of such undivided devotion.

Steadfast love is not a feeling or an emotion. It is a deliberate choice to remain loyal, especially when your emotions don't line up with your commitment. On days when you are tempted to choose a different path yet remain faithful to God's purposes, your faith will be strengthened more than in times of ease. Your love for God will surely be tested, but He will give you the fortitude you need to remain steadfast.

God, thank You for Your steadfast love. Help me remain loyally committed to You even when I don't feel like it. Keep me from following my whims and emotions. Instead, give me the fortitude to choose You and Your purposes even when it's hard.

SEPTEMBER 16

Worthy of Praise

I will praise you, Lord, among the nations;
I will sing of you among the peoples.

PSALM 108:3 NIV

When we praise God, we have the opportunity to do it with everything we have. We can posture our body in worship to Him and command our spirit to praise Him. We don't just give Him lip service, but we offer Him the entirety of our soul despite our circumstances. It's easier to praise God on days when we are joyful or when things are going our way. It's more difficult to praise Him when we are impatient, frantic, angry, or irritated.

The call to praise God came at a time when the Israelites had been released from captivity and were seeing the destruction of their homeland. You can imagine the wide range of emotions they must have been feeling. Even so, they were instructed to turn their hearts toward the King. God knows the complexity of every single one of your emotions. He knows that on some days, it takes extra effort to posture yourself in an attitude of worship. You can either allow yourself to be a slave to your emotions, or you can accept the challenge of praising God no matter what.

God, help me praise You in every circumstance. Give me fortitude to turn toward you even when I am struggling emotionally. You are worthy of everything I have.

SEPTEMBER 17

Work of Restoration

*Save us and help us with your right hand,
that those you love may be delivered.*

PSALM 108:6 NIV

We can always praise God for the restorative work He does in our lives. At the same time, it's okay to acknowledge that restoration isn't always easy. The work involved might be difficult, complicated, or hard. When we walk through trials or experience hardship, God generously gives us grace to navigate whatever we are facing. However, this doesn't mean that it won't take fortitude, endurance, or dedication on our part.

God is your Savior and your Deliverer. When you call upon Him, He will rescue and redeem you. His ability to do that isn't diminished by the way He chooses to do it. His restorative work in your life might be painful, but that doesn't mean it isn't good. The path He has you on might cause growth and be difficult at the same time. Your relationship with Him is meant to be a partnership. If you are expecting Him to magically fix everything that is wrong, you will likely be left disappointed. Instead, as you partner with Him, He will help you rebuild what is broken.

God, I want to be on Your team. Give me grace to be obedient when You call me to action. Even when restoration is difficult, I want to honor You.

SEPTEMBER 18

Divine Assistance

*Give us aid against the enemy,
for human help is worthless.
With God we will gain the victory,
and he will trample down our enemies.*

PSALM 108:12-13 NIV

When Israel returned from exile, they still faced opposition from the nations around them. Their trials weren't over, and they still desperately needed God's help. After walking through their past experiences, they knew that without God, they were helpless. It didn't matter if men stepped in to help them; they needed God's intervention. They acknowledged that He was the only one who could truly rescue them from their enemies and give them victory.

God is the one who restores your soul. He might lead you to pursue various kinds of help, but at the end of the day, He is the one who does the impossible work of changing your heart and healing your wounds. Without Him, you will constantly seek after a version of healing that doesn't exist apart from Him. While therapy and medical intervention are wonderful gifts, they aren't the only thing you need. You need divine assistance and the merciful redemption that only God can provide.

Heavenly Father, thank You for leading me along a path of healing. Help me to continuously acknowledge that Your help is far more valuable than human help. I need You to move on my behalf more than I need anything else.

SEPTEMBER 19

All of You

*I am poor and needy,
and my heart is full of pain.
I am fading like a shadow at dusk;
I am brushed off like a locust.*

PSALM 109:22-23 NLT

If we're honest with ourselves, we've all been in situations where we've wondered if we can really be honest with God. We have thoughts or emotions that we categorize as bad, and sometimes, our response is to hide them in shame. We assume that God would be disappointed with us or that His response would be harsh and reprimanding. The reality is that God already knows our hearts. He is well aware of the worst parts of who we are.

You have the freedom to pour your heart out to God. You don't have to sort through your emotions before you present them to God. In Psalm 109, the writer offers Him his heart with abandonment. He doesn't filter through his emotions or give God a guarded version of what he's feeling. He unashamedly presents the whole picture to Him because he knows that God alone can make things right. You can follow his example and give God the most honest version of yourself. He wants every part of your heart and life, not just the ones you've decided are good enough.

God, give me boldness and help me share every part of my heart with You. I trust You with my failures, weaknesses, and frustrations. You alone can heal my heart.

SEPTEMBER 20

One True King

*"Sit in the place of honor at my right hand
until I humble your enemies,
making them a footstool under your feet."*

Psalm 110:1 nlt

Throughout this Psalm we see a parallel between David's rule and the prophesied rule of Jesus. It's a prophetic Psalm that describes how Jesus will one day rule and reign. Every description written about David is fulfilled in Christ. One day, all of Jesus' enemies will be like a footstool under His feet. He will sit enthroned at the right hand of God, and we will engage in worshipping Him for all eternity.

As the resurrected King, Jesus will have all authority and dominion. There is no enemy who will be able to stand against Him. When He returns, He will take His rightful place as the one true King. Until that day, you can watch and wait. You can remain vigilant and dedicated to honoring Him with the life you have. It won't always be easy to follow Him, but it is worth it to be in relationship with Him. As you faithfully commit your days to Jesus and His ways, He will equip you to remain loyal and devoted until the end.

Jesus, You are my King and are worthy of all my praise. Give me grace to stay devoted to You and Your ways. Help me remain faithful until You return. I can't wait for the day that You rule and reign forever!

SEPTEMBER 21

Fear of the Lord

*The fear of the Lord is the beginning of wisdom;
all who follow his precepts have good understanding.
To him belongs eternal praise.*

PSALM 111:10 NIV

Fear of the Lord is not a matter of cowering or bowing down to a dictator. True fear of the Lord is founded in awe, reverence, and respect. When we fear God, we recognize His provision and our role within creation. We acknowledge that He is our creator, and we owe everything to Him. He is sovereign, worthy, and holy. Our submission to Him has nothing to do with being dominated, subdued, or diminished in any way. We bow in worship to the King, and in exchange, He showers us with mercy and grace.

If you've ever experienced the awe of standing on the edge of the Grand Canyon or overlooked the majesty of the Great Rift Valley, you might understand a small glimmer of what it means to be in awe of God. The feeling you get when you are overcome by the wonder of creation is the same feeling that fear of the Lord stems from. Your reverence for Him is meant to come from a place of experiencing His wonder, beauty, and might.

God, I want to properly fear You. Soften my heart and fill me with fresh admiration and wonder for who You are. Help me understand what it really means to be in awe of You.

SEPTEMBER 22

Take Delight

Happy is the person who fears the Lord,
taking great delight in his commands.
His descendants will be powerful in the land;
the generation of the upright will be blessed.

Psalm 112:1-2 csb

Inevitably, we all go through dark seasons. No matter how long our trials last, we can find hope in the promises of God. Psalm 112 assures us that light shines in the darkness for the godly. If we have surrendered our lives to God, we can trust that He will keep His promises to us. We can rely on the Word even when everything around us seems unreliable.

If you fear the Lord, you won't fear life's circumstances. This doesn't mean that your days will always be easy or seamless. It also doesn't mean that you won't experience the full spectrum of human emotions. Rather, it means that you will continue to trust in God's Word even when things don't go the way you want. You won't despair when you encounter difficulties because you know that God will do what He says. If your life is based on fearing the Lord, you won't have room to fear your circumstances.

God, give me a holy and right fear of You. As I read Your Word, give me grace to understand it and apply it to my life. Fill me with love for Your commands and help me honor You for all my days.

SEPTEMBER 23

A Secure Heart

The righteous one will be remembered forever.
He will not fear bad news;
his heart is confident, trusting in the Lord.
His heart is assured; he will not fear.

PSALM 112:6-8 CSB

Life is full of potential pitfalls and threats. Hardly a day goes by that we don't hear about another crazy story on the news or even personally observe something disheartening in our own communities. If we are wise, we will face this world full of confidence because of our steadfast relationship with God. He is our protection and security. He keeps us steady even when our circumstances warrant fear or doubt. No matter what, God is our anchor and our hope.

Through Christ, you can face bad news and remain trusting and faithful. The longer you follow Him, the more you'll settle into the identity of being a child of God with unwavering confidence. Your confidence doesn't come from the details of your day but from the unchanging nature of your Heavenly Father. He will be with you every step of the way, protecting, guiding, and strengthening you.

God, I trust You to keep me steady. When circumstances cause me to waver, help me to find my confidence in who You are. Fill my heart with peace and help me trust You more today than I did yesterday.

SEPTEMBER 24

Never Enough

*The wicked one will see it and be angry;
he will gnash his teeth in despair.
The desire of the wicked leads to ruin.*

Psalm 112:10 csb

People who are living under the illusion that they can exploit and oppress others will eventually come to ruin. They seek material gain, power, or fame unto their own demise. They will spend their whole lives searching for more but will never be fulfilled. The message of Psalm 112 is that eventually, the blessings of the righteous will far exceed the temporary gain of the wicked. In other words, we shouldn't compare our current struggles with the perceived success of those who don't follow God.

If you live with an eternal perspective, you won't fall into the trap of comparison. You'll be able to remain steadfast even when the world does its best to convince you to be dissatisfied or disappointed. Remember that anything you gain on earth is temporary. Instead of collecting worldly treasures, it's much more important to know God and pursue His values. Those things cannot be taken away from you. Regardless of what you experience in this life, the blessings you will receive after devoting your life to God will be eternal and truly satisfying.

God, knowing You is more satisfying than anything else I could pursue. Remind me of this when I am tempted to give my affection to anything less worthy than You.

SEPTEMBER 25

None Like You

*The LORD is exalted over all the nations,
his glory above the heavens.
Who is like the LORD our God,
the One who sits enthroned on high,
who stoops down to look
on the heavens and the earth?*

PSALM 113:4-6 NIV

The original audience of this Psalm would have understood God as the creator. They were familiar with the idea that someone bigger than them was responsible for every pattern and situation under the sun. The part of this Psalm that would have been revolutionary was the idea that God wants to be part of our lives. God is the creator, and He remains involved with His creation. He is not distant or removed from the happenings of earth.

God cannot be compared to any other false god in history. He stands alone in His power, love, mercy, and grace. He is personally concerned with every detail of your life. He is not aloof or uninvolved when it comes to His children. He is worthy of your worship, and He longs for a relationship with you. He is seated on high, yet He willingly meets you when you are at your lowest. There is no one else like Him.

God, thank You for Your presence in my life. Thank You for being mighty, glorious, and powerful yet kind, gentle, and attentive. There is none like You. Help me understand the fullness of Your character as I read through the Psalms.

SEPTEMBER 26

No Discrimination

*He raises the poor from the dust
and lifts the needy from the ash heap;
he seats them with princes,
with the princes of his people.*

PSALM 113:7-8 NIV

It is a misconception that it's optional to care for the needy, the poor, and the widow. Scripture is clear that it's a non-negotiable part of being a Christian. Throughout the Old and New Testament, we see that God always pays attention to people who are vulnerable. If caring for those who are needy is on God's heart, it should also be on our hearts. We reflect His love to the world when we love others without discrimination.

God doesn't hold Himself back from anyone. It doesn't matter if you are financially stable, socially accepted, influential, or successful in your career. God's love does not discriminate between status, gender, ethnicity, or class. He is equally available to everyone who calls on His name and surrenders to His plan. He offers salvation graciously to anybody who is willing to accept His gift. When you care for people based on their innate value as humans rather than their differences, you love like God does.

God, thank You for offering Your love freely and equally to everyone. Help me love others the same way You do. Show me opportunities to care for the needy and give me grace to be obedient when You call me to action.

SEPTEMBER 27

He Sees

He settles the childless woman in her home as a happy mother of children.

PSALM 113:9 NIV

Psalm 113 gives special hope to those who are socially vulnerable. In particular, it focuses on women who are childless or widowed. Scripture is full of stories of how God opened the wombs of barren women. We can read about Sarah, Rebecca, and Rachel in Genesis. In Luke we can read about how God blesses Elizabeth with her son Samuel. From these stories, we can learn that God cares about our broken parts. He pays attention when we are lacking or grieving.

God lifts up the poor and needy. He is attentive toward you when you are hurting and in pain. When you grieve, He sees you. When the longings of your heart are unfulfilled, He does not turn away. He knows exactly how to provide for you. Your life might not look exactly how you expected it to, but if you are following Him, not a moment will be wasted. Even in the midst of circumstances that shouldn't exist, God is sovereign and faithful.

God, I trust You to care for me when I am vulnerable and needy. Help me turn to You when I am overwhelmed by my circumstances. Even if the longings of my heart are never satisfied, You are worth pursuing for all my days.

SEPTEMBER 28

Set Free

*Tremble, earth, at the presence of the Lord,
at the presence of the God of Jacob,
who turned the rock into a pool,
the hard rock into springs of water.*

Psalm 114:7-8 niv

In Psalm 114 the writer is celebrating God's victory over Egypt. He highlights the provision the Israelites received in the wilderness and their eventual entry into the promised land. There's a lot of poetic personification in this passage, and it gives vibrancy to the historical events that are referenced. It allows us to easily remember how God operated in the past. This gives us a strong foothold to stand upon as we look toward the future.

Just like God delivered Israel from Egypt, He has delivered you from the power of sin and death. He has set you free from a prison you could not break yourself out of. Let the truth of your salvation stir within you a desire to worship. He was faithful then, He is faithful to you now, and He will be faithful in all the days to come.

God, thank You for the picture of Your faithfulness seen in the Psalms. Remind me of Your goodness and how Your character never changes. Thank You for redeeming me and setting me free from bondage.

SEPTEMBER 29

All the Glory

> Not to us, O Lord, not to us,
> but to your name goes all the glory
> for your unfailing love and faithfulness.
>
> PSALM 115:1 NLT

Sometimes, it's really difficult not to brag about the things we've accomplished in our lives. Especially for those of us who are hard workers, it can be tempting to take credit for the goals we've met or the challenges we've faced. Today's Psalm helps us remember that all praise belongs to God. He is the one who has elevated us and put us in the positions we are in. Every good gift we have comes directly from His hands.

Praising God for what He's done in your life doesn't discredit your hard work. Giving Him all the glory doesn't mean you were passive or uninvolved in your successes. It simply means that you have remained humble despite your success. It means that you understand God's part in your life, and you are willing to submit yourself to His ways. Worship Him for who He is and remember all He has done for you. Focus on the way He has moved in your life and refuse to take credit for things that are only possible through His blessing and faithful provision.

God, You alone are worthy of all my praise. Keep my heart soft and forgive me for the times I have pridefully taken credit for my success. Every good thing I have is from You. You deserve all the glory.

SEPTEMBER 30

Aware and Involved

> O Israel, trust the LORD!
> He is your helper and your shield.
>
> PSALM 115:9 NLT

The writer of Psalm 115 is urging the Israelites to trust God. He is reminding them that they don't serve a God who is uninvolved or aloof. The gods of other nations were useless and made by men, but the God of Israel is alive and well. He is aware of His people and intricately involved in their lives. He longs for relationship, and He wants to bless them with His presence. He wants to shower them with good gifts and give them the fullness of His love.

God has good things in store for you. Scripture is full of promises He has made. He is a kind, attentive, and involved father. He wants so much more than obedience from you. Your relationship with Him is meant to be interactive on both sides. It is meant to be a twofold relationship with a back-and-forth dynamic. He doesn't want you to simply follow the rules until you are in heaven. He wants to have communion with you for all your days.

God, I put my trust in You. Help me cultivate a meaningful and fruitful relationship with You. I want more than a life of following the rules. Help me to surrender my whole heart to You each day.

OCTOBER 1

Attentive Father

*I love the Lord because he hears my voice
and my prayer for mercy.
Because he bends down to listen,
I will pray as long as I have breath!*

PSALM 116:1-2 NLT

Prayer is a two-way dialogue. When we engage in prayer, we are not simply talking about our issues and then walking away. The beauty of prayer is that He hears us. He pays attention to what we say, and He moves on our behalf. He knows what each voice sounds like, and His ears are always turned to us as we pour our hearts out to Him. We don't pray out of duty, obligation, or religious practice. Instead, we have the privilege of participating in a mutual exchange with the creator of the universe.

God hears you. He bends down and listens when you speak. He is a kind and attentive father. When children are little, parents often kneel and pull their faces close in order to hear their sweet voice. Even when the words are jumbled or aren't pronounced correctly, the parent does their best to meet the child where they are. This is similar to how God communicates with you. With great love and patience, He hears your words. Even when you don't know the words to use, He hears your heart, and He is present with you in your need.

God, thank You for hearing me. Thank You for being a God who is personal, attentive, and kind. May I always remember the gift of talking with You. As I pour my heart out, give me grace to hear Your response.

OCTOBER 2

I Told You So

> Death wrapped its ropes around me;
> the terrors of the grave overtook me.
> I saw only trouble and sorrow.
> Then I called on the name of the LORD:
> "Please, LORD, save me!"
>
> PSALM 116:3-4 NLT

We've all gotten ourselves into situations that we can't handle. We think we can manage on our own, but sooner or later we are in over our heads. When we cry out to God in desperation, He hears us. Even when we've caused the mess ourselves, He does not turn us away. Even when we've been naïve in thinking we don't need His help, He offers us grace and mercy when we turn back to Him. He is not prideful, and He is not manipulative. His love is always gracious and compassionate.

Turning to God for help is always the right answer. He exchanges peace for our hopelessness even when our situations don't immediately change. When you run to Him, He will not shame you for your mistakes or belittle you for your weakness. He is not a God who says *I told you so* with disdain or a prideful need to be right. Instead, He welcomes you in and equips you to live in a way that honors Him.

God, You are so gracious and kind! Thank You for helping me even when the mess is my own. When I am prideful, You are patient. When I am stubborn, You are compassionate. Thank You for always answering me when I call.

OCTOBER 3

After Sorrow

Let my soul be at rest again,
for the Lord has been good to me.
He has saved me from death,
my eyes from tears,
my feet from stumbling.

Psalm 116:7-9 NLT

God is the one who designed our nervous system, and He knows exactly how our emotions affect us. Psalm 116 is a glimpse into what it can look like to regulate troubled emotions. We know that the psalmist has experienced a lot of anxiety, sorrow, and sadness. On the other hand, he is exhorting himself to find rest in God. We can imagine him taking a deep breath, acknowledging what he's been through, and doing his best to find solace in the only place it can really be found.

Learning how to deal with your feelings will have a lasting impact on your life. Everyone's path is different, but you can trust the Lord to show you the way forward. No matter which tools you utilize, it all starts with finding rest in your relationship with the Lord. You can throw a myriad of solutions at an emotional problem, but none of them will truly satisfy your soul like time with the one who made you.

God, when I am overwhelmed with my emotions, help me turn to You. When I look for other ways to deal with my feelings, remind me that You are who I need most.

OCTOBER 4

Trustworthy

*I believed in you, so I said,
"I am deeply troubled, Lord."*

PSALM 116:10 NLT

Even when the psalmist was in the middle of a crisis, he trusted that God would help him. He knew that God was reliable, so he poured his heart out to Him. We can turn to God for guidance, especially when we don't have answers or solutions. When we don't understand, we can trust the one who always does. As we posture our hearts toward Him, He gives us wisdom and comforts us as we walk through our situation.

God is more trustworthy than anyone you know. No matter how close your relationships are, you cannot trust others the way you trust God. Especially when you've been close to someone for a long time, it's only natural to elevate their opinion above others. It's important to remember that God's voice is always meant to have top priority. Your allegiance belongs to Him above all else. Allow His voice to be the one that speaks the loudest.

God, everything You say and do is trustworthy. I want to elevate Your voice above all others in my life. You are the one I want to honor and praise for all my days. Deepen my trust in You.

OCTOBER 5

All Nations

Praise the L<small>ORD</small>, all nations;
Sing His praises, all peoples!

P<small>SALM</small> 117:1 <small>NASB</small>

Psalm 117 is essentially a hymn that calls on everyone to worship the Lord, who demonstrates perpetual love and loyalty to all. The call to worship does not exclude anyone. Every nation, tribe, and community are to acknowledge that Jesus Christ is Lord to the glory of God the Father. Jesus is available to all people everywhere, and one day, every nation will exalt His perfect name. As we reflect His character and love to the world, our lives should also reflect His heart for all people.

It's normal to view the gospel through your own cultural lens. Your perspective is based on how you view the world and the challenges you face on a consistent basis. It's easy to forget that your reality is not the only one. One day, everyone will worship together, and you will see the perfect picture of God's creation. He is delighted by the differences between cultures and people. Each one is equally valuable to Him. Imagine the day when we all worship in perfect unity.

God, help me see the beauty found in different cultures. When I begin to value my way of living above others, remind me that all people reflect who You are.

OCTOBER 6

Better than Before

*The stone the builders rejected
has become the cornerstone;
the Lord has done this,
and it is marvelous in our eyes.*

PSALM 118:22-23 NIV

Psalm 118 compares the Israelite people to a stone the builders rejected. They were tossed aside and presumed to be useless and unimportant. Everything changed when God intervened on their behalf. Instead of being rejected, they became like a cornerstone. The cornerstone is the most important part of a structure. A cornerstone cannot be just any stone found in a field. It is well cut and precise, and the stability of everything else depends on it.

God is an expert at repairing what is broken and making it even better than it was before. He has done this throughout history, and He can do it with you. The broken parts of your life are opportunities for God to work and move in ways that only He can do. He has proven that He can transform brokenness into something beautiful. Don't write off the things you struggle to change. Continue offering what you have to God and trust His perfect timing to make all things new.

God, You redeemed the Israelites in a miraculous way, and I trust You to redeem me as well. Thank You for transforming the broken parts of my life into something beautiful.

OCTOBER 7

Delight in the Word

*I delight in your decrees;
I will not neglect your word.*

PSALM 119:16 NIV

We all know that we should value God's Word. Most people who follow Him don't argue about the importance of Scripture. At the same time, knowing the truth and applying it to our lives are two different things. We say that we delight in God's law, but do our lives reflect it? There are some practical ways we can live out the truth found in today's Scripture.

You can't delight in God's instructions if you don't know what they are. Spend time reading the Word and studying it. Let the truth of God's story settle into your heart and mind. Studying God's word will be a life-long journey. The goal of reading the Word is to understand its author. When you read God's words, you learn the sound of His voice.

God, thank You for Your Word. Give me a new desire to study and read Scripture. As I read it, give me understanding and wisdom. Show me how I can apply the Word to my life and help me honor You with all I do.

OCTOBER 8

In Distress

*In my distress I called to the LORD,
and he answered me.*

PSALM 120:1 CSB

In this situation, the psalmist is about to begin his journey to Jerusalem. He is in a distant land that is foreign and dangerous. As he prepares to begin, he calls upon the Lord to help him. God is with him even though he is far from home and far from the temple. This is a reminder to us that we can call upon God in all circumstances. No matter how far we are from home, God is our refuge and strength.

Call out to the Lord, and He will answer you. He hears your prayers and never leaves you alone. Suffering cannot be avoided on this side of Heaven, but God promises to be with you no matter how much distress you are in. You can have confidence that He will show up when you need Him. Developing the habit of calling to God at the first sign of trouble will help cultivate peace in your life, even in the midst of chaos.

God, thank You for always being available to me. Help me develop the reflex of asking You for help as soon as trouble comes up.

OCTOBER 9

Messy Emotions

*"What misery that I have stayed in Meshech,
that I have lived among the tents of Kedar!
I have dwelt too long
with those who hate peace."*

PSALM 120:5-6 NIV

As we read through Psalm 120, it might seem like the writer is constantly complaining. It's important to notice the difference between complaining to God and complaining about God. Through Scripture, the psalmist is complaining to God. He is presenting his emotions to the Lord because he knows He can handle them. He trusts God's character, so he is comfortable sharing the deepest and most raw parts of his heart.

When you take your complaints to God, you can trust Him to give you mercy and grace. There isn't an emotion that is too much for Him. You can complain to Him, and He will comfort you. He will help you sort through your emotions or circumstances when you cannot do it alone. He longs to be involved in every aspect of your life. When you boldly bring Him your messiest emotions, you acknowledge He can handle whatever is going on. He is big enough to carry even your heaviest burdens.

God, thank You for being big enough to handle my complaints. Thank You that I don't have to hide my emotions or figure them out alone. When I feel overcome by my feelings, help me to turn to You with confidence.

OCTOBER 10

Mountain Maker

I will raise my eyes to the mountains;
From where will my help come?
My help comes from the LORD,
Who made heaven and earth.

PSALM 121:1-2 NASB

Psalm 121 is a declaration that the psalmist knows exactly what to do when he's in trouble. He knows where to look, and he is confident in his decision. He is not worried because he knows that God, creator of the heavens and earth, will help him. He sees the mountains, and he understands how they got there and who sustains them.

If God can create the heavens and the earth, He can help you in your time of need. If He can form the mountains with His own hands, He can help you navigate the problems you face. There is nothing you can encounter that is too difficult for Him. The mundane tasks of your daily life, the trauma of unexpected grief, or the sting of disappointment are all well within His capabilities. When you face trouble of any kind, turn your eyes toward the one who made the mountains.

God, if You can make mountains, I know You can move them in my own life. I trust You to help me when I need it most. Thank You for being my refuge and strength. No matter what I face, You are faithful to provide for me.

OCTOBER 11

Sure Footing

He will not allow your foot to slip;
He who watches over you will not slumber.
Behold, He who watches over Israel
Will neither slumber nor sleep.

PSALM 121:3-4 NASB

The Israelites traveled on a pilgrimage to Jerusalem. The people would have been traveling there, likely by foot, to encounter the presence of God in the temple. Their journey would have been difficult and taxing. The psalmist is reminding the people that God will watch over them. He is encouraging them that God will keep their steps steady even when the road is rough or unmanageable.

If you've ever walked a difficult path, you know that footing is important. Loose gravel, slippery mud, or steep terrain can all make progress difficult. The way you walk is dictated by the condition of the road in front of you. Even when you have to walk across wild or difficult land, God is with you. Even when it doesn't make sense for you to be steady, God will uphold you. There is no path that is too tangled or confusing for Him. In all situations, He is capable of keeping you from slipping. God will give you sure footing on the path of your life.

God, keep me steady and secure. Help me trust in You with each step I take. Help me look to You with confidence when I am unsure which way to go. Thank You for giving me sure footing even in difficult circumstances.

OCTOBER 12

He Brings Relief

The LORD is your protector;
The LORD is your shade on your right hand.
The sun will not beat down on you by day,
Nor the moon by night.

PSALM 121:5-6 NASB

We all know what it's like to get sunburn. It's uncomfortable, frustrating, or even miserable. Protecting ourselves from the sun is in our best interest. In Psalm 121, we see a metaphor that compares God's mindfulness to being safe from the harsh effects of the sun. God is the one who watches over His people. He protects us when we need it, and He ensures we are taken care of.

God is your shade. He provides relief and safety when you need it most. He watches over you, and He knows what is best for you. He knows each challenge you face, and He readily equips you to face each of them. When you feel like you cannot stand another moment in the blazing heat, allow Him to be your refuge. He will shelter you, and He will give you what you need. You don't have to muster up strength on your own. Instead, remember His promise to protect you and keep you safe.

God, You are my shade and my shield. When life feels too harsh to manage, You are the one who rescues me. When I can't stand on my own, You are the one who gives me strength. Thank You for protecting me at all times.

OCTOBER 13

Always Seen

> The Lord will protect you from all evil;
> He will keep your soul.
> The Lord will guard your going out and your coming in
> From this time and forever.
>
> PSALM 121:7-8 NASB

God is aware of His people. He is attentive, capable, and kind. There is nowhere we can go that is too far away from Him. He watches over and protects His people because He is a loving and faithful creator. He made each of us with purpose and intention. We are incredibly valuable to Him, and it wouldn't make sense for Him to abandon His most precious possession.

Think of something you value. Maybe it's something extravagant like a piece of heirloom jewelry, or maybe it's simple like your phone or even your car keys. You are likely mindful of its location and the state it's in. You know exactly what is going on with your most precious possessions. On an infinitely larger scale, God is mindful of you in the same way. There is nowhere you can go to escape God's presence. He is with you even when you feel lost, helpless, or alone.

God, thank You for Your watchful eye over my life. Thank You for seeing me and knowing me perfectly. Thank You for protecting me and keeping my soul secure. Give me grace to remember that You are always near when I need You.

OCTOBER 14

Holy Places

*Jerusalem is built like a city
that is closely compacted together.
That is where the tribes go up—
the tribes of the LORD—
to praise the name of the LORD
according to the statute given to Israel.*

PSALM 122:3-4 NIV

In ancient times, Jerusalem was considered to be the center of the world. The Israelites felt God's presence was isolated to the temple located there. Pilgrims would travel to that city, and they would pray for its peace and security. Christ's death, resurrection, and the outpouring of the Holy Spirit marked the first time in history that God's presence permeated the world all at the same time. He is not limited to one location, and there are no longer specific holy places we need to travel to.

You are not made holy because you do certain things or go specific places. You cannot attain holiness no matter how many rules you follow perfectly. Your only avenue for holiness is to humbly accept the mercy and grace Jesus offers you. Even if you never step foot in another church building again, your righteousness is secured.

God, help me remember that holiness comes from You alone. Your Spirit is within me, and I don't have to search the world to find it.

OCTOBER 15

Submission and Surrender

As the eyes of slaves look to the hand of their master,
as the eyes of a female slave look to the hand of her mistress,
so our eyes look to the Lord our God,
till he shows us his mercy.

PSALM 123:2 NIV

Sometimes, the idea of submission is difficult for us. Some of us have a history of unhealthy relationships or experiences when authority has been abused. We might view submission as giving up our own rights or individuality for the sake of someone else. It's important to realize that submitting and surrendering to God is not the same thing as giving up. Instead, it's giving control to someone we trust.

When you have confidence in God's character, submission to Him isn't an issue. When you understand God's nature and intentions, it becomes easier to give Him control. You can trust Him with every aspect of your life because He has your best interests in mind. He doesn't want you to give up your independence, but He wants you to experience the peace that comes from surrendering to Him, especially in situations you cannot manage alone.

God, help me submit to You in obedience. When my flesh rises up, and I want to take control, give me wisdom to surrender to You. I trust You with every aspect of my life.

OCTOBER 16

When It Hurts

He poured water into a basin and began to wash his disciples' feet, drying them with the towel that was wrapped around him.

JOHN 13:5 NIV

One of the most important aspects of the Gospel is that Jesus becomes a servant on our behalf. He washes His disciple's feet, and Paul goes on to call Christians to adopt the same attitude. We are to have a humble posture of surrender, submission, and humility. As Christ's followers, we are meant to love each other with the same sacrificial love He displayed for us.

Life is filled with opportunities to serve others. If you want to love like Jesus, there will be times that you deliberately go against the desires of your flesh. You can't love well and also try to always get your own way. Service to others is often inconvenient and messy. It means laying aside your comfort and pride for the sake of someone else. Sharing your time, money, and emotional bandwidth often means experiencing a personal level of sacrifice.

God, help me love like Jesus even when it hurts. Open my eyes to see opportunities to serve others. As I lay my life down, I trust You to give me what I need.

OCTOBER 17

In Battle

*"Had it not been the Lord who was on our side
When people rose up against us,
Then they would have swallowed us alive."*

PSALM 124:2-3 NASB

Sometimes, it's easy for us to forget that the world that we live in is not neutral. It's evil. The prince of this world hates believers, and we're always under spiritual attack. It's impossible for us to fight this battle alone. We need God's help, and He is happy to give it. Without Him, we would be hopelessly lost. Instead, He gives us resources to fight successfully. He is the reason we can have hope for victory.

God is on your side. He will not leave you alone, no matter how desperate your situation might seem. There is no battle He won't fight on your behalf. Not only is He able to secure victory for you, but He longs for you to depend on Him. Don't fight alone when the King of Kings can strengthen you and fight alongside you. No matter what you are facing, you have the resources of His kingdom at your disposal.

God, You are the one who secures my victories. Remind me to call on You when I am in battle. Instead of fighting alone, I will depend on Your strength. Thank You for equipping me and carrying me through.

OCTOBER 18

Strong and Able

Take up the full armor of God, so that you will be able to resist on the evil day, and having done everything, to stand firm.

EPHESIANS 6:13 NASB

When we surrender our lives to God, He equips us to follow Him. He gives us everything we need to be victorious against the plans of the enemy. He knows that life will be full of suffering, trials, and temptation, but He does not leave us empty handed. We are able to escape spiritual danger because of His help and intervention. Without Him, we would be helpless and lost.

God offers you His full armor. When you are in a battle, you have more at your disposal than you might realize. Through Christ, you already have what you need to resist temptation and stand firm in your faith. Though you might feel weak, the reality is that you are strong. Remember that you belong to the God who created the world. He is on your side, He is fighting for you, and He will strengthen your weakest parts. You are not helpless, and you are not alone.

God, thank You for the reminder that I am strong and equipped. When I am in battle, open my eyes to all You have done for me. Strengthen me from the inside out and encourage me when I forget the truth. Thank You for the victory I have through Jesus.

OCTOBER 19

Healing and Stability

Those who trust in the LORD are like Mount Zion.
It cannot be shaken; it remains forever.

PSALM 125:1 CSB

Psalm 125 is a community psalm that reminds us of the confidence we can have in our relationship with God. The psalmist is writing on behalf of the Israelite people. He is requesting that God uphold retribution toward the wicked people who oppose them. He wants peace and prosperity for Israel. The mention of Mount Zion indicates that the writer is already in the city of Jerusalem. They've already been through an incredible journey, and Psalm 125 is an expression of hope for stability and rest. He reminds His people that trusting Him is the only way they will find the peace they are looking for.

It's not likely you've experienced the same turmoil that Israel did, but you've certainly got your own list of battle scars. When you're on the other side of trauma or suffering, it can be tempting to lick your wounds or try to heal them on your own. Without a foundation of trusting in God, true healing, recovery, or stability isn't even possible. Run to Him first and allow Him to lead you on a path of healing that is based in His love and strength instead of your own.

God, You know exactly what my mind, body, and spirit need. Lead me along a path that honors You. When I need healing, You are the one who provides it best. Remind me to run to You instead of my own comforts.

OCTOBER 20

Restoration Process

When the LORD restored the fortunes of Zion,
we were like those who dream.
Our mouths were filled with laughter then,
and our tongues with shouts of joy.

PSALM 126:1-2 CSB

When the Israelites finally reached Jerusalem, they had a lot to be thankful for. They had finished their pilgrimage, and they were joyfully praising God for all He had done. At the end of their journey, they began the difficult work of restoration. Just because we reach a long-awaited destination doesn't mean we don't need to process what happened along the way. It can be healing and therapeutic to remember the highs and lows we've been through.

Life is a constant mix of peaks and valleys. When you find yourself in a positive place, it can be beneficial to think about what brought you there. As you remember God's faithfulness, you will be strengthened. As you process through your experience, sorrow and joy can exist simultaneously in your heart. If you let Him, God will faithfully lead you toward restoration. He will be by your side as you lament what was lost and look forward to the future.

God, thank You for walking alongside me. Thank You for reminding me of the wonderful things You've done while holding me as I grieve. Thank You for walking me through restoration whenever I need it.

OCTOBER 21

Read and Do

Don't just listen to the Word of Truth and not respond to it, for that is the essence of self-deception.

JAMES 1:22 TPT

If we read God's Word and don't apply it to our lives, we are missing the point. We can't limit our relationship with Him to a time of devotion in the morning while the rest of our day is devoid of His presence. Instead, He invites us to have a continuous relationship with Him through the Holy Spirit. If we allow Him to, the Spirit will constantly teach us how to live in a way that honors God and His purposes.

Be wary of reading the Word without integrating it into your daily life. Honoring God is about obeying His instructions, not just listening to them. Reading the Word is the starting place for living in a way that actively reflects God's character. From that point, the Holy Spirit will teach, guide, and convict you when needed. He will bring to mind the truth you've learned and help you apply it to your life. He will encourage you with it when you are weary, and He will gently remind you of it when you begin to walk astray.

God, help me apply Your Word to my life. Fill me afresh with the Holy Spirit and help me live a life that honors You. Soften my heart and keep me sensitive to Your voice of correction and encouragement.

OCTOBER 22

His Kingdom

*Unless the Lord builds the house,
the builders labor in vain.*

PSALM 127:1 NIV

We live in a culture that loves to hustle, and it's easy to get wrapped up in our own egos. If we claim that the good things in our lives are the result of our own efforts and resources instead of gifts from God, we've wandered away from the truth. Everything we enjoy, from the food we eat to the safety of our families, comes from His hands. When we take credit for His blessings, we lose sight of His sovereignty and provision.

God has provided every good thing in your life. Even your ability to work hard, persevere, or use your intelligence for financial gain comes from Him. As your creator, He is responsible for all of it. This isn't meant to spark a debate about the success of believers compared to unbelievers. Worldly or material success is not the point. Instead, switch your perspective to eternal versus temporary gain. If God is building your life, it will be eternal. If you are building a personal kingdom apart from Him, it will only last as long as your days on earth.

God, I don't want to build my own kingdom. Instead, help me walk confidently according to Your plans. I commit my day to You, and I invite You to have Your way in my life.

OCTOBER 23

Precious Gifts

> Children are a heritage from the Lord,
> offspring a reward from him.
> Like arrows in the hands of a warrior
> are children born in one's youth.
>
> PSALM 127:3-4 NIV

Children are a gift and a blessing from God. Some of the most precious gifts in our lives can be wrapped up in the tiny hearts of the children around us. God sees each child as incredibly valuable. He delights in children, and He grieves when they are mistreated. As His followers, we can reflect His character to the world by embracing and cherishing the little ones we are blessed to have in our lives.

While you may not be a mother right now, you are not exempt from God's call to love His children. You can build His kingdom by acting lovingly and patiently toward any children you come across. If you are a parent, take a moment to remember that it is a great and wonderful gift. Despite the hardships it may bring, mothering is a blessing. Ask God to soften your heart in the hard moments and remind you of the gift you have been given.

God, thank You for the children in my life. Give me Your heart for them and teach me how to value them like You do. Give me words to encourage them and teach them about You. Help me build a legacy of faith that will be passed down through generations.

OCTOBER 24

Different Roles

> We have many parts in one body, and all the parts do not have the same function, in the same way we who are many are one body in Christ and individually members of one another. According to the grace given to us, we have different gifts.
>
> ROMANS 12:4-6 CSB

There isn't one singular way to follow God's purposes. God has given each of us different gifts and roles. There can be a tendency within the church to view ministry or missions as the epitome of godly work. That isn't how God views it. God has given some people certain skills that will never be used in a traditional ministry setting. We don't need to force ourselves to fill a role that doesn't fit the way God made us.

You can be faithful to God and never get on a plane to a foreign country. You can honor Him with your career and never work in a Christian setting. Your title is significantly less important than your character and your willingness to reflect His love to the people around you. If you use the opportunities you have to honor Him to the best of your ability, you are doing the very thing He has called you to do.

God, show me how to live up to Your standards. Help me develop the gifts You have given me without comparing myself to others. Give me confidence in the role I'm in and give me guidance when I need to redirect my steps.

OCTOBER 25

Right Perspective

Blessed are all who fear the Lord,
who walk in obedience to him.
You will eat the fruit of your labor;
blessings and prosperity will be yours.

PSALM 128:1-2 NIV

The prosperity gospel teaches that Christians are guaranteed material blessings on earth. It says that we can expect God to grant our wishes and bless us with wealth and material gain. Sometimes, in an effort to shy away from false teaching, we forget that Scripture teaches us that God blesses those who follow Him. The biggest difference lies in the type of blessing we can expect to receive.

God longs to give you good gifts. When you follow His path, He loves to bless you. The rewards and gifts that He gives can come in many different forms. Sometimes they are physical, and sometimes they are spiritual or emotional. In some cases, you'll be rewarded now, and there are some gifts you won't receive until the other side of heaven. Either way, every good thing comes directly from His hands. Rather than expecting to get what you want, trust that God knows exactly what you need and is capable of giving it to you in His perfect timing.

God, I don't want to have false expectations, but I also don't want to limit You. Help me see You rightly and give me a spirit of thanksgiving no matter what I receive from You.

OCTOBER 26

Unnecessary Burdens

Do not be anxious about anything, but in every situation, by prayer and petition, with thanksgiving, present your requests to God.

PHILIPPIANS 4:6 NIV

If we stuff down our emotions and frustrations, they will come back stronger. The right way to deal with our feelings is to bring them to God. In prayer, we can come before Him and give Him our burdens. We can offer Him our frustrations and ask Him to handle the things we can't. When we present our struggles and requests to God, He gives us peace.

When the Bible commands you not to be anxious, don't view it as one more thing you must master. It's not a to-do item on a list of good Christian behaviors. Instead, it's more like an invitation to take advantage of God's great compassion for you. He longs for you to give Him your burdens. Why carry something that He is more than willing to carry for you?

God, show me any burdens in my life that I am stubbornly or unknowingly carrying alone. Teach me how to readily give You my frustrations. I trust You to help me navigate even my messiest emotions.

OCTOBER 27

Chaos of Sin

Out of the depths I have cried to You, Lord.
Lord, hear my voice!
Let Your ears be attentive
To the sound of my pleadings.
Psalm 130:1-2 nasb

The Hebrew word used for *depths* is often connected with words for water or the sea. This is usually a metaphorical reference to chaos. In Psalm 130, the psalmist is crying out for help because he's lost in the chaos of his sin. We can relate to him because we all know what it's like to feel out of control. Sometimes, the consequences of our own sin might make us feel hopeless or like we cannot get our heads above water. This is not how God wants us to live. Through Christ, He pulls us out of our own messes and restores us.

God has lifted your soul out of the depths and called you His own. He is your rescuer and your salvation. No matter the circumstances of your testimony, the miracle is the same. If God kept a record of your sins, you would be hopeless. The good news of the gospel is that He has heard your cries and given you a path toward redemption.

God, thank You for pulling me from the depths. Thank You for the miracle of my salvation. Keep me from the chaos of sin and give me grace to be quick to repent when I make mistakes.

OCTOBER 28

Guilt-Free Restoration

I wait for the LORD, my soul waits,
And I wait for His word.
My soul waits in hope for the Lord.

PSALM 130:5-6 NASB

When we fall into sin, it can feel difficult to reconcile our hearts with God. We allow our guilt to get in the way of restoring our relationship with Him. Even when we are ashamed, God's invitation for grace and mercy hasn't changed. Psalm 130 is a lament where the psalmist expresses his distress from knowing he did the wrong thing. He doesn't run and hide. Instead, he waits with expectation, knowing that God alone can restore him.

While there might be consequences for your sin, being abandoned by God is not one of them. His love is unfailing, and He never leaves you alone. The instant you turn back to Him in repentance, He welcomes you with abundant mercy and grace. He never expects you to wallow in guilt. He doesn't want you to pay penance for your sin when He has already done that work through Christ. The work of getting back on track isn't always easy, but it is never full of shame.

God, You are unlike anyone else. You forgive, heal, and restore even when I think I don't deserve it. Keep my heart soft and help me to always be aware of my need for forgiveness.

OCTOBER 29

Like a Mother

*I have calmed and quieted myself,
I am like a weaned child with its mother;
like a weaned child I am content.*

PSALM 131:2 NIV

As believers, we were made in the image of God. This means that both men and women perfectly reflect who He is. Together, we are a complete representation of God's character and nature. He is a culmination of masculine and feminine traits. This means that some of His attributes are seen more commonly in women. He is caring, nurturing, gentle, and attentive. He can be compared to a mother without that comparison suggesting that He is a woman.

You can interact with God like a child interacts with her mother. You can find comfort and contentedness in His arms. Like a good mother, God is quiet, calm, and reassuring. His presence is a place where you can rest comfortably. God is not limited to your ideas about His character. Everything about Him is perfect, complete, and whole.

God, thank You for the perfection of Your character. Teach me more about who You are. Give me an accurate perspective of Your nature. Don't let my own mental blocks keep me from experiencing Your parental love.

OCTOBER 30

Always Available

*"You will seek me and find me
when you seek me with all your heart."*

JEREMIAH 29:13 NIV

Each one of us has the capacity to hear Jesus. He is not hiding from us, and He is not difficult to find. If we are relying on our feelings, we will definitely experience seasons when we think He has abandoned us or isn't paying attention. If we rely on the truth of Scripture, we will be confident in the fact that He is always nearby. He promises us His presence when we give Him our hearts. When our desire is to be close to Him, He will not let us be disappointed.

Through the gift of the Holy Spirit and the truth found in Scripture, you have everything you need to follow God. You are not lacking anything. God promises He is with you, so you can depend on it. Turn your heart toward Him and faithfully keep looking no matter how you feel. Let your faith be based on truth rather than emotions and it will last until the end.

God, give me confidence in Your Word. When I begin to doubt Your presence, remind me of Your promises. Strengthen my faith and give me perseverance.

OCTOBER 31

Unity

*Behold, how good and how pleasant it is
For brothers to live together in unity!*

PSALM 133:1 NASB

There's an overall sense of disunity within the Body of Christ, at least within the American church. It's not typical to see churches working together toward any type of goal, even within the same town. We like to find a place to be comfortable and stay there. Imagine what could be accomplished if we were to pool our resources and work together. With so much technology at our fingertips, there are fewer barriers than ever before.

Unity brings peace. Without unity, relationships can be unpleasant and difficult to navigate. When two or more people have a common goal, the road to reach that goal becomes significantly less bumpy. It's not uncommon for churches to get hung up on theological differences when, in reality, everyone should have the same goal. We've all been given the same set of instructions by the same God. Until the day we are perfectly unified under Christ, we can continue striving to work together as His body.

God, thank You for the gift of the Church. Help me to live in unity with the believers around me. Give me wisdom to know when to speak and when to listen. Teach me how to encourage those around me as we work together to further Your kingdom.

NOVEMBER

NOVEMBER 1

Unseen Service

Bless the Lord,
all you servants of the Lord
who stand in the Lord's house at night!

Psalm 134:1 csb

Psalm 134 is a picture of the superior blessing the inferior. God blesses those who praise Him. Specifically, He is blessing those who minister to Him by night in the house of the Lord. The psalmist is exhorting the night shift workers at the tabernacle who are lifting up praise and worship to God. The Levites who worked in the temple at night would have kept the lamp stand lit and the sacrifices burning when no one else was around. Their worship, though quiet and unseen, mattered immensely to God.

God notices when you minister to Him in hidden places. He blesses you when you offer Him your service, whether it is seen by others or not. Just like the Levites kept the sacrifices burning when everyone else slept, you might have seasons when the work you do for God isn't acknowledged in the light of day. This doesn't mean that it is less important than the work that is obvious or noticeable. Everything you offer to God counts.

God, thank You for equipping me to serve You. Thank You for the blessings that come from laying my life down for Your purposes. When I am weary, give me the strength to keep going. When other people don't notice my sacrifices, help me to persevere.

NOVEMBER 2

In Control

*The LORD does whatever pleases him,
in the heavens and on the earth,
in the seas and all their depths.*

PSALM 135:6 NLT

God is the highest authority over the heavens and earth. He does exactly what He wants to. He is not swayed by our opinions, and He is not shaken by our failures. His character is steady, and His power is unwavering. There is nothing we can do to change Him or diminish Him. His steadiness, especially when the world feels chaotic, brings us great peace and comfort. When everything around us is constantly changing, we can rely on His unchanging nature.

You don't need to micromanage your life. You are not the one who is in control anyway. If you have surrendered your life to the Lord, you can rest in His presence. You can trust Him to orchestrate and manage your days with more proficiency than you could ever achieve. You can take a deep breath and give Him your burdens. The stress of trying to make sure that everything is perfect is not necessary. He is the Lord, and He does what He pleases.

God, thank You for being steady when life feels chaotic. Thank You for being reliable when my circumstances feel shaky. I trust You to be in control. Help me surrender to Your plans each day.

NOVEMBER 3

False Gods

*The idols of the nations are merely things of silver and gold,
shaped by human hands.
They have mouths but cannot speak,
and eyes but cannot see.*

PSALM 135:15-16 NLT

The original hearers of this Psalm 135 would have been familiar with the many gods who were worshipped in their surrounding area. The psalmist would have been encouraging people to choose the one true God instead of the many false gods that others were turning to. In their culture, every aspect of their lives was attributed to the various higher powers they believed in. It was counter-cultural to suggest that one Creator was behind everything.

Your life isn't filled with false gods who control the sun or the moon, but there are other things you might give your time and devotion to. Careers, money, social media, relationships, or addictions can all take the form of idols in your life. It's healthy to evaluate your heart every so often and question if your priorities are in order. Is the majority of your time and resources spent on things that have eternal value? Or are you chasing after comfort and personal satisfaction?

God, be lifted high in my life. You are the one true God, and You deserve all my praise. Bring conviction when I give too much of my time, heart, or resources to other things. Draw me back to You and help me keep my priorities in line.

NOVEMBER 4

Powerful Liturgy

*Give thanks to the LORD, for he is good!
His faithful love endures forever.*

PSALM 136:1 NLT

If you didn't grow up in a church that used liturgy, you might not be familiar with its purpose or power. Basically, liturgy is the repetition of scriptural truth. It's a form of public worship where the leader or pastor recites a biblical truth, and it is repeated by the congregation. Repetition allows it to be rooted in our hearts and memories.

Psalm 136 is a liturgical psalm. The specific truth of God's love enduring forever is repeated twenty-six times. From creation to the cross, God's story is perfectly interwoven with His love. God's love endures forever. It's the foundation for everything He does, and it must be your starting point as well. Unless you grasp how great His love is, you won't have an accurate understanding of His character or His purposes. Today, let God's love be a constant refrain within your heart. Remind yourself of it and declare it over your life.

God, thank You for Your enduring love. Remind me of it as I go through the mundane tasks of my day. May Your love for me and others permeate everything I do.

November 5

Chaos into Order

*Give thanks to him who alone does mighty miracles.
His faithful love endures forever.
Give thanks to him who made the heavens so skillfully.
His faithful love endures forever.*

Psalm 136:4-5 NLT

God is a skilled creator. From the beginning of time, we have seen His amazing ability and creativity. Everything He has done fits perfectly into His plan. Each intricate system speaks of His brilliance and how He created all things to work together. The sun warms the earth to a very specific degree, and tiny seeds grow into plants that produce fruit. Every corner of creation is orderly and ideal. He laid the foundations of the earth with wisdom, and He established the heavens with intention.

If God created the world with such intention and purpose, He is capable of doing the same thing with your life. If He can manage the stars and the cosmos, He can give you what you need to navigate whatever you are facing. He is an expert at turning chaos into order. There isn't anything beyond His ability. When you surrender your life to Him, you are placing yourself in expert hands.

God, thank You for turning chaos into order. I trust You with the details of my life. When I look at creation, remind me of all You have done.

NOVEMBER 6

Backward and Forward

*Give thanks to him who parted the Red Sea.
His faithful love endures forever.
He led Israel safely through,
His faithful love endures forever.*

PSALM 136:13-14 NLT

Psalm 136 is a great example of what it means to look backward and forward at the same time. The Israelites had experienced many miracles, and they had a lot to thank God for. At the same time, they had hope for the future. God redeemed them and gave them freedom. He promised them His enduring and faithful love for all of their days. He rescued them, but that was not the end of their story.

God's story is not complete. The work of Jesus did not end with the cross. While Christ's death and resurrection were a fulfillment of God's promises, there is still more to come. There will be a day when everything is made perfect once and for all. You can look at the amazing things God has done while still having an incredible amount of hope for the future. There are better things coming than anything you've already experienced.

God, thank You for the redemption I have through Jesus. Thank You for the wonderful things You've done in my life. Give me hope that the best is yet to come. When I am weary, remind me that Your story isn't finished yet.

NOVEMBER 7

Continuous Sanctification

I am certain that God, who began the good work within you, will continue his work until it is finally finished on the day when Christ Jesus returns.

PHILIPPIANS 1:6 NLT

Israel's story is full of waiting. They waited to be rescued from slavery. They waited through seasons of exile, and they waited for the hope of the promised land. They were familiar with trusting God for a promise to be fulfilled. Seasons of waiting look different for us but the general concept is the same. God's promises do not always follow our timelines, but our faith will remain steady if we trust His Word.

If you have surrendered your life to Jesus, you are already justified before God. You have been redeemed. At the same time, you are waiting for the fulfillment of God's promises. Until you are with Him in heaven, you will experience a continuous process of becoming more like Him. You will make mistakes, ask God for forgiveness, gain wisdom, and likely make mistakes again. Growth and change are part of life. As you surrender to Him, God will continue His good work in your life until you make it across the finish line.

God, as I live in the tension of waiting for eternity, remind me that You are constantly working in my life. When I am weary, remind me of Your faithfulness.

NOVEMBER 8

True Home

*How can we sing the songs of the Lord
while in a foreign land?
If I forget you, Jerusalem,
may my right hand forget its skill.*

PSALM 137:4-5 NIV

Being part of God's family makes us strangers among the world. We are foreigners who are waiting to inhabit our eternal home. We belong with God, and one day, we will be with Him face to face. Until then, we wait. Like the Israelites, we don't want to forget our true home. There is nothing worse than forgetting who we are and where we are meant to be.

You are a child of God. You are His chosen and cherished possession. Until you are home with Him, you will always feel a little bit out of place. This is not a bad thing. On days when nothing seems to be going right, remember that you were not made for this world. You were created to live in a place of perfection with God. May the Lord fill your heart with songs of praise while you wait in a place that may never truly feel like home.

God, thank You for preparing an eternal home for me. As I wait for You, fill me with hope. Remind me daily who I am and where I belong.

NOVEMBER 9

Don't Quit

> By the rivers of Babylon we sat and wept
> when we remembered Zion.
> There on the poplars
> we hung our harps.
>
> PSALM 137:1-2 NIV

When Israel was held captive by Babylon, they struggled to worship. They hung up their harps in the midst of their sorrow. They were far from home, and they didn't want to sing. These are very relatable circumstances. When we are filled with sorrow, longing, and grief, songs of praise aren't easy to sing. When we lose hope or can't see how our situation will be redeemed, it takes discipline and intention to worship with joy and thanksgiving.

Even if you are in a difficult season, don't allow it to keep you from worshiping. Your worship isn't tied to a location or a particular set of circumstances. The Holy Spirit is within you, and Jesus is interceding on your behalf. Even when you can't utter anything coherent, the Holy Spirit can draw you to worship. He will remind you of truth and help you turn your eyes toward God despite your situation. No matter how far away you feel from God, He never leaves you alone.

God, fill me with hope as I worship You. Help me develop the habit of praising You no matter what my circumstances are. Help me depend on what is true rather than how I feel.

NOVEMBER 10

He Wants To

*As soon as I pray, you answer me;
you encourage me by giving me strength.*

PSALM 138:3 NLT

God answers the prayers of His people. He answered David's prayer in Psalm 138, and He answers our prayers today. We know that God is able to respond to us, but do we believe He is willing? Our confidence in His desire to answer our prayers will have a direct impact on the way we pray. If deep down we think He doesn't care, our prayers will be limited and empty. If we are convinced that His ears are turned toward us out of love and faithfulness, we will approach Him boldly with the expectation that He will respond.

God answers your prayers because He loves you. He knows your thoughts and every desire of your heart. He sees you, and He wants to help you. If you let Him, He will encourage you and strengthen you. You might find it easy to believe in God's power but difficult to believe in His affection and kindness. He is a mighty King, and He is an attentive Father. Challenge yourself to grasp the full character of God and watch your prayer life be transformed.

God, show me which aspects of Your character that are difficult for me to grasp. Help me see You rightly. I want to approach You knowing that You can hear me and that You are willing to respond to me.

NOVEMBER 11

Even Kings

*Every king in all the earth will thank you, LORD,
for all of them will hear your words.
Yes, they will sing about the LORD's ways,
for the glory of the LORD is very great.*

PSALM 138:4-5 NLT

Psalm 138 expresses David's hope that his praise to God will go beyond himself. He wants God to be worshipped throughout the entire world. His desire is to see every king in all the earth bow down in thanksgiving to the one true God. David knows that God deserves not just the praises of His people in Israel but the praises of people everywhere. This longing stirred David toward evangelism.

David's heart for evangelism is a reminder that God's glory is worth everything despite your level of privilege. Even kings and great rulers cannot be compared to God. The most valuable earthly positions still cannot compete with God's power, authority, and goodness. There is no one else like Him. When you recognize that there is nothing worth having if you don't have Jesus, it will change the way you approach life. Your previous pursuits become less important as you acknowledge that God's glory is worth everything you have.

God, I want to worship You all of my days. I want my life to be defined by a relentless pursuit of Your glory. No matter how much power, privilege, or possessions I collect, may I always be more in awe of who You are.

NOVEMBER 12

God Knows

> O LORD, you have examined my heart
> and know everything about me.
> You know when I sit down or stand up.
> You know my thoughts even when I'm far away.
>
> PSALM 139:1-2 NLT

We sometimes forget that God knows us intimately. He knows the good, the bad, and the ugly. There is nothing about us that is hidden from Him. He knows exactly what each of our days will look like. He is not surprised by a single detail of our stories. He has been everywhere we've been and everywhere we will ever be. His power knows no limits.

God is acutely aware of you. He sees your past, present, and future clearly. He doesn't see your life split into seasons or situations like you do. While you might be concerned or overwhelmed with the details of your days, He sees your heart. He wants a relationship with you more than anything. He cares about the ins and outs of your life, but they are not what grabs His attention when He thinks of you. He is drawn toward you by His pure and perfect love.

God, thank You for seeing me. When I get caught up in details that don't matter, remind me that my relationship with You is most important. When I am overly concerned with what my life looks like, remind me that knowing You and being known by You is my top priority.

NOVEMBER 13

Fully Known

*You know what I am going to say
even before I say it, Lord.*

PSALM 139:4 NLT

There are three concepts about God described in this psalm. As we read, we learn that He is omniscient, omnipresent, and omnipotent. This means that He knows everything, He is everywhere, and He has power over everything. Psalm 139 gives us a picture of what it means for God to be all-knowing in relation to us.

God's omniscience is especially meaningful in regard to prayer. God knows your heart. He knows what you think before you even say it. He understands your intentions and motives. You cannot hide anything about yourself. He is not fooled by your inconsistencies or the version of yourself you present to others. He knows the real you, and He loves you. Having this understanding changes how you approach Him. You lose the need to puff yourself up, defend yourself, or hide your weaknesses. Instead, you can enter His presence and experience the peace that comes from being fully known and fully loved.

God, thank You for knowing me and loving me. Thank You for the freedom that comes from not having to hide or project a specific version of myself. Teach me how to walk confidently in a way that honors You.

NOVEMBER 14

Hemmed In

*You hem me in behind and before,
and you lay your hand upon me.*

PSALM 139:5 NIV

God hems His people in. He goes before us and after us. He surrounds us on all sides. This does not mean that we are confined or suffocated. Because of God's love and watchful care, we are secure. He wraps us in His arms, and He protects us. He has the perfect vantage point over our lives. There isn't a single threat He cannot see coming.

You are held and secure in God's love. You are never alone, and you are always within reach of His care. He longs to be intimately involved in your life. He doesn't want to observe you from a distance, but He wants to walk with you through each and every situation you face. When you're on a path you've never traveled before, you can have confidence because God has already gone before you and prepared the way.

God, thank You for the way You protect me. No matter what I am walking through, You are by my side. Thank You for the comfort and safety I find in Your presence.

NOVEMBER 15

Search and Know

*Search me, O God, and know my heart;
test me and know my anxious thoughts.
Point out anything in me that offends you,
and lead me along the path of everlasting life.*

PSALM 139:23-24 NLT

The invitation for God to search our hearts should not be intimidating. We are not meant to be afraid of Him finding out our secrets or exploiting our weaknesses. We have nothing to be embarrassed of. He is already aware of our greatest failures. The beauty of the gospel is that He redeemed us while we were still sinners. He reached down into our messy lives and created something beautiful.

As you follow God, you can confidently ask Him to search your heart. As you give Him permission to access your entire life, your heart will stay soft and humble. The moment you begin to hide your failures is the moment pride and shame begin to creep in. The act of inviting God into your life, even though He already has a comprehensive understanding of you, creates space for an ongoing relationship with Him.

God, search and know my heart. Show me anything that doesn't line up with Your character or Your purposes. Keep my heart soft and humble. Help me to respond to Your correction with a willing and humble heart.

November 16

On Your Side

If God is for us, who can be against us? He who did not spare his own Son, but gave him up for us all—how will he not also, along with him, graciously give us all things?

Romans 8:31-32 NIV

Everywhere we go, God is present with us. He walks with us, defends us, protects us, and equips us. There is no guarantee that we won't face suffering and hardship. In fact, the opposite is true. Pain cannot be avoided in this life. Our guarantee as believers is that no matter what kind of pain we walk through, God will be with us. He will not allow us to be defeated or destroyed. We might be tested, and we might experience pain, but we will not be left alone to manage it.

Whatever you are facing right now, God wants to help you. He longs to guide you through the daily activities of your life, and He promises to give you what you need. He cares about the things that cause you stress. When you are overwhelmed or anxious, He offers you rest. Let Him reach into the chaos you feel and bring peace and confidence. If you let Him, He will steady your steps and make your path straight before you.

God, I'm so thankful I don't have to face my life alone. Thank You for equipping me and fighting alongside me. Thank You for giving me strength where I am weak. Help me rely on You instead of floundering in stress.

NOVEMBER 17

God Alone

Be imitators of God, as beloved children.

EPHESIANS 5:1 NASB

There are no heroes of the Bible besides God. It's His story, and everything we read is meant to point us back to Him. Each victory, encouraging anecdote, correction, and piece of wisdom teaches us about His character and His purposes. If we read the Word and elevate people over God, we've missed the point. Each person, no matter how admirable, is imperfect. It's dangerous to get into the habit of putting specific people on pedestals they are bound to fall from.

Ask yourself if your desire to emulate other believers has overcome your desire to emulate God Himself. There are some practical ways you can evaluate your heart in this area. Are you consuming more Christian content than reading the Word? Are you searching for ways to get your life on track more than you are spending relational time with God? Are you following the recommendations or preferences of people without asking God for guidance? Above all else, God is the hero of your story.

God, You alone are my Savior and Redeemer. You are the one I want to imitate. Show me if there are people I have put on a pedestal. I turn my eyes toward You because You are the only one worthy of my worship.

NOVEMBER 18

Persevere in Love

> I know that the LORD secures justice for the poor
> and upholds the cause of the needy.
> Surely the righteous will praise your name,
> and the upright will live in your presence.
>
> PSALM 140:12-13 NIV

God protects the vulnerable and weak. He cares for those who are poor and in need. As His followers, this should be important to us as well. We don't get to pick and choose who is worthy of God's love or who deserves His attention. Caring for others isn't typically convenient or comfortable because sacrificial love is costly. If we only lay our lives down when it feels good, comes easily, or makes us look good to others, our hearts aren't in the right place.

God doesn't ask you to only love people who are easily loved. Typically, those who need God's grace and mercy the most are difficult, frustrating, and messy. In those moments, the Holy Spirit can equip you with patience, kindness, and gentleness. God's love is truly reflected when your ability ends, and you must rely on His strength. Caring for others out of your own strength will only take you so far. Eventually, you will have to press into His presence and lean on Him.

God, give me strength to love those the world considers unlovable. Give me strength to those the church considers unlovable. Keep me from picking and choosing who I care for. Give me boldness, perseverance, and fortitude in the way I love the needy.

NOVEMBER 19

In Desperation

*I call to you, LORD, come quickly to me;
hear me when I call to you.*

PSALM 141:1 NIV

It's okay to approach God with a sense of urgency. If we take our cues from David's example, we can see that no matter how frantic we are, God is steady. No matter how chaotic our emotions seem, God is unwavering. He is able to take our stress and turn it into peace. He does not match our frenzied spirits; He transforms them. He is big enough to hold our storms in His hands and create something beautiful out of them.

God hears you when you posture yourself in prayer and lift your hands toward the heavens. He responds to your desperation with competence and calmness. You are not too much for Him. Your heart, exactly as it is, is not beyond His ability to redeem. Don't hold back because you have come to believe that you are overwhelming or difficult to handle. His presence is the perfect place for your desperation to be turned into peace.

God, thank You for hearing my desperate cries. Thank You for welcoming me into Your presence. Help me approach you boldly, just as I am. I trust You to transform my life in Your perfect timing.

NOVEMBER 20

Heart Reflection

Set a guard over my mouth, L ORD;
keep watch over the door of my lips.

P SALM 141:3 NIV

Having self-control over what we say isn't always easy. Our culture praises loud opinions and divisive words, and it can be difficult to have a quiet tongue. Even when our words are typed, they have the power of life or death. The way we communicate matters because it is a direct reflection of our hearts. If the words we say are harsh, unloving, or judgmental, that is the picture others will have of us. Our words should be kind, truthful, honest, and compassionate because that's how God communicates with us.

Commit your words to the Lord and allow Him to transform the way you speak. Maybe you default to being quiet when you should speak up. Or maybe you default to speaking harshly when gentleness is needed. Either way, transformation and obedience to God are necessary. It isn't only loud or obnoxious people who need to control their tongues. In every situation, despite our natural tendencies, we should bring our communication into alignment with God's character and purposes.

God, may my words honor You. Teach me when to speak and when to be silent. Help me to be sensitive to Your guidance. Help me to reflect You in everything I say.

NOVEMBER 21

Godly Correction

Let a righteous man strike me—that is a kindness;
let him rebuke me—that is oil on my head.
My head will not refuse it,
for my prayer will still be against the deeds of evildoers.

PSALM 141:5 NIV

Godly discipline is a blessing and a mercy. It is better to learn and grow now than be held accountable for our mistakes later. When God gives us an opportunity to change, we should welcome it with an open heart and mind. This doesn't mean that we need to accept corrections from just anyone. The stipulation in Psalm 141 is that we welcome correction from people who are righteous. This means that we accept godly discipline from people who faithfully follow Jesus and live according to His Word.

God's correction, and the correction from godly people, should always be kind and life-giving. It should be patient, gentle, truthful, and aligned with Scripture. If you receive correction that doesn't fit those criteria, it may not be from God. Follow the guidance of the Holy Spirit and allow Him to keep your heart soft. Humbly receive a gentle rebuke and don't give time or energy to the criticism of the world.

God, bless me with the gift of discernment when it comes to correction and discipline. Soften my heart and give me grace to respond well to godly correction.

NOVEMBER 22

Every Season

*When I am overwhelmed,
you alone know the way I should turn.*

PSALM 142:3 NLT

David cried out to God in many different circumstances. He called upon Him in battle, in the throes of emotional distress, in shame over sin, and even while hiding in a literal cave. His life was never dull and contained a whirlwind of circumstances. He knew the importance of leaning on God's strength no matter what was happening. He trusted God to intervene every time.

You don't need to walk through any season alone. Whether you are experiencing grief, celebration, or are simply getting through each day, God is with you. When you are overwhelmed, He is the one to turn to. When you are bored, He is worthy of your praise. In each and every circumstance, He is your refuge and strength. Lean on Him in trauma, delight in Him in the mundane, and rejoice when blessings are abundant.

God, permeate my life with Your presence. Teach me to lean on You through every season of the soul. When I am overwhelmed, remind me to look to You. When I am at peace, stir my heart to praise You. Keep me close through every high and low.

NOVEMBER 23

Your Portion

I cry to you, LORD;
I say, "You are my refuge,
my portion in the land of the living."

PSALM 142:5 NIV

When the psalmist uses the word *portion*, he is talking about an inheritance or the plunder that each person would have received after a victory in battle. To declare that God is our portion is to say that He is our ultimate inheritance. His presence is what makes us rich. He is exactly what we need. Being in communion with Him is our greatest prize and reward.

God is your portion. He is exactly what you need in every situation. He provides for you and faithfully cares for you in every circumstance. You can cry out to Him and know that He is with you and will remain with you throughout every season of your life. In His presence, you are not lacking anything because He is enough for you.

God, You are my portion. In Your presence, I have everything I need. You are my reward and my greatest gift. When I am tempted to chase after worldly desires, remind me that You are the only one worthy of my affection.

NOVEMBER 24

Only Option

*Listen to my cry,
for I am in desperate need;
rescue me from those who pursue me,
for they are too strong for me.*

PSALM 142:6 NIV

In Psalm 142, we see David's plea to God for help in the midst of trouble. He knows he does not have the ability to rescue himself. He doesn't have the resources to survive, and he is pleading with God to intervene on his behalf. He has been through enough in his life to know that God will rescue him. He has confidence based on his previous interactions with God.

The longer you follow God, the more clearly you will see His hand in your life. Your confidence will grow as you see proof of His ability to rescue you. You will move from a place of hoping God will intervene to knowing He will. There's a comfort that comes from the longevity of relationships. Your expectations are no longer based on what you are told but on what you've experienced yourself. Faith grows in situations where God is your only option.

God, strengthen my confidence in You. As I cry out to You, remind me of all You've done in the past. Take my doubts and replace them with steadfast faith. Your ability to rescue me is limitless.

NOVEMBER 25

No Comparison

Answer me because you are faithful and righteous.
Don't put your servant on trial,
for no one is innocent before you.

PSALM 143:1-2 NLT

In Psalm 143, the psalmist appeals to God because he knows He will be gracious. He is asking God not to judge him because He has an understanding that no one can compare to God's perfect standard. He acknowledges that if he is compared to God, he will fall short. He is fully aware of his weaknesses and failures.

You cannot follow God and be unaware of your need for Him. If you don't understand your own inadequacy, you won't see the need for forgiveness. If you can't admit when you are wrong, you won't understand God's redemptive plan. Don't allow pride to get in the way of humbly accepting Christ's offer of redemption. Awareness of your sin is the first step of laying your life down at the cross.

God, keep me from being blind to my sin. Help me see my need for You at all times. Keep my heart soft and open to Your correction. Thank You for being gracious and kind when I make mistakes.

NOVEMBER 26

The Only Way

We know that no one receives God's perfect righteousness as a reward for keeping the law, but only by the faith of Jesus, the Messiah!

GALATIANS 2:16 TPT

It's so easy to fall into the trap of trying to manage our own righteousness. We easily get hung up by checking off our to-do lists and making sure that our Christian life looks exactly right. We measure our success by our own human ability, and we hold others to standards that we've created ourselves. It's good to follow God's instructions, but Scripture constantly warns against following the letter of the law without engaging in a heartfelt relationship with God.

There is no way for you to earn God's approval. Nothing you can do makes you good enough. Even if you could follow every rule perfectly, none of it has any value without Jesus. His sacrifice is the only path to God. You cannot add to the gospel, and you cannot take anything away from it. Find freedom in the knowledge that you cannot pay the price for your own sin.

God, keep me from striving for Your approval. Remind me of the gift I have been given through Christ. Teach me how to walk in freedom and live in a way that honors You.

NOVEMBER 27

Tear and Repair

> Blessed be the LORD, my rock,
> Who trains my hands for war,
> And my fingers for battle.
>
> PSALM 144:1 NASB

We've all experienced trials and spiritual attacks. If we're not currently in one, it's usually only a matter of time before something comes up. The time when we are waiting is the perfect time for God to prepare us for what's to come. Waiting time is training time. He gives us skills to manage the problems we face, and if we let Him, He will give us what we need to stand strong against the enemy.

God often gives you the tools for battle before you realize you need them. He responds and rescues you when you struggle, but He also trains you in advance and strengthens you to persevere. He offers His followers preemptive protection. Spiritual training is difficult, just like physical training. Growth comes when muscles tear and repair. The same concept can be true spiritually. The next time you feel like your spiritual muscles are being torn, remember that God might be preparing you for something that is coming.

God, You see every struggle I will face. Thank You for training my hands for war and my fingers for battle. Thank You for equipping me even when I don't realize You are doing it.

NOVEMBER 28

Wonder and Awe

*L*ORD*, what is man, that You look after him?*
Or a son of man, that You think of him?

PSALM 144:3 NASB

God's desire to be with us is worth marveling at. We can echo David's sense of awe that a holy God would be so attentive toward flawed and broken humans. In spite of the fact that we are a temporary creation, like a breath or a passing shadow, God is intimately aware of us. When we recognize who God is compared to who we are, the only appropriate response is wonder.

God's concern for you is nothing short of miraculous. From the heights of the heavens, He is aware of you during every single moment of your day. He sees each tiny detail of your life, and He cares about all of it. Your relationship with Him is beautifully out of balance. You cannot compare what He has done for you to what you are capable of doing for Him. Let your heart be filled with wonder as you recognize how small you are and how great He is.

God, it's incredible that You are mindful of me. Thank You for seeing me and loving me so perfectly. Fill me with a sense of wonder and awe as I look to You.

NOVEMBER 29

He Rescues

God, I will sing a new song to You;
On a harp of ten strings I will sing praises to You,
Who gives salvation to kings,
Who rescues His servant David from the evil sword.

Psalm 144:9-10 nasb

Even though David is talking about literal war, we can relate because we are always in a spiritual battle. Whether our struggle is with our finances, jobs, or relationships, it's important to recognize that God is our protector. He is present in the middle of every battle we face. If we are surrendered to Him, He will faithfully bring us through to the other side. He longs to restore us to a state of peace.

Psalm 144 can be used as a prayer when you are suffering with the everyday struggles of life. No matter what your fight looks like, God wants to help. If you ask Him to rescue you, He will. Think about situations in your past that seemed hopeless at the time. Notice how God carried you through when you didn't think it was possible. Praise Him for how He has already rescued you and look toward the future with confidence, knowing He will do it again.

God, fill my heart with songs of praise. Thank You for all the ways You've rescued me. Thank You for bringing me through each trial I've faced. My trust is in You alone.

NOVEMBER 30

Exalt the King

*I will exalt you, my God and King,
and praise your name forever and ever.*

PSALM 145:1 NLT

Sometimes, it's easy to get caught up with everything that is going on around us. We get lost in our personal lives or the cultural and political climate of the day. It's helpful to remember that God is King. He's not just the king of Israel or the people who choose to follow Him; He is the one true King with authority over all the earth. There is nothing that is out of His jurisdiction. He is the creator and ruler of all things. He provides not just for His people but for vulnerable people everywhere.

When things seem most out of control, God is the King. When life is going exactly how you want it to, God is the King. He is worthy of your praise in all circumstances. No matter how chaotic the world feels, God is still sovereign. He sees everything, knows everything, and is mindful of you in the midst of it. Let His proven faithfulness in your life stir you to praise Him with all you have. Look at what He has done in the past and trust that He can handle your future.

God, You are my King. I praise You because You are worthy, and You have proven to be faithful. Remind me of all You have done and build up my confidence. Strengthen my faith and help me lean on You when the world seems out of control.

DECEMBER

DECEMBER 1

Covenant Love

*The LORD is merciful and compassionate,
slow to get angry and filled with unfailing love.
The LORD is good to everyone.
He showers compassion on all his creation.*

PSALM 145:8-9 NLT

God is gracious and compassionate. He is slow to anger and quick to love. His love is loyal and based on the covenant that He made with us. It's a promise He will not break. His covenant is displayed in the Old Testament, fulfilled in Christ in the New Testament, and is at work in our lives today. The closest example of God's covenant love that we have is marriage. Even so, we can't wrap our minds around the permanence of God's promise to us.

God's promises to you are not temporary or able to be broken. They are not dependent on your ability to be faithful, and they are not based on your actions. His promises are eternal and untouchable by humanity. There is nothing you can do to cause Him to be less faithful. His response to you will always be the same. The defining factor in your relationship with God is your response to Him. He will be merciful and compassionate toward you if you turn to Him.

God, thank You for Your kindness and compassion. Thank You for having mercy on me when I don't deserve it. When I waver, remind me of the covenant You've made with me.

DECEMBER 2

First and Foremost

> Praise the Lord
> Praise the Lord, my soul!
>
> PSALM 146:1 NASB

In Psalm 146 the psalmist is calling the people around him to worship God. He begins by commanding his own soul to praise the Lord. Even though he is the one responsible for leading the community into praise, he starts by posturing his own soul rightly. This is a great example of how our own relationship with God must be prioritized before we attempt to lead others. There is often a temptation to pour ourselves out for others while neglecting our own connection with God.

The most important part of your life is the connection between you and God. The pursuit of Him should be your priority. This goes beyond doing it because you should or because it is right. His presence is where you belong. Knowing Him and being known by Him is the greatest gift you'll ever have. When you start to feel in over your head with the responsibilities of life, take inventory of your personal relationship with God. Has it taken a lesser seat because you've prioritized tasks over connection?

God, when I get distracted or become too busy, draw me back to You. Help me prioritize my own connection with You before I try to lead others. Keep me in the place where my acts of service are an overflow of what I experience with You.

DECEMBER 3

His Plans

I will praise the LORD while I live;
I will sing praises to my God while I have my being.

PSALM 146:2 NASB

The psalmist expresses several times that his desire is to give everything he has to God for all of his days. We all know that our time on earth is limited, yet it's easy to get caught up in the busyness of life. If we don't prioritize praising God, we will find ourselves pursuing goals that don't have eternal value. We can't take the possessions we collect, the plans we make, or the kingdoms we build with us. The only thing that has eternal value is God's love and the kingdom He builds.

If your hopes and dreams are resting on your ability to achieve them, you'll be disappointed. If your highest goals are based on your personal satisfaction, you'll be disappointed. Instead, turn your attention to God's heart. When you commit your ways to Him and follow His plans, you'll find true fulfillment. He is the foundation of your hope, and His plans are the ones that will last. This applies not only to the ways you serve Him but also to your daily life.

God, thank You for the time You've given me. Help me use it to honor You and Your plans. As I commit my ways to You, show me each step I should take. I trust You to lead me well.

DECEMBER 4

Beginning and End

> The Lord will reign forever,
> Your God, Zion, to all generations.
> Praise the Lord!
>
> Psalm 146:10 NASB

Psalm 146 begins and ends with a call to praise God. The same thing should be true about our pursuits, our days, and the span of our lives. Everything should begin and end in worship and service to God. He is the Alpha and the Omega, the creator of all things, and the one who will redeem all that is lost. Everything we have and anything we can create belongs to Him. He is the author of each of our stories, and He is the one who will hold all things together until the very end.

God is worthy of all your praise. Worship is meant to be like bookends for all that you do. When you begin your day by praising Him, you set the tone for the rest of the day. When you end your day by praising Him, you give Him the credit He is due. This doesn't mean that you must set aside hours for intense or perfectly organized worship. It's more about the posture of your heart and your willingness to give what you have, no matter how feeble, to God.

God, thank You for all You have given me. Thank You for the way You have orchestrated my life. Every good thing I have is from Your hands. Give me grace to posture my heart before You in worship. Remind me each morning to devote myself to You and Your purposes.

DECEMBER 5

God Alone

> Was Paul crucified for you?
> Were you baptized in the name of Paul?
>
> 1 Corinthians 1:13 NIV

People are not always a great representation of who God is. We make mistakes, misjudge situations, and sometimes purposefully do the wrong thing. It's important as believers to be able to separate God's character from the downfalls of His people. If we look to others to show us who God is, we will be disappointed and won't have an accurate picture of His character. No matter how impressive they are, we are called to follow Jesus rather than people.

People in your life can absolutely give you glimpses of who God is, but they should not be the ultimate authority on your opinion of Him. When you elevate others and hold them to a standard they cannot keep, you set yourself up for bitterness or grief. Scripture is God's story. He is the main character and the one you should always turn to. It's good to be inspired by others, but they should inspire you to draw nearer to God rather than imitating their actions.

God, I want to have an accurate perspective of Your character. Show me if there are any people in my life who I have elevated above You. Your ways are the only ones I want to copy and reflect.

DECEMBER 6

Build and Gather

The LORD builds up Jerusalem;
He gathers the outcasts of Israel.

PSALM 147:2 NASB

We serve a God who builds and creates. He does not leave His children in a state of brokenness or disrepair. God's faithfulness to rebuild Jerusalem after the Israelites returned from Babylon echoes His faithfulness to repair our own brokenness. He offers us restoration when we surrender our lives to Him. We will experience full healing when we join Him in heaven, but until then, we can experience glimpses of the perfection He has promised.

There might be pain, suffering, or brokenness you carry with you for all your days. This doesn't mean that God isn't rebuilding your life. From the moment you surrendered to Him, He has set you on a path toward full restoration. A day is coming when everything He promised you will be fulfilled. He might heal certain things along the way, but even that can't compare to the glory of what is coming. Don't lose heart on days when things seem extra broken. The Lord will build you up in His perfect timing.

God, I trust You to build my life exactly how it should be.
I surrender to Your ways, and I look to You for guidance.
When I experience brokenness, help me run to You for
comfort and healing.

DECEMBER 7

He Heals

*He heals the brokenhearted
And binds up their wounds.*

Psalm 147:3 nasb

God binds up our wounds. He takes care of us with purpose and intention. If we picture someone dressing a wound, we might see them gently clean it, address any infections, deal with pain, and apply a bandage with just the right amount of pressure. This is how God manages our hurt as well. He doesn't brush over it, tell us to deal with it, or care for it improperly. He knows exactly what we need, and He is capable of doing it.

If you allow Him to, God will heal your wounds. There are some things in your life that might receive miraculous and immediate attention. Other situations might require a process or a journey of healing that takes work and dedication. In both instances, God deserves the glory. Praise Him for the wounds in your life He has already healed and look toward the future with hopeful expectation that He will continue healing you. His work in your life is not done.

God, thank You for healing my wounds when I come to You. I trust You to take care of me perfectly. When I try to bandage myself up, remind me that You give the greatest care.

DECEMBER 8

By Name

He counts the number of the stars;
He gives names to all of them.

PSALM 147:4 NASB

If God knows each of the stars in the sky personally, we can be assured that He knows the hurts of each one of His people. If He calls each star by name, He must be aware of us. We serve a God who willingly reaches into each of our lives and gives us peace, mercy, and grace. He intervenes when we need it most, and He offers us His unending love.

Look up at the sky tonight and take in the vastness of the heavens. What you can see is barely a glimpse of the contents of the universe. Even what's visible to you is too big to count, catalog, or understand. Yet, God knows each star by name. He is fully aware of every corner of His creation, and you hold His attention above everything else. His love for you goes beyond the edges of the universe. He knows your hurts, and He knows your joy. He knows the things that you're struggling with emotionally, physically, and spiritually.

God, thank You for the beauty of the heavens. Thank You for how they remind me of Your faithful love and attentiveness. Thank You for seeing me and knowing exactly what I need.

DECEMBER 9

Creator and Sustainer

It is He who covers the heavens with clouds,
Who provides rain for the earth,
Who makes grass sprout on the mountains.
It is He who gives an animal its food,
And feeds young ravens that cry.

PSALM 147:8-9 NASB

We serve a God who provides. He is the creator of every system and cycle on earth, and He holds them together perfectly. He makes the rain fall, and He provides food for every animal. Every single aspect of creation is attributed to Him. There isn't a single detail that falls between the cracks. If He can manage the complexity of creation, He can certainly manage our lives.

If God feeds the ravens, He will feed you. If He provides refreshing rain for the earth, He will not let your heart go dry. He knows what you need, and He is capable of providing it. Today, spend some time thinking through all the details that make your life work. From the bed you wake up in to the air you breathe and even your ability to cook a meal, God is the author of everything. There are countless details that you don't even think of on a daily basis, yet God orchestrates it all perfectly.

God, I worship You as my Creator and Sustainer. You hold my life together in ways I can't even understand. You deserve all the glory. Help me remember all of the good gifts You are constantly providing me with.

DECEMBER 10

Impossible Standard

He does not delight in the strength of the horse;
He does not take pleasure in the legs of a man.
The Lord favors those who fear Him,
Those who wait for His faithfulness.

Psalm 147:10-11 NASB

God loves those who fear Him. He is not impressed by our skills or our strength. All He asks for is a heart that is devoted to Him. He wants us to put our hope in His unfailing love rather than offering Him the impressiveness of our abilities. When we try to clean ourselves up or behave a certain way because we think He'll accept us, we've missed the point. God is not swayed by our attempts to impress Him.

God's steady love and unending grace are not meant to excuse incorrect behavior. Instead, they are meant to free you from striving to meet an impossible standard. There is absolutely no way for you to compare to His perfection. This is why you need Jesus. Through Christ, you are made perfect. Through Christ, you have freedom because you no longer have to uphold the law in order to gain access to God. No matter what your opinion is of yourself, Jesus' sacrifice is what makes you worthy.

God, keep me from finding confidence in my own strengths or abilities. Help me humbly offer any skills I have to You. The hope I find in You is the only thing that will last.

DECEMBER 11

Weakest Point

*Praise your God, Zion!
For He has strengthened the bars of your gates.*

PSALM 147:12-13 NASB

In ancient times, the gate would have been the most vulnerable part of the city. Bars held it in place, and it kept enemies out. If someone were going to attack, the first place they would weaken would be the gate. When the psalmist told Israel that God strengthened the bars of their gates, they would have understood exactly how strategic and important that move was. They would have felt comforted and safe knowing that God was not only aware of their weak points but willing to strengthen them as well.

God knows where you are lacking. In your greatest weakness, He is made strong. The areas of your life where you feel the most frustration and shame are exactly the areas where you need Him most. If you let Him, He will protect you when you cannot protect yourself. When the enemy tries to strategically exploit your downfalls, God will fight for You. You are His child, and He longs to defend you. As you surrender to His ways and seek to honor Him with all you have, He will not let you fall.

God, thank You for protecting me just like You protected Israel. I trust You to strengthen me where I am weak. Instead of living in shame, help me turn to You. You are the only one who can protect me and keep me safe.

DECEMBER 12

The Heavens Declare

Praise him, sun and moon!
Praise him, all you twinkling stars!
Praise him, skies above!
Praise him, vapors high above the clouds!

PSALM 148:3-4 NLT

In Psalm 148, the psalmist calls for all of creation to worship God. He calls for everyone and everything to acknowledge that God is our Creator. The earth is filled with His fingerprints, and we were all made to praise Him. Everything on the earth is the work of His hands, and each corner of the universe belongs to Him. Out of His creativity and genius, He made the heavens and everything below them.

The heavens and everything in it declare the glory of God. While people may try to manipulate messages of the stars, we recognize that God is their author. He is the one holding them together, and they were made to worship Him. Let the beauty of the night sky stir your heart to praise the one who made it. Let its vastness fill you with wonder and remind you of His greatness.

God, thank You for the way creation declares Your glory. Thank You for creating the heavens for me to marvel at. Fill me with wonder and awe when I see the work of Your hands.

DECEMBER 13

His Victory

The horse is prepared for the day of battle, but the victory belongs to the Lord.

PROVERBS 21:31 NLT

Throughout the Old Testament, we see many references to battle. Without fail, it's clear that God is the one who establishes victories for His people. This can encourage us today because it reminds us that it isn't our job to win the wars we face. This doesn't mean we don't have a responsibility to stand up as believers in a dark world, but it does take the pressure off. At the end of it all, we aren't in control. God is the one who fights for us and with us. Without Him, we are helpless.

It's easy to feel powerless when the world feels chaotic, and the darkness of our culture is overwhelming. Remember, you are not alone. God is in control, and He is the one who will execute judgment. You don't have to carry that burden. Your job is to trust His plans and do your best to live in a way that displays His love and character to a hurting and broken world. Turn your eyes toward Him and follow His ways, but don't be burdened by something that isn't yours to accomplish. At the end of the day, God is the one who will defeat the evil in this world.

God, thank You for being strong in battle. Thank You for equipping me to follow You. When I am tempted to take control or responsibility, remind me that You are the one with all authority.

DECEMBER 14

Humility First

> The LORD takes delight in his people;
> he crowns the humble with victory.
>
> PSALM 149:4 NIV

Humility is a specific element of worship that opens up our hearts and puts us in a posture of praise. Only when we are humble can we come before the Lord with sincere hearts. God deserves our devotion not only because He created us but because He is our king. Our response to Him should be an enthusiastic outpouring of thanksgiving. We cannot put Him in His rightful place in our lives if we don't approach Him with humility.

Being humble does not mean thinking less of yourself. Instead, it means acknowledging that God is always greater. Humility does not mean ignoring your gifts and talents. Instead, it means giving God the credit He is due. When you are humble, you admit your desperate and continuous need for God. The humble are given victory because they make space for God to fight for them. On the other hand, the prideful often fall because they insist on fighting their battles alone.

God, thank You for fighting with me and for me. Soften my heart and help me to always acknowledge my need for You, my Creator, and my King. Be lifted high in my life and turn my heart toward You in worship.

DECEMBER 15

Don't Hide

*Praise God in his sanctuary;
praise him in his mighty heaven!
Praise him for his mighty works;
praise his unequaled greatness!*

PSALM 150:1-2 NLT

One of the things we learn throughout the book of Psalms is that it is essentially a place for our hearts to gather. We can speak freely and worship in the presence of God, despite how we feel. Our praise is not limited to our emotions. Sometimes, we worship Him in moments of sorrow or depression, and sometimes we are overcome with celebration or joy. Every emotion and expression is welcomed by God.

You can praise God regardless of what's going on in your life. As you bring what you have to Him, He responds with mercy and grace. As you pour out your heart to Him, He transforms you in His presence. Don't let anything hold you back from approaching Him with confidence. He has invited you to dwell with Him, and He will not turn you away. He has made it clear that your humanity is not too much for Him. Allow Him full access to your heart and you will not be disappointed. He holds everything together, and He can hold you together as well.

God, thank You for speaking to me through the Psalms. Thank You for showing me that You can handle even my messiest emotions. When I am tempted to hide, remind me that You have welcomed me into Your presence.

DECEMBER 16

Delayed Obedience

*I will hurry, without delay,
to obey your commands.*

PSALM 119:60 NLT

Doing the right thing isn't always easy or natural. There are times in our lives when we would rather go our own way or do things according to the timeline we prefer. We must remember that delayed obedience is disobedience. If we know what God wants but are dragging our feet or trying to put our own twist on it, we are allowing time to be wasted. Our faith is strengthened when we follow His ways even when we don't want to or it isn't easy.

If something in your heart feels uncomfortable with the word *obey*, it might be time for some self-evaluation. Your perspective is off when you equate obedience to God with control or the misuse of authority. God's desire for you to obey His commands comes from a foundation of love. Everything He asks you to do has a purpose. He doesn't ask you to follow a list of rules simply for the sake of order or obedience. He does it because He knows what is best, and you can trust His perfect plan.

God, Your ways are higher than mine. Remind me of Your goodness when I am tempted to be disobedient. Teach me how to obey Your commands quickly and without delay.

DECEMBER 17

Every Opportunity

"Who knows if perhaps you were made queen for just such a time as this?"

ESTHER 4:14 NLT

If we read through the book of Esther, we will quickly see that God is at work. Though He isn't specifically mentioned by name, His character is seen through Esther's bravery and selflessness. When her people were at risk, she willingly laid her life down for them. She knew that her actions could end in death, but she did the right thing anyway. Her heroic behavior saved an entire race of people. Instead of shying away from the opportunity she was given, she embraced her privilege and used it for God's glory.

The way you conduct yourself matters. Even if you aren't standing on a stage boldly proclaiming the gospel, your life and actions can reflect God's love and character. The way you respond to stress or injustice can show the people around you what God stands for. Your life is filled with opportunities to share who He is, spoken or unspoken. God has placed you in a specific season or place for a reason. Ask Him for courage to make the most of the opportunities you have.

God, help me be brave like Esther. Show me how I can share Your character with the people around me. Teach me when to speak and when to let my actions speak for me. May everything I do declare Your goodness and truth.

DECEMBER 18

Give Generously

*The generous will prosper;
those who refresh others will themselves be refreshed.*

PROVERBS 11:25 NLT

The story of the widow of Zarephath is found in 1 Kings 17. Through her example, we see that God graciously gives good gifts to those who selflessly serve others. Even though she herself is starving, she gives what she has to Elijah. She would be perfectly justified to refuse him, yet she obediently answers his request. She makes him something to eat, and that's when God intervenes. Not only is there enough for Elijah but there is also enough for her and her starving son to survive for a year.

Even in times of famine and drought, God can provide. You can serve Him through generosity and kindness even when it doesn't make sense. When your physical circumstances seem dire, He can still move. His intervention in times of desperation brings strength and hope. He is the God who can take deserts and turn them into lush gardens. When you put your faith in Him, generosity becomes second nature. When you remember that He is the one who provides for you, it becomes much easier to hold what you have with an open grasp.

God, I put my faith in You as the one who provides for me. You are a God of abundance and generosity. Help me reflect this part of Your character to each person I encounter. I surrender my gifts to You and put all of my blessings back into Your hands.

DECEMBER 19

Compassion Over Judgment

He is so rich in kindness and grace that he purchased our freedom with the blood of his Son and forgave our sins. He has showered his kindness on us.

EPHESIANS 1:7-8 NLT

Scripture is full of examples of imperfect people encountering the grace of God. Tamar's story, found in Genesis 38, is a great example. Even though she is typically seen as prostitute and a liar, reading her story shows that she is actually in the lineage of Christ. Despite her past, He redeemed her story. This reminds us that no one is excluded from God's offer of grace and forgiveness.

It's impossible to know what your circumstances will drive you to do. Instead of allowing yourself to be critical or prideful, it's important to remember that there isn't a situation in existence that God cannot redeem. Everyone justifies their sins for different reasons, yet all are offered equal grace at the foot of the cross. God has purchased freedom for all without exception. When you are tempted to write someone off or call their situation hopeless, realize that without Jesus, we are all separated from God's grace.

God, open my eyes to the reality of Your redemptive power. I don't want to limit Your ability to miraculously turn a situation around.

DECEMBER 20

Death Doesn't Win

Elisha turned away and walked back and forth in the room and then got on the bed and stretched out on him once more. The boy sneezed seven times and opened his eyes.

2 Kings 4:35

The story of the Shunammite woman illustrates for us that even when it looks like we should give up, God can intervene. She held her lifeless son in her arms, yet she called upon God for a miracle. Through the prophet Elisha, God answered her prayer. Her great faith led to a miracle. Death did not have the final word, but it became just one more opportunity for God to display His power and attentiveness to the needs of His people.

There are many ways to experience death in this life. Maybe you've walked through the immense grief of losing someone. Maybe you've navigated the death of a dream, expectation, or relationship. No matter the circumstances, death does not win. Though it feels crushing, death can stir up your faith. It can draw you to the feet of Jesus as you call upon Him to intervene. Don't give up because the final victory belongs to God.

God, thank You for giving me victory over death through Jesus. When I am weary of the losses I've experienced, draw me closer to Your heart. Comfort me when I weep and strengthen me to persevere.

December 21

Final Authority

The midwives feared God and did not do what the king of Egypt had told them to do; they let the boys live.

Exodus 1:17 NIV

In an effort to secure his throne, the king of Egypt decided to eliminate any baby boys who were born. He knew that the King of the Jews was coming, and he used his authority to command the midwives of the day to kill any baby boys they delivered. Shipra and Puah were two midwives who bravely refused to listen. They knew that God was their final authority. They allowed each baby to live despite the instructions they were given. As a result, the lineage of Christ was protected.

Shipra and Puah probably didn't know that their actions would have an impact on the life of the eventual Messiah. All they knew was that they feared God, which meant standing up to Pharoah. There might be times in your life when God calls you to take a stand. There is no way for you to understand the ripples your decisions will have. It's not your responsibility to have all the details or a clear picture of God's plans. It's your responsibility to respond with obedience when He calls you to be steadfast.

God, teach me how to be brave like Shipra and Puah. Help me to boldly take a stand when You ask me to. Give me the right words to say and the courage to follow Your instructions. I trust You to lead me even when I don't know all the details.

DECEMBER 22

Patiently Waiting

By faith even Sarah, who was past childbearing age, was enabled to bear children because she considered him faithful who had made the promise.

HEBREWS 11:11 NIV

God made a promise to Abraham and Sarah that they would have many children. The details of that promise didn't make sense from a human perspective. It's understandable why Sarah thought she needed to take matters into her own hands. She was determined to fulfill God's promise herself. Despite her disobedience, God blessed her. Even though she grew tired of waiting and was disobedient to God, He did not abandon her. Sarah's story is a great example of what God can do in our lives despite our faults and mistakes.

If you are someone who finds comfort in control, you can likely relate to Sarah's situation. Waiting for the fulfillment of a promise is not easy, especially when you think you can do something about it yourself. Waiting on God's timing is just as important as believing what He said He would do in the first place. Sarah's story isn't meant to give us an excuse to micromanage our faith. Rather, it's a reminder that God's ability to redeem us goes beyond our ability to do everything correctly.

God, help me remember that waiting on You, no matter how long it takes, is always the best plan. Teach me how to trust Your promises, especially when I am weary and impatient. You know what is best, and I don't want to take matters into my own hands.

DECEMBER 23

Each Step

"Praise be to the Lord, who this day has not left you without a guardian-redeemer. May he become famous throughout Israel!"

RUTH 4:14 NIV

Throughout the genealogy of Jesus, we see a picture of broken, hurting people who have been redeemed by the Lord. People who we wouldn't expect to be in the lineage of Christ are prevalent and highlighted. God redeems all things, including His family line. He takes what is broken and patches it together in a way that is beautiful and full of purpose. The story of Ruth is a great example of how nothing is beyond God's ability to repair.

Read Ruth's story and be encouraged by her faith. She trusted in God when she didn't know the outcome, and you can do the same. You can rely on Him to tell you the next right thing to do, even when your situation seems hopeless. If you call on Him for help and submit to His leadership, He will be with you through each step. Instead of giving in to anxiety or sorrow, let God gently guide you through whatever you are facing.

God, thank You for Your faithfulness displayed in Ruth's story. I trust that You will also redeem the broken or hopeless parts of my life. When I am tempted to sit in my sorrow, turn my eyes toward You. Show me what to do next because I know You know best.

DECEMBER 24

Gracious Redeemer

If we confess our sins, he is faithful and just and will forgive us our sins and purify us from all unrighteousness.

1 John 1:9 NIV

Many of us have had scenarios where we start off with good intentions, and then somewhere along the line, everything falls apart. If we read the story of Rebecca, we can see the same thing happening. She wanted to ensure that her son Jacob received his birthright, so she deceived her husband into giving it to him. She started out with a desire to follow God and do the right thing for her family. In the end, her behavior got out of hand, and she didn't finish strong. Instead of maintaining her trust in God, she took matters into her own hands and created division.

Rebecca's choices did not honor God, yet He includes her child in the lineage of Christ. He honors and redeems Rebecca's family even though she made mistakes. In the same way, your poor choices do not exclude you from God's family. Despite your faithlessness, sin, or brokenness, you have a God who redeems all things. When you are honest with Him, He graciously offers you forgiveness and freedom.

God, help me to follow You well. Keep me on the path You have chosen for me. When I am tempted to create my own way, remind me that Your plans are best.

DECEMBER 25

In Weakness

One thing I do: Forgetting what is behind and straining toward what is ahead, I press on toward the goal to win the prize for which God has called me heavenward in Christ Jesus.

PHILIPPIANS 3:13-14 NIV

There are probably times in all of our lives when we have disqualified ourselves from being used by God because of current or past sin. The reality is that God often uses people who are weak, inadequate, and underqualified. Our definition of being fit for use is not the same as His. Our weakness only magnifies His strength and perfection. His faithfulness matters more than our faithlessness.

If you look at the story of Rahab, you'll find a woman who, despite her mistakes, had a deep affection for her family and wanted to protect them. Even though she was a prostitute, God used her to hide Israelite spies in Canan. Her obedience to God, even though she didn't know Him well, illustrates that it's never too late to follow God. It's never too late to devote your life to Him and be obedient to His instructions. No matter how you have failed in the past, God is worthy of all you have.

God, thank You for the reminder that You are bigger than my past. As You call me to action, give me strength to answer with obedience. Increase my faith as I depend on You.

December 26

More than Beauty

*Charm is deceptive, and beauty is fleeting;
but a woman who fears the Lord is to be praised.*

PROVERBS 31:30 NIV

If we read Rachel's story in Genesis 30, we will learn that she allowed her competitive spirit, anger, and bitterness to dictate her life. She is described as incredibly beautiful, but her beauty actually made her life more complicated. Beauty is not a guarantee of success or blessing. Our culture might be obsessed with outward appearances, but we know that the state of our heart matters much more.

There isn't anything wrong with being beautiful or paying attention to the way you look. The problem is that outward perfection can never be attained. Standards continuously shift, and the desire for youth, attention, or attractiveness cannot be met forever. It takes courage to stand strong in a culture that is so focused on outward appearances. This life is fleeting, and the only thing with eternal value is your relationship with God. Spend your days trying to live up to His standards rather than the world's.

God, help me have a balanced perspective when it comes to outward beauty. Help me honor You with the gifts You've given me. Have mercy on me when I become distracted by what the world says is beautiful.

DECEMBER 27

Great Lengths

When the queen of Sheba heard of Solomon's fame, which brought honor to the name of the LORD, she came to test him with hard questions.

1 KINGS 10:1 NLT

The Queen of Sheba traveled all the way from southwestern Arabia to experience the rumored wisdom of King Solomon. She heard that he was blessed with incredible wisdom from God, and she wanted to hear for herself. She met him, brought him extravagant gifts, and questioned him extensively. She went to great lengths to get what she wanted.

You don't have to travel across the globe to find God. He has gone to great lengths for you to experience His presence without limitations. The Holy Spirit is equally accessible to everyone. God can speak the same thing to you on a Tuesday in your living room as He can on the mission field or at a conference. You don't have to book plane tickets, block out days from your work schedule, or even set aside your daily life to seek God. You can turn your heart toward Him in any circumstance. He will meet you wherever you are whenever you approach Him with humility and a willingness to acknowledge His presence in your life.

God, thank You for Your great wisdom, which is always available to me. Thank You for being accessible and available whenever I need You. Remind me again that You are always near.

DECEMBER 28

Inspire Praise

Then Miriam the prophet, Aaron's sister, took a tambourine and led all the women as they played their tambourines and danced.

Exodus 15:20 NLT

Many of us know Miriam from her involvement in Moses's story. We may not realize Miriam was one of the few women in Scripture who was called a prophet. In her later years she walked the Israelites across the Red Sea with her brothers. God miraculously saved them from their enemies, and Miriam responds by leading the women of Israel to sing and praise God. She knew that God's hand was the reason for their deliverance, and she inspired everyone around her to give Him the credit He was due.

Not only did Miriam inspire people to worship, but she prepared them for it. The Israelites crossed the Red Sea with instruments in their hands. It can be assumed that someone told them they should bring them. Like Miriam, you can impact the atmosphere around you. You can encourage others to worship when you see Him at work. Your willingness and enthusiasm to praise God in all circumstances is contagious.

God, teach me how to approach my life in a posture of praise. Fill my heart with worship and open my eyes to all You are doing. As I praise You, help me inspire others to do the same.

DECEMBER 29

Fully Surrendered

Lot's wife looked back as she was following behind him, and she turned into a pillar of salt.

GENESIS 19:26 NLT

Sodom and Gomorrah were known for being immoral. It's likely that Lot chose to live there because of the business opportunities it provided, even though it wasn't the best place for his family in a spiritual sense. When God destroyed it, He gave Lot and his family a chance to escape. They were specifically instructed not to turn back and look at the destruction. Unfortunately, Lot's wife didn't obey, and she was turned into a pillar of salt. We only see this small piece of her life, but we can glean a lot from it.

Lot's wife knew the city would be destroyed. She received the message, and she believed it. She was faithful to God's Word, but her heart was divided. Some people think that she ached for her former home, a potential life of ease, or the people she had come to know. Either way, her longing was her downfall. The same thing is true now. It's impossible to follow God with a divided heart. You can't be aligned with God and obedient to His ways while still having allegiance to the world. God asks you to fully surrender your heart to Him. As you give Him your life, He meets you with mercy and grace.

God, thank You for the lessons I can learn from Lot's wife. Give me an undivided heart. I surrender all I am and all I have to You. Help me to follow You closely and be obedient to Your Word.

DECEMBER 30

Everyone Counts

Abraham took another wife, whose name was Keturah. She bore to him Zimran, Jokshan, Medan, Midian, Ishbak, and Shuah.

GENESIS 25:1-2 NASB

Keturah was Abraham's wife during the last years of his life. We don't know very much about Keturah other than the fact that she had six sons with Abraham. This is significant in a culture when sons were an incredible blessing. She was obviously a big part of Abrahams life, and her sons went on to become leaders of six different nations. From reading about Keturah, we can remember that God sees us. Our stories are important to God.

God saw Keturah. He knew how many hairs were on her head, and He valued her. Just because her appearance in Scripture is short doesn't mean her life was overlooked. Her influence and participation in the life of Abraham had long-term consequences. In the same way, you don't know the impact your life will have. If you feel overlooked, remember you are important to God. Your sphere of influence may be large or small, but size isn't what gives it meaning. God can do so much with a heart that is yielded to Him.

God, You saw Keturah, and You see me. You used her life to have an impact on Your kingdom, and I know You can use me. Give me grace to be obedient to Your call.

DECEMBER 31

Your Contribution

When she could no longer hide him, she got him a papyrus basket and covered it with tar and pitch. Then she put the child in it and set it among the reeds by the bank of the Nile.

EXODUS 2:3 NASB

Jochebed was the wife of Amram and the mother of Moses. She was an extraordinary woman with extraordinary faith. While we only have a handful of verses that teach us about her, we can see her influence throughout the entire Old Testament. Her children followed in her footsteps and lived faithfully unto the Lord. She's a reminder that the way we choose to live will have an impact for generations to come.

Your life matters in God's story. The choices you make and the way you live mean more than you will ever know on this side of heaven. You have incredible worth as a child of God. Like Jochebed, you can lean on the stories of faith from those before you and step out boldly when God calls you. Simple obedience has ripple effects beyond your ability to understand. Acts of faith, like placing a baby in a basket, can change the world. The legacy of faith you are leaving will have an eternal impact.

God, I want my life to have a positive impact on Your kingdom. Give me grace to be obedient to You even when it's hard. Teach me how to honor You in big and small ways. I trust You to perfectly weave my life into Your story.

Author Bio

Rachael Groll is an author, speaker, Bible teacher, and host of the *Hearing Jesus* podcast, where she helps women grow in their faith by learning to recognize God's voice. With a master's degree in Bible Exposition from Biola University and years of experience in ministry, she is passionate about making Scripture accessible and practical for everyday life.

Rachael has served in a variety of ministry roles, from pastoring in the local church to working in global orphan care. Her heart is for equipping women to hear from God, walk in obedience, and experience the fullness of a life rooted in Christ.

Through her books, teaching, and podcast, she creates space for women to explore their faith, deepen their understanding of Scripture, and develop a personal relationship with Jesus. Whether she's speaking at events, writing devotionals, or sharing insights on her podcast, Rachael's mission is to encourage and empower women to walk confidently with God.

Rachael lives in Pennsylvania with her family, where she continues to write, teach, and lead others in their faith journey.